"This is a wonderfully creative and fascinating read that reveals hints of the divine all around us—in what we believe, what we love, what we have, and what we know. Rick's carefully reasoned yet whimsical approach to apologetics is more about engaging in better conversations than about arguments. And for skeptics who read this book, they may find they are closer to faith than they had ever imagined."

Terry Glaspey, author, *75 Masterpieces Every Christian Should Know* and *Not a Tame Lion: The Spiritual Legacy of C.S. Lewis*

"This excellent book deals with topics that matter to all of us and uncovers, hidden within those topics, surprising clues to God's existence. *31 Surprising Reasons to Believe in God* will be encouraging for believers and eye-opening for those who are not, and hopefully will open conversations between them. It meets people where they are, like the apostle Paul did with the Athenians. I'll be picking up multiple copies for my friends."

Francine Rivers, *New York Times* bestseller author; recipient of American Christian Fiction Writers Lifetime Achievement Award

"In a breezy, genial style that combines engaging story-telling with acute cultural analysis, Rick uncovers proofs of God's existence and reality in everyday situations and experiences to which all people, believers, seekers, and skeptics alike, have access. God is all around us, if only we will have eyes to see and ears to hear. I hope this fine book reaches a wide audience."

Dr. Louis Markos, professor in English and scholar in residence, Houston Baptist University; author, *Apologetics for the 21st Century*

"Descartes might have meant *ego miror, ergo credo*: *I wonder, therefore I believe* when, in his *Discourse on Method*, he wondered about the complexity and beauty of the world around him and the dark night soul's doubts within himself. It was through these wonders, then, that he found a way back to God, a way filled with surprise and awe.

"Stedman's book takes us down Descartes's path by detailing some 31 ways that we wonder about the world. His delightfully rich writing points us back to an unavoidable belief in God and His ways."

Dr. Don Thompson, professor of Great Books & Mathematics, Pepperdine University

"It is rare to come across a book that deals with profoundly philosophical issues yet is true to Scripture and written with such clarity that a person of any age could understand it. This is one of those books. In the style of C.S. Lewis, Rick has given us a gift by pointing out the evidence for God's existence that can be found all around us if we know where to look. Drawing from contemporary culture to the most respected writings in human history, Rick makes the teleological argument for the existence of God so abundantly clear."

Dr. Mark W. Baker, psychologist, executive director, La Vie Counseling Centers, CA

"Once the existence of God (or the gods) was taken for granted. Today it is otherwise. Yet we still enjoy music, detest animal cruelty and human trafficking, and defend our inalienable right to free speech and the pursuit of happiness. Rick Stedman has written 31 delightful and slightly whimsical essays showing how these common beliefs and attitudes make today's atheism dubious. One need not find all of the essays equally persuasive to be convinced that belief in God is still a rationally defensible position."

Ric Machuga, professor of philosophy, Butte College, CA;
author, *Life, the Universe, and Everything*

"Rick provides a helpful entry point to cultural apologetics, with his multifaceted exploration of how film, stories, music, art, morality, and human experience all contribute to a cumulative case for the existence of God."

Dr. Holly Ordway, Houston Baptist University, author, *Not God's Type: An Atheist Academic Lays Down Her Arms*

"This book will rock your world! Could sex, zombies, art, nature and music all be neon signs pointing to the existence of God? Atheists, agnostics, skeptics and Christians alike will be challenged by the thoughtful and well-reasoned arguments in this book."

Erik Neilson, senior pastor, McMinnville Christian Church, McMinnville, OR

"If you want an intelligent, relevant, and gracious appeal to believe in God, look no further! With the mind of a scholar and the empathy of a friend, Rick reveals clues to God's existence, hidden all around us. Devour *31 Surprising Reasons to Believe in God,* and give copies to your friends so they too can enjoy the feast."

Caleb Kaltenbach, lead pastor, Discovery Church; author, *Messy Grace*

"This amazing book has echoes of C.S. Lewis. Comprehensive and easy to read, Rick takes the wonders of everyday life and reveals the fingerprints of God. Learn from Rick, and your soul will thank you for bringing out insights that are often overlooked."

John Seitz, senior pastor, Antioch Christian Church, IA

"This is the first book I have read that explains apologetics in a way that relates to the perspective of today's nonbeliever. The author's connecting examples and expressed humility will compel even the most cynical to keep reading. I intend to use this as my primary evangelism tool."

Brad Dacus, president and founder, Pacific Justice Institute

"Rick Stedman sails the readers across the sea of scientific mysteries regarding the origin of the universe and the information needed for life, a sea that deepens each decade with far more questions than answers. He exposes either the flippant foolery of some scientists, or the respectful awe of others, while gently guiding the reader to an accurate yet simply packaged presentation of the problems faced by the pondering researcher. As only a philosopher and theologian can do, Stedman then brings the reader back to the fundamentals: reason, humanity, and the love of God."

Dr. James M. Tour, professor of NanoEngineering, Chemistry, Applied Materials and Computer Science, Rice University

"The fraction of people who are atheists remains tiny. However, several of the more outspoken ones have recently become media darlings. Thus there is a need for fresh approaches to the fact that ultimately nothing makes sense apart from a belief in the sovereign God of the universe. Rick tackles this important challenge very effectively."

Dr. Henry Schaefer III, professor and director, Center for Computational Quantum Chemistry, University of Georgia; five-time Nobel Prize nominee

"My friend Rick has made a huge impact for Jesus as a pastor-philosopher, church planter, and Christian leader. He has found a way to communicate the good news that makes sense across a spectrum of cultural contexts. This book will help you do the same!"

Cam Huxford, senior pastor, Compass Christian Church, Savannah, GA

"Rick Stedman's *31 Surprising Reasons to Believe in God* is engaging and thought-provoking as he uncovers clues that point unexpectedly (and convincingly) toward the existence of God."

Rodney L. Morris, Morris Editorial, Eugene, OR

"Rick obviously has his eyes wide open watching for the whispers of heaven here on earth. He writes with an understanding that there is indeed a 'God-shaped hole' at the center of every human heart and all creation is pointing us toward our Creator. No matter where you are on the spectrum of belief, this book will resonate with your soul."

David Garison, Lead Pastor, Northside Christian Church, Spring, TX

"Life is full of mysteries and wonders. Rick takes what is familiar to our own personal experience and opens our eyes to the personal touch of God in them. In a culture that has blinded itself to God, Rick's 31 reasons help restore our vision to see and experience the wonders and mysteries of God in our everyday experience."

Randy Watson, former missionary to Chile, founder/senior pastor, Gateway Christian Church, Rhonert Park, CA

"Rick has taken a palette of 31 colors and designed a picture that clearly presents God in ways one might expect Him to be found and ways that will surprise you. In any case, one finds themselves 'without excuse.'"

Ken Long, senior pastor, Northshore Christian Church, WA

"Rick Stedman is a man and pastor I can relate to. He likes great movies, classic rock, and sports. Not coincidentally, Rick uses these same things to prove the existence of God. Now *that* is a great apologetics book! More importantly, Rick's common-man, creative approach to biblical proofs is exactly the kind of material I can use to meet people in a street-level way."

Alan Scott, lead pastor, Cumberland Community Church, Smyrna, GA

"Rick captivates us to visualize the presence of God in everyday life. In your hands you have a treasure that points surprisingly and delightfully toward God's existence. Read this book, and your perceptions of God and this world will never be the same."

Tim Boyles, lead minister, Church of Christ South Hayward, Hayward, CA

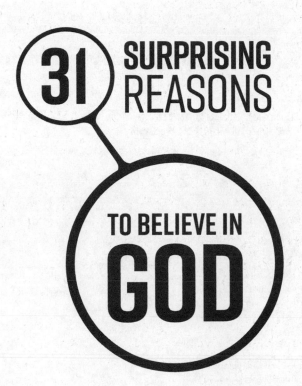

31 SURPRISING REASONS TO BELIEVE IN GOD

RICK STEDMAN

HARVEST HOUSE PUBLISHERS
EUGENE, OREGON

Cover by Bryce Williamson, Eugene, OR

Cover Image © Marvid / iStock

Published in association with the Books & Such Management, 52 Mission Circle, Suite 122, PMB 170, Santa Rosa, CA 95409-5370, www.booksandsuch.com.

31 SURPRISING REASONS TO BELIEVE IN GOD

Published by Harvest House Publishers
Eugene, Oregon 97402
www.harvesthousepublishers.com

ISBN 978-0-7369-6983-3 (pbk.)
ISBN 978-0-7369-6984-0 (eBook)

Library of Congress Cataloging-in-Publication Data
Names: Stedman, Rick, author.
Title: 31 surprising reasons to believe in God : how superheroes, art, environmentalism, and science point toward faith / Rick Stedman.
Other titles: Thirty-one surprising reasons to believe in God
Description: Eugene, Oregon : Harvest House Publishers, 2017. | Description based on print version record and CIP data provided by publisher; resource not viewed.
Identifiers: LCCN 2017001283 (print) | LCCN 2017015667 (ebook) | ISBN 9780736969840 (ebook) | ISBN 9780736969833 (pbk.)
Subjects: LCSH: Christianity and culture. | Faith.
Classification: LCC BR115.C8 (ebook) | LCC BR115.C8 S7322 2017 (print) | DDC 239—dc23
LC record available at https://lccn.loc.gov/2017001283

Printed in the United States of America

17 18 19 20 21 22 23 24 25 / BP-SK / 10 9 8 7 6 5 4 3 2 1

To Don and Gay Stedman,
Whose blood flows in my veins,
Whose values have shaped my mind,
And whose God fills my spirit.

CONTENTS

Introduction: Surprising Reasons to Lean Toward Theism 9

PART ONE: THE ECSTASY AND AGONY OF BEAUTY

Chapter 1: Superhero and fantasy movies aren't just for kids, *therefore God exists* 17

Chapter 2: Horror movies and books are shockingly popular, *therefore God exists* 23

Chapter 3: Music moves my soul like nothing else, *therefore God exists* 31

Chapter 4: I love beauty and art, *therefore God exists* 37

Chapter 5: Sports fanatics can't help themselves, *therefore God exists* 43

Chapter 6: Happiness is a moral responsibility, *therefore God exists* 49

Chapter 7: Sex can be out of this world, *therefore God exists* 55

PART TWO: YEARNINGS FOR A BETTER WORLD

Chapter 8: Human trafficking is a vile evil that must be stopped, *therefore God exists* 63

Chapter 9: Cruelty to animals is detestable, *therefore God exists* 67

Chapter 10: I'm embarrassed by the bad behavior of believers, *therefore God exists* 73

Chapter 11: Protecting our environment is a moral issue, *therefore God exists* 79

Chapter 12: I despise needless violence and cruelty, *therefore God exists* 85

Chapter 13: I deeply value free speech and self-expression, *therefore God exists* 91

Chapter 14: I believe in the justice of seeking justice, *therefore God exists* 97

PART THREE: SHAFTS OF GLORY

Chapter 15: I'm amazed at the existence of existence, *therefore God exists* 107

Chapter 16: I'm staggered by the glory of our universe, *therefore God exists* 113

Chapter 17: The marvel of language can't be put into words, *therefore God exists* 119

Chapter 18: Mathematics and numbers are no mere games, *therefore God exists* 127

Chapter 19: The scientific method is fabulously effective, *therefore God exists* 133

Chapter 20: I need reasons to trust my own reason, *therefore God exists* 139

Chapter 21: Truth is more real and important than preference, *therefore God exists* 147

PART FOUR: THE MIRACLE THAT IS ME

Chapter 22: I wonder about the wonder of the self, *therefore God exists* 157

Chapter 23: I wonder about the wonder of free will, *therefore God exists* 163

Chapter 24: I wonder about the wonder of doubt, *therefore God exists* 169

Chapter 25: I wonder about the wonder of emotions, *therefore God exists* 173

Chapter 26: I wonder about the wonder of compassion, *therefore God exists* 179

Chapter 27: I wonder about the wonder of hope, *therefore God exists* 187

Chapter 28: I wonder about the wonder of human dignity, *therefore God exists* 193

PART FIVE: FEELING HOMESICK AT HOME

Chapter 29: I long for a world without pain and suffering, *therefore God exists* 203

Chapter 30: I long for lasting love and community, *therefore God exists* 211

Chapter 31: I long for immortality and eternity, *therefore God exists* 217

Conclusion 225

Acknowledgments 229

Endnotes 231

INTRODUCTION

SURPRISING REASONS TO LEAN TOWARD THEISM

Can you imagine finding, hidden in your backyard, $11 million in buried treasure?

In February 2013, a family on rural property in northern California literally found this to be true. While walking their dog, the couple noticed the top of an old, rusted can protruding near their well-worn path. They wondered if someone, years ago, had buried old garbage—tin cans and such—on their property.

Piqued by curiosity, the husband used a stick to free the can, which turned out to be much heavier than expected. Inside they discovered gold coins. After searching the area, they eventually unearthed eight cans containing 1427 coins—worth an estimated $11 million. Experts concluded the coins were probably buried in the 1850s during the early years of the California Gold Rush. Ever since purchasing their home on this property in the foothills of the Sierra Nevada Mountains, the couple had been fabulously rich—but also totally unaware of their fortune.[1]

Asked if they had any clue, before the find, of the treasure buried on their land, they said no. But in hindsight they remembered noticing, years before, a tin can that was tied to the tree beside the treasure, but it was so old that the wood had grown around part of the can.[2] Could it be, they now wondered, a marker placed by the person who buried the treasure, a reminder so he could locate the correct tree in the future? Had they noticed the very sign designed to reveal the buried treasure, but were unaware that it was a clue?

Since our family home is also on property in the same foothills, I now tend to look down more carefully as my wife and I walk together (after all, maybe the prospector buried his gold in two different places). And I also tend to look more carefully and think deeper about peculiar things that strike me as beautiful, odd, or exceptional because not all treasures are made of gold, and I'm convinced that reality is more than meets the eye.

HIDDEN SPIRITUAL REALITIES

"More than meets the eye" is not just a tag line for the popular Transformers toys and movies (though I enjoy them both!); it's a profoundly meaningful insight. I think the phrase first appeared in W.H. Auden's poem "At Last the Secret Is Out." A similar idea was expressed by World War II hero Antoine de Saint-Exupéry:[3]

> [The little prince] went back to meet the fox.
>
> "Goodbye," he said.
>
> "Goodbye," said the fox. "And now here is my secret, a very simple secret: It is only with the heart that one can see rightly; what is essential is invisible to the eye."
>
> "What is essential is invisible to the eye," the little prince repeated, so that he would be sure to remember.[4]

The fox's secret is a proverb all of us should remember: what is essential is invisible to the eye. Just as we shouldn't judge a book by its cover nor people by their looks, so too we must learn that the important stuff in life is hidden behind the ordinary, the material, the mundane.

The theme of this book is that the essential realities in life reveal themselves to us in the things we love—and loathe—most in life. If we have eyes to see, the very things we love so passionately and hate so fiercely are markers, clues to hidden treasures of deep importance. For instance, on the positive side we humans seem to have an insatiable appetite for beauty, music, justice, and a host of other wonders. And on the negative side, we are united in our revulsion over cruelty to animals, destruction of the environment, the trafficking of innocents, and the violence of war. In the end, I think all of these point us toward life's most important issue: whether God exists. Those things that move us most in life are *signposts*, I will suggest, to *spiritual* realities of our existence that are often invisible to the eye, buried treasures that we were intended to find.

Has God secreted himself within the glories of life and shrouded himself behind its horrors? Could both the magnificence of our existence, as well as its maleficence, be telling us that, indeed, there is more to life than meets the eye? For those of us who treasure life in all its fullness, I think that both our joys and pains say, "Look closer here. Like an iceberg, there is much more beneath the surface."

Or, as Rainer Maria Rilke, the twentieth-century German poet, wrote, "If your daily life seems poor, blame not life. Blame yourself that you are not poet enough to call forth its riches."[5] When facing difficult times, I often have repeated those lines to myself as a challenge.

In a similar fashion, this book is a challenge for you, dear reader, to call forth the spiritual treasures hidden in the normalcies of life, both delightful and difficult, which you know to be true in your heart. Ask why you are so moved by music, stirred by sports, angered by injustice, and maybe even drawn to unusual pleasures like sci-fi and zombie movies—and you may find that a *surprising* result emerges.

The importance of *surprise* in philosophy

"The beginning of all philosophy, according to both Plato and Aristotle, lies in the experience of wonder. One might go further and say that the beginning of all serious thought—all reflection upon the world that is not merely calculative or appetitive—begins in a moment of unsettling or delighted surprise...the astonishing recollection of something one has forgotten only because it is always present...an abiding amazement that lies just below the surface of conscious thought and that only in very rare instances breaks through into ordinary awareness."[6]

—DAVID BENTLEY HART

CARDS ON THE TABLE

Just so you know where I'm coming from, let me clearly show my hand: I am a convinced theist, a Christian, and a pastor. I am not a professional philosopher, though I have graduate degrees in philosophy and theology. Actually, I'm a very normal man—I love my wife and kids, my collection of classic rock 'n' roll LPs, my books (to be really honest, I'm a book-a-holic), and my workshop.

In addition, I'm not writing for academic philosophers since I'm not a member of their guild. Instead, I'm writing to everyday people, trying to suggest that the reality of God can be inferred from common parts of *their everyday lives*, rather than from topics one hears only in a university classroom. This is because I believe God intended that normal people could actually discern his existence from the normalcies of their lives. Though I think higher education can be a great good, it is not a necessary prerequisite in order to grasp the reality of God's existence.

For these reasons I present, in the pages to follow, only one side of the case for believing in God—the theistic side. I have chosen thirty-one aspects of life that theists and atheists can both easily identify (out of a list of about a hundred that I have compiled), features that, I believe, reveal deep convictions that *lean* us either *toward* or away from belief in God. I emphasize "lean toward" because the essays in this book do not contain watertight or irrefutable arguments, but instead uncover clues or signs that point toward the existence of God. I am not presenting proofs of God's existence; instead, I'm simply suggesting that our loves and loathings have significant support within a theistic worldview, whereas within atheism they may not.

These thirty-one essays—designed to be read in the course of a month—are intended to stimulate thought, provoke discussion, and introduce different ways of looking at common values and valuables in everyday life. You might even consider forming a study group to discuss each essay in a coffee shop or a home group.

A philosophy professor reflects about hidden glory:

"As I look at my universe and walk among my fellow humans, I have the deep belief that hidden realities are all around us. These hidden realities are there in the physical world; and they are there, also, in the human world. If I'm foolish enough to think that I see all there is to be seen in front of my eyes, I simply miss the glory...When we are aware that there are glories of life still hidden from us, we walk humbly before the Great Unknown."[7]

—PROFESSOR HARRY A. OVERSTREET

DECIPHERING THE DOUBLE CODING

Like my neighbors who discovered buried gold, musicologist Helga Thorne made a startling discovery while studying Bach's *Partita for Unaccompanied Violin in D minor*. Thorne found, ***hidden in the musical notes themselves***, "a remarkable double coding." According to Oxford mathematician and philosopher of science John Lennox,

> [T]here appears the following ancient proverb: *Ex Deo nascimur, in Christo morimur, per Spiritum Sanctum reviviscimus* ["In God we are born, in Christ we die, through the Holy Spirit we are made alive"]. Clearly, one doesn't have to know about this hidden text in order to enjoy the Sonata—it has been enjoyed for hundreds of years without people having any idea that the message was there. But it was Bach's genius to encode a completely different kind of message in music.[8]

That's exactly it—God has double coded (and maybe triple, quadruple, etc.) evidence of his own reality and presence within our world, albeit in very subtle forms. To those who say, "If God exists, why doesn't he say something?" my answer is: He has spoken, but it is double coded. We have to look for it and learn how to decipher it, hidden as it is in the glory and gore around us.

I hereby invite you to join with me as we try to crack the double codes of existence itself, much like the cryptologists in the 2014 movie *The Imitation Game* sought to break military codes. Or, to switch metaphors, join me as we embark on a voyage of discovery. Like arctic cruises that navigate between icebergs, we will sail between our likes and dislikes while paying special attention to what lies beneath the surface.

Taken together and honestly considered, I believe the collective weight of the treasures revealed in these chapters, their gravitas, add up to pretty good reasons to believe in God—and ultimately will be worth far more than gold.

Rick Stedman
Auburn, California

PART ONE

THE ECSTASY AND AGONY OF BEAUTY

Why are some aspects of life so heartpoundingly beautiful? And why, since such beauty exists, is it so heartbreakingly temporary? Why are roses, songs, and kisses so lovely? And why do roses have to wilt, songs reach their last note, and lovers' lips part?

A portion of the answer may be in the synonym, used above, for beautiful: *lovely*. A beautiful moment, object, or person isn't just a thing we rationally appreciate, it's something (or someone) we *love*. Beauty is a reality, a quality of existence that we grasp not with our heads but with our hearts. As Helen Keller said, "The best and most beautiful things in the world cannot be seen or even touched—they must be felt with the heart."[1]

So what is an encounter with beauty? Is it something that can be explained away as a mere evolutionary vestige, glandular response, or a set of synaptic firings in our brains? Aesthetics scholar David Bentley Hart says no: "Beauty is something other than the visible or audible or conceptual agreement of its parts, and the experience of beauty can never be wholly reduced to any set of material constituents. It is something mysterious, prodigal, often unanticipated, even capricious." This is why evolutionary materialism cannot completely explain beauty: it is not utilitarian. As Hart says, "Beauty is gloriously useless; it has no purpose but itself."[2]

If materialism can't fully explain beauty, can theism? When we truly love, and especially when we love the beautiful, do we rise above all physicalist explanations and enter the realm of the metaphysical? In other words, when we encounter the beautiful, do we begin to see traces of divinity?[3]

In Christian theology, both the givenness of beauty and its heart-rending impermanence are seen as gifts from God. C.S. Lewis expressed this in a brilliant phrase: "Thou gavest man the tether and pang of the particular"[4] (which pilgrim John sings to God in Lewis's *The Pilgrim's Regress*). As we grasp both the tether and pang of the beautiful, do we at last begin, as Shakespeare said, "to feelingly see"?[5]

Theism makes sense not only of the *tether* (the connection we feel with beauty) but also the *pang* (the sorrow we feel over the loss of beauty). Beauty is ethereal (a delicacy that seems almost too perfect for this world), but also ephemeral (it's gone before we know it). The tether points to the hint of the divine in each particular, and the pang to the hint of the eternal. There is a profundity in pleasure, of which the experience of beauty is one aspect.

In Part 1, we will survey six beauties (and one anti-beauty) common in our postmodern culture: superhero and fantasy movies, horror novels, art, music, happiness, sports—and even sex. It's a wild ride, like a roller coaster rushing through the ups and downs of life, but it's a revealing ride. So buckle your seat belts and keep your hands inside the car as our beautiful adventure begins.

CHAPTER 1

SUPERHERO AND FANTASY MOVIES AREN'T JUST FOR KIDS, THEREFORE GOD EXISTS

"I put the Force into the movie to awaken a certain kind of spirituality in young people, more a belief in God than in any particular religion. I wanted to make it so that young people would begin to ask questions about the mystery [of our existence]."[1]

GEORGE LUCAS (1944–)

As a kid I loved superhero comic books and slowly amassed a small collection. In college, my interests switched to fantasy heroes like Frodo in *The Lord of the Rings* and Ransom in *Out of the Silent Planet*. But my world was rocked when *Star Wars* hit movie screens in 1977—here was swashbuckling action and sci-fi adventure, superheroes and supervillains, all expressed through thrilling music, heart-moving storylines, and breakthroughs in computer cinematography. But for me the biggest surprises were the spiritual matters that dominated the movie: good versus evil, self-sacrifice, redemption, life after death, and—above all—the belief that there is more to reality than mere materialism. I felt like I was watching a paraphrase of the Bible, written for the scientific generation, whose real agenda was subtly disguised within alien disguises. What a marvel!

What I never imagined was that this movie was also a harbinger, a herald of a cultural trend that would come to dominate movie theaters in the twenty-first century. I never dreamed superheroes would become super popular.

Think back over the movies you last saw in theaters. Were they superhero movies (like *The Dark Knight*), science fiction (a la *Star*

Wars), or fantasy flicks (*The Hobbit*)? If so, you have plenty of company. Supernatural thrillers rule movie box offices today.

But why is this the case in our postmodern, secular society? Why, in the materialist twenty-first century, are *Lord of the Rings*, *X-men*, and *Harry Potter* so loved? Why are the fans so devoted? Why do normally rational adults pay to see comic books on the big screen, including characters such as Superman, the Joker, and Wolverine? What are we—teenagers again?

Honestly, would anyone have predicted fifty years ago that grownups would flock to see movies about a Jedi knight or a teenager with spider abilities? The *Batman* TV show of the 1960s was a campy, comedic farce. (As also was, to a lesser degree, the 1950's *Adventures of Superman*. After all, how could mere glasses hide the identity of anyone?) But the *Dark Knight* movie of 2008 was no joke, and Heath Ledger's role as the Joker won critical acclaim, was lauded for its analysis of anarchy, and won Ledger a posthumous Academy Award for Best Supporting Actor.

One would think that as society became increasingly secular, the popular interest in supernatural heroes would have diminished. Surprisingly, the opposite has been the case. Think about it: Belief in the supernatural is supposedly on the decline, yet we flock to see movies about heroes and villains with superhuman or magical powers. Seven out of the top ten highest grossing films of all time (not accounting for inflation) are science fiction or fantasy, as are over thirty of the top fifty. There are no biographies, no documentaries, and very few action films or romances (*Titanic* is a notable exception) in the top fifty. The best-grossing film is *Avatar*, which brought in almost $2.8 billion worldwide (two-thirds of its sales were overseas). Chew on that last fact a while: the hunger for sci-fi and the supernatural is a global obsession. Could it be that this transcultural phenomenon reveals a spiritual longing within us all?

Some nontheists demur: these are just meaningless entertainment trends, nothing more and nothing less. Yet we are not talking here about occasional diversions or infrequent appetites. Instead, we are noting that specific genres comprise the *majority* of our movie ticket purchases. Could it be that the movies we watch reveal clues as to our longings for a world that is more than physical? That is, could our entertainment choices be telling us something about our need for God?

A provocative answer to these questions is provided by E. Michael Jones in *Monsters from the Id.*[2] Jones argues that as society has become more and more materialistic and has pushed the supernatural world further from the conscious mind, our subconscious need to acknowledge the existence of the supernatural realm is being satisfied through sci-fi and fantasy genres—and especially through horror films and novels, which we will discuss in the next chapter. Like Freudian impulses that resurface elsewhere when denied, so too our spiritual impulses, when repressed, sublimate and reappear in other arenas.

This explains to me the phenomenal success, in both print and film, of J.R.R. Tolkien's *The Lord of the Rings*. Published in three volumes in 1954 and 1955, it became one of the bestselling novels of all time (over 150 million copies sold), and scores high on lists that attempt to rate the best novels of the twentieth century. *The Lord of the Rings* movies, directed by Peter Jackson and released in 2001, 2002, and 2003, were major successes both financially and critically (the films won seventeen Academy Awards). What explains these extraordinary successes?

The Lord of the Rings is essentially Christian moral philosophy written via the vehicle of myth, for Tolkien believed myth to be a better conveyer of truth than mere discourse. Like *The Chronicles of Narnia*, written by Tolkien's friend C.S. Lewis, *The Lord of the Rings* is a profoundly spiritual book.

In one of his letters Tolkien states, "*The Lord of the Rings* is of course a fundamentally religious and Catholic work; unconsciously so at first, but consciously in the revision. That is why I have not put in, or have cut out, practically all references to anything like 'religion', to cults or practices, in the imaginary world. For the religious element is absorbed into the story and the symbolism."[3]

Yet the work is brimming with theological realities, as philosopher Peter Kreeft points out in *The Philosophy of Tolkien*.[4] Especially evident is the reality of good and evil, along with the inability of good intentions to overcome evil—since in the end even Frodo himself cannot withstand the evil influence of the ring. It also portrays the Christlike value of self-sacrifice (seen in Gandalf, Aragorn, and especially in the humble Sam, who, Simon the Cyrene-like, carries not just the cross but also the cross-bearer up the final hill). The comparisons go on and on, but here one more will have to suffice: *fellowship* (of the ring) is also a distinctly Christian term and, in fact, is another name for the church itself.

Thus, in Tolkien's *The Lord of the Rings*, as in the superhero and science fiction movies today, the constant yet concealed theme is clear: there are spiritual elements in life, and indeed they are the most important elements of all. To state this in naturalistic terms, what really matters in reality is not just matter.

Another example of this is the greatest science fiction creation of our era, *Star Wars*, which, according to creator George Lucas, is also fiction with a clear spiritual element. Lucas confessed that he created the Force to awaken spirituality in his audiences. (Lucas was raised a Methodist but abandoned the idea of a personal God, so he now identifies with what he calls Buddhist Methodism.) For Lucas, the Force was a way in which he could inculcate belief in the existence of a non-personal, nondenominational God to secular moviegoers, as well as belief in the real existence of good and evil.

At the very least, the Force is a denial of brute materialism. Plus, it illustrates the polarity of the spiritual world: good and evil, dark and light. Luke Skywalker must not give in to the "dark side" of the Force, but must learn to have faith and find strength in the "light side" of the Force. Plus, the self-sacrifice of Obi-Wan Kenobi is very Christlike, and his existence beyond death is another subtle affirmation of the existence of metaphysical realities.

As opposed to Lucas's subtle intention to encourage belief in the existence of God, *Star Trek* creator Gene Roddenberry based his sci-fi world on a more rigid humanism. Even so, Roddenberry also claimed he was not an atheist. Even in the *Star Trek* universe, there were subtle spiritual suggestions, such as that the ultimate goal of evolution is divinity.[5] In addition, the crew values traits such as honesty and self-sacrifice (clearly Christian values), and are certain of the rightness of their mission and the wrongness of their enemies'.

References to Christian doctrines can also be seen in C.S. Lewis's *Chronicles of Narnia* and even in the massively popular Harry Potter series by J.K. Rowling (what is it with the British preference for initials, anyway?). In the Potter series, subtle references to Christianity include "Gryffindor," Harry's team, which is symbolized by a Griffin—a mythical animal that is part lion and part eagle. These represent the two-sided nature of the incarnation: The lion on Christ's human side (lion of Judah[6]), and the eagle on his divine side (it soars to heaven and is not blinded when looking at the sun).[7] Harry's nemesis is Draco Malfoy of the "Slytherin" house, symbolized by a snake, which is clearly a satanic reference (and "malum" is the Latin root for evil). Plus, the only way to defeat evil is through self-sacrifice, seen in Harry's parents and even in his own death and resurrection. After Pope Benedict XVI condemned the Harry Potter books, Rowling asserted in a 2007 interview that not only was she a Christian, but the books themselves were heavily influenced by her Christian faith and echo her own struggles with faith.[8]

To sum up this chapter: though today we have knowingly denied the existence of the supernatural realm and the moral order it brings to our world, we are unable to live in the merely material world we have arbitrarily delimited for ourselves. As a result, we are left with a metaphysical vacuum, a spiritual void that seeks to be filled. One of our culture's subconscious solutions to meet this need for the supernatural is to fill the gap with sci-fi and superhero movies and books.

Thus, superhero comics, fantasy books, and their associated movies are clues pointing to our need for the supernatural and to the emptiness of materialism. The existence and popularity of these genres, if we are willing to discern those clues and follow them where they lead, may surprisingly lean us toward the existence of God.

When I was a child, I enjoyed reading comic books. As I grew older, I put them aside thinking they were only for children. How wrong I was. I am just now seeing the profundity of these recreations—for in our world that has killed God (Nietzsche), our lay psychologists (Stan Lee and others) are re-creating him. It seems that even in the escapist world of movies, we just can't escape the supernatural.[9]

Can a science fiction writer believe in God? Ray Bradbury

The New York Times called science fiction writer Ray Bradbury, most known for his novels *Fahrenheit 451* and *The Martian Chronicles*, "the writer most responsible for bringing modern science fiction into the literary mainstream."[10] Interestingly, Bradbury was also a believer in God.

During some interviews Bradbury occasionally appeared to be pantheistic. But to those close to him, Bradbury was no pantheist since he clearly drew a distinction between himself and God. Sam Weller, who was both a friend and the biographer of Bradbury, remembers that Bradbury would often declare his thankfulness toward God. Weller wrote that Bradbury once remarked, while rereading his own work, "I sit there and cry because I haven't done any of this. It's a God-given thing, and I'm so grateful, so, so grateful. The best description of my career as a writer is, 'At play in the fields of the Lord.'"[11]

CHAPTER 2

HORROR MOVIES AND BOOKS ARE SHOCKINGLY POPULAR, THEREFORE GOD EXISTS

"Horror movies are the best date movies. There's no wondering, 'When do I put my arm around her?'"

FILMMAKER ELI ROTH (1972–)

Since our society is so increasingly secular, have you ever wondered how horror novelist Stephen King could become one of the bestselling authors of all time? Why movies based on the *Vampire Chronicles* of Anne Rice raked in huge profits? Even popular teen romance novels and movies (such as the *Twilight* series) now include vampires, werewolves, and other such supernatural themes. And what is it with all the sudden interest in zombies? (I'm referring here to reanimated corpses, aka the walking dead, not the rock group behind the 1970 hit "Time of the Season.") Does the fact that King has sold more books worldwide (400 million) than John Grisham and Tom Clancy combined tell us something about ourselves, something spiritually important?

The explosion of interest in horror films and books in the last several decades is especially remarkable. Why is our postmodern, irreligious society so taken by the occult and still so surprisingly superstitious? (Friday the thirteenth is a spooky day in horror movies, and many hotels still don't have a thirteenth floor.) To put this more philosophically, how can we reconcile the rise of interest in horror themes with the concurrent rise of secularism in media and academics?

As was mentioned in the previous chapter, E. Michael Jones, whose PhD in American literature is from Temple University, provides an intriguing answer to this question in *Monsters from the Id*. Jones argues that as society has become increasingly materialistic and has repressed belief in the supernatural world, those beliefs inevitably resurface in other arenas. In the previous chapter we looked at the supernatural resurfacing in superheroes and fantasy works. In Freudian psychology this is called *sublimation*, the attachment of our denied emotions and beliefs onto a positive substitute such as comic books and fantasy heroes.

In this chapter, we will focus on the darker side of this phenomenon—the surprising reappearance of the supernatural in horror genres. Psychologically this is called *displacement*, wherein one attaches one's repressions to negative substitutes. Thus, horror products reveal another hint toward the existence of God, but they also add a huge twist: the destructive consequences that result when we try to deny belief in God's existence.

Let's begin our investigation with what has been called the first truly science fiction novel—*Frankenstein* by Mary Shelley, née Mary Godwin. As Michael Jones meticulously documents, Shelley was an early victim of the Enlightenment, especially the Enlightenment myth of morality through naturalism, that is, the liberty of following one's own nature. "Since there was no such thing as original sin, since man was 'naturally' good, one need only remove external restraint [and] virtue would flourish."[1]

However, the opposite was the gruesome reality, as Mary's parents saw firsthand in the French Revolution of the 1790s. Rather than begetting a free-love utopia, this product of Enlightenment philosophy spawned rivers of blood and suffering for thousands—as well as Mary herself (literally, since she was conceived in France just before her mother returned, broke and broken, to England). But Mary's parents, especially her father, William Godwin (himself a famous libertine English philosopher), were unable to admit the error of their materialist philosophy. As a result, Mary would have to repeat their tragic sufferings and learn that 'natural moralism' is basically another word for selfishness, and when given free rein ultimately leads to disappointment, violence, and even death.

Young Mary Godwin was seduced, both in mind and in body, by Percy Shelley. Though a married man, he eloped with her—and her younger sister Claire!—from England to the continent to explore the wonders of naturalistic amoralism or, to be less discreet, sexual license. But everyone touched by Shelley's bohemian ethic was eventually destroyed. His first wife, Harriet, called Shelley "a vampire" and committed suicide.[2] Mary, eventually abandoned by Shelley and thoroughly dismayed with the outcome of their philosophy, lived a life of regret and remorse. She wrote, "Polluted by crimes and torn by the bitterest remorse, where can I find rest but in death?"[3] Mary's eyes were opened to the failure of naturalism, but because she "spurned Christianity and any possibility of repentance," she condemned herself, in her own words, to a life of "remorse, hatred, grief, misery."[4]

So her solution was to transform her own story into a mythic tale, a novel that also revealed her judgment on godless morality. As Jones puts this, "The moral order, when suppressed, reasserts itself as an avenging monster," and "The monster in *Frankenstein* is largely remorse personified."[5]

This is why horror genres are so filled with monsters—literally speaking. Werewolves and vampires. Zombies and ghosts. Freddy Krueger and Hannibal Lecter. The monsters are the result of rebellion against the moral order, which in essence is rebellion against God. Jones concludes, "The calamities described in horror fiction are really repressed moral truths. Horror is morality written backwards."[6]

According to Jones, it is crucial to understand that the monsters of horror and fantasy are no mere characters—they are the *very product* of the secular-driven Enlightenment:

> Horror haunts the Enlightenment as its uncanny doppelganger. Frankenstein is the inchoate protest of someone who accepts the premises of the Enlightenment but who recognizes that they do not work, and what is worse cause horrific suffering and death when implemented. So the culture is locked in a curious dialectic: It keeps producing horror, because it cannot understand the horror, and that, in turn, is because it cannot understand the cause of horror.[7]

The monsters of horror, to sum all this up, are the result of the secularization of society. They are warnings, from deep within our subconscious, that the alluring path we are following is dangerous—and maybe even demonic. As we have removed God from the scene, we have birthed our own Frankensteins, our own cultural monsters, which are wreaking havoc on the very parents who gave them birth. Ours is now a horrific society that produces more horror because it cannot understand the source of its current horror, and on and on, not just ad nauseam but ad mortem—to death.

So here is the grand surprise: horror books and movies are not mere entertainment. Instead, they are indictments on the ghastly results of Enlightenment scientism. In Jones's words, "Reliance on 'scientific' reason leads not to light and peace but to ruin and darkness."[8]

As all that the scientist, Victor Frankenstein, loves is destroyed by the very monster he created (who, by the way, is never called Frankenstein but only "the creature"), so too the abandonment of the sacred has sired another consequence: the destruction of our world at the hands of science itself, which we can see in today's many dystopian movies. Whether as a result of nuclear war, chemical toxins, harmful viruses, or the hubris of industry (Mordor in Tolkien's Middle-Earth or the Terminators from James Cameron's sci-fi future), nature is eventually destroyed by the child of naturalism itself—science.

So horror movies are messages from our subconscious selves to wake up before it's too late; they are heralds warning of our impending self-destruction. Plus, they tend to portray Christian themes in unusual manners, as if Christian theology were being taught on a subliminal level through, for instance, ghosts and zombies. Yes, even zombies! Really, could there be any more unanticipated trend than the popularity of zombies in movies and TV shows in our scientific society?

But maybe—again!—our pastimes are evidence, deep revelations within us, of spiritual realities that can't be buried (forgive the pun), for aren't zombies crude characterizations of the Christian doctrine that the dead will truly be made alive again, and some of them to a grisly existence? Might our fascination with the walking dead actually reveal a deep, tacit awareness that death is not really the end and for some humans the afterlife won't be pleasant? Could horror and zombie movies be subconsciously warning us about something few of us want to discuss; might they be spiritual intuitions of the possible existence of hell?

Or how about vampires and their blood-drinking obsession? Could these be inversions of the Eucharist, the celebration that Christ gave his blood on the cross, or of his instruction that Christians are to drink his blood and eat his flesh (John 6:53-55)? Or consider ghosts. Could they be an effort to depict what C.S. Lewis in *The Great Divorce* envisioned as the less-than-real existence of the inhabitants of hell? After their bus ride to heaven, the inhabitants of hell appeared to him as

> transparent—fully transparent when they stood between me and [the light], smudgy and imperfectly opaque when they stood in the shadow of some tree. They were in fact ghosts: man-shaped stains on the brightness of the air. One could attend to them or ignore them at will as you do with the dirt on a window pane. I noticed that the grass did not bend under their feet: even the dew drops were not disturbed.[9]

In Lewis's imagination, a spirit from hell is not a full person and lacks physical solidity. It is literally a phantom. So again I ask, could the portrayals of ghosts be a subconscious effort to warn us of what eternal existence outside heaven is like?

Atheist readers may consider much of what I have written in this chapter to be hogwash. I admit that, in the end, they may turn out right. Materialism might be true, in which there is no life after the grave. In that case, no one will know who is right or wrong, for in the atheist worldview there will be no consciousness after death, much less any afterlife. But if they are right, the question still lingers: why are horror movies and books so popular in our secular culture? Why all this interest in the supernatural, in angels and demons, in ghosts and zombies and vampires?

I know of no compelling explanation for this from the atheist perspective. But from the theist viewpoint, the reasons are psychologically profound. Our spiritual impulses, when denied and repressed, are displaced and reappear in other guises—which is an appropriate word if we consider how Halloween is the annual celebration of horror.

In a nutshell, we have denied the existence of anything supernatural but can't live with the destructive, evil consequences of materialism. We avoid the frightful consequences of our secularism by enjoying artificial, frightful entertainment. We have tried to bury God, but he has climbed out of the grave and onto our TV and movie screens—in disguise.

Fascinating converts from atheism to theism: Anne Rice

Anne Rice, the bestselling author of *The Vampire Chronicles* and whose many novels have sold almost 100 million copies, was an atheist for most of her adult life. Then, as she wrote in her memoir *Called Out of Darkness: A Spiritual Confession,* "In the moment of surrender, I let go of all the theological or social questions which had kept me from [God] for countless years. I simply let them go. There was the sense, profound and wordless, that if He knew everything I did not have to know everything, and that, in seeking to know everything, I'd been, all of my life, missing the entire point."[10]

Her personal website offers this profession of faith, "After years of pondering and searching, the great gift of faith in our Lord Jesus Christ, our Savior, came back to me on a December afternoon, and I went home to the church of my childhood, becoming a member and supporter of it with my whole soul."[11]

Then, on July 28, 2010, Rice abruptly announced that she had left the Roman Catholic Church, posting this on her Facebook page: "Today I quit being a Christian. I'm out. I remain committed to Christ as always but not to being 'Christian' or to being part of Christianity. It's simply impossible for me to 'belong' to this quarrelsome, hostile, disputatious, and deservedly infamous group. For ten years, I've tried. I've failed. I'm an outsider. My conscience will allow nothing else."

Does this mean Rice is an atheist again? No. In her words, "Certainly I will never go back to being that atheist and that pessimist that I was. I live now in a world that I feel God created, and I feel I live in a world where God witnesses everything that happens...That's a huge change from the atheist I was when I wrote the vampire novels."[12]

CHAPTER 3

MUSIC MOVES MY SOUL LIKE NOTHING ELSE, THEREFORE GOD EXISTS

"Music expresses that which cannot be put into words and cannot remain silent."[1]

VICTOR HUGO (1802–1885)

A delightful event happened with my teenage boys a few years ago: as lovers of music, they discovered that some of the old rock 'n' roll bands were pretty cool, and—shock of all shocks—these were the groups their dad had listened to as a kid. In fact, I still owned the records, buried away in boxes. Could it be that their dad at one time had been—gasp!—cool? This was all the motivation I needed to dig into those boxes and recover my vinyl albums.

So I got out the old LPs and set up my stereo system, complete with my Bang and Olufsen turntable, only to discover that the needle had long ago broken off. Big problem, since Bang and Olufsen no longer makes replacements. Long story short, I was able to find an aftermarket stylus through the miracle of the Internet. Yes! I was back in business.

I then began to notice, during forays to the local thrift stores, the occasional record for sale that was still in great shape. I found some fantastic first-edition albums, like the Jimi Hendrix Experience, Bob Dylan, and a rare Pink Floyd. And so began what has become a compulsion for me, maybe even an addiction. I have a hard time passing thrift stores without wandering in to quickly check out their records. I bought so many during one visit that I felt obliged to hide them from my wife (confession!). Another time, I left a memorial luncheon to slip quickly in and out of the thrift store next door (mea culpa).

I love music, though I am a listener, not a producer. My singing is pitiful, so I keep quiet even in the shower. In college I heard a music professor say that anyone could learn to sing, so I signed up for his course to remedy this malady. Well, let me just say that I am the only student for whom he ever waived the solo requirement in end of the semester vocal recitals. Neither of us wanted to go public with our lack of progress. So when people ask me if I am musical, I usually respond, "Yes, I play the turntable."

Of course, I am not alone in my love of music. Archaeologists claim that music has been part of every human culture since human history began. For instance, a prehistoric Mousterian flute made of a cave-bear bone has been found (purportedly, since archaeologists argue over whether the bone fragment is indeed a flute) in a cave site in Slovenia, estimated to be forty-five thousand to fifty thousand years old.[2] Another flute, made from a swan's wing bone discovered in a cave in Germany, is judged to be about thirty-six thousand years old.[3] And my teens thought my music was old!

Today, music is a huge industry and musical stars are the demigods of our culture. The Beatles played to tearful, ecstatic fans who idolized them, leading John Lennon to infamously declare, "We're more popular now than Jesus."[4] His statement produced an uproar in Bible-belt America, but not in England. In the midsixties, a graffiti artist wrote on a London wall, "Clapton is God," which sent guitarist Eric Clapton's fame into orbit, and American Christians again into fits.

But there was no stopping the music juggernaut. Music stars today are our cultural idols, treated with such a high level of reverence, awe, and worship that even the mythological Zeus would be jealous. Maybe this is why many people think we don't need God in our culture any longer: the need for worship is more than satisfied through the music and celebrity industry. Perhaps this is why William Michael Albert Broad renamed himself Billy Idol and the TV show *American Idol* was so popular. Humans love music so much that they tend to idolize the best musicians.

Why is this so? Why do atheists and theists both love music? We often sit together in concert halls, appreciating the same artists. We buy many of the same albums (or rather download the MP3 files). We appreciate the talents of musicians regardless of their theological or moral positions. As Arturo Toscanini once said about Richard Strauss when Strauss accepted a position from the Nazis to the *Reichsmusikkammer*, the State Music Bureau, "To Strauss the musician I take off my hat; to Strauss the person I put it back on again."[5]

What is there about music that is so special, so comforting and delightful to the soul? What makes Pachelbel's *Canon in D Major* so evocatively lovely, Bach's fugues so intricately beautiful, and Mozart's *Requiem* so moving? Why is music such a huge part of contemporary life and such a transcultural phenomenon? The Beatles were loved in Britain and Boston, from Beijing to Bangkok. Today kids around the world can identify American rock stars in a heartbeat, yet may be clueless of the identity of our senators or vice president.

Take a moment to think of your favorite songs. Why do harmonies please and dissonant notes displease? Why do minor chords sometimes emotionally touch us in ways that major chords do not? Why do some sounds soothe us and others irritate? Why do we call some music good and some bad?

I think part of the answer is that music is *structurally complex* and not random. Some people enjoy the sounds of city life, such as traffic noise (the same people wear T-shirts that say "I love NY"), but these noises pale in comparison to composed music. The avant-garde musician John Cage experimented with musical randomness in the 1950s and 1960s, but his "music" never caught on and was never really considered music by ordinary people. The difference is that Cage's faux music,[6] like traffic sounds, was random, whereas real music is highly ordered.

From a theistic perspective, the structure inherent in music is reflective of the structured, law-abiding universe that was created ex nihilo by a supernatural, law-giving, and orderly God. There is an order to planetary and galactic movement (some scientists call them "the music of the spheres"), and also to microscopic and even subatomic particle behavior. There is order that follows the laws of physics (such as $E=mc^2$), as well as moral order that follows the character of God himself. For theists, we humans love music because God created an ordered universe, and music meets our deeply inborn design that resonates with order and harmony.

A classical music composer on his music and God

No prophet I, no warrior bold
No learned mantle wearing
But as I go my harp I hold
The grace of God declaring.[7]

SERGEI RACHMANINOFF

Yet real music is about much more than just the experience of order, which leads us to the second reason humans love music: it's all about tension and resolution. As Jeremie Begbie put this, "Music lives with a sense of endings. It operates in a kind of permanent sonic future tense, always pushing toward endings."[8] All sorts of tensions ebb and flow in good music, through such devices as meter, rhythm, timbre, volume, and harmonics. As Begbie summarized, "everything depends upon how and when we resolve our tensions."[9]

Wow!—that statement applies not just to music but abundantly to life itself. Thus music is an analogy to life, which also is composed of discordant parts that lead us toward a final resolution. In other words, music is an instrument of hope, a reminder of the resolutions that will come at different stages of our lives and also of a cosmic resolution that will come at the end. We love music so much because music is a patient pedagogue that teaches us to expect the sense of an ending. Of course, this makes sense only within a theistic perspective, for atheism has jettisoned all notions of *teleos*, a purposeful end that human life is aimed toward. The theistic universe, in contrast, is awash with hope plus it possesses a rationale for that hope (more on "hope" can be found in chapter 27).

But there is a third reason also: God seems to really like music!

This is seen in the prominent role music and musical instruments play in the Bible. The first reference to a musician is Jubal, who is only seven generations removed from the first man, Adam. As early as the fourth chapter in Genesis we are informed, "Jubal...was the father of all who play stringed instruments and pipes."[10] So the ancient Hebrews already used both stringed and wind instruments at a very early date, and the rest of the Bible follows suit. Moses gave instructions[11] in the Law for the use of trumpets after the Exodus, and David played his lyre[12] to soothe King Saul (possibly the first case of music therapy). In addition, many instruments[13] are mentioned in the psalms (including trumpets and harps), hymns were sung[14] by the early church, and in heaven a new song will be sung and instruments will be played. In fact, God himself gives instruments to be played in heaven[15] and the song of the redeemed is received with God's approval, since God found them, after singing, to be "blameless."[16] This is why music has flourished in Jewish worship for four thousand years, and why it always has been an integral part of Christian worship.

Let me sum this up: both atheists and theists love music, and the rationale for why humans love music so intensely is quite understandable from within the theistic perspective. However, it remains rather pragmatic within the atheistic position, whose main claim is that music was once a helpful adaptation that aided evolutionary development. Its real value is utilitarian, its real worth in what it produces for humans rather than what it is in itself.

Ask yourself the next time you are profoundly moved by a musical piece: was this an experience of the order I desire to find in nature, or was this an experience in which something, someone, somewhere was speaking to my very soul? Furthermore, when I listen to this music, am I filled with a subconscious hope that, just as this piece was beautifully resolved, so too will my problems and life as a whole have a resonant and peaceful ending? Could it be that all of life—all of existence—is a score written and being performed by our Cosmic Conductor, and we are little—yet important—notes and phrases that contribute our parts to the glorious whole?

For me, music is neither pointless entertainment, a manipulative marketing tool, nor a mere evolutionary vestige; instead, music is a clue to the very heart and meaning of existence. You and I are not insignificant notes in a sea of cacophonic, cosmic noise. That's why I believe that if one loves music deeply, that is a sign that points toward the existence of God rather than away from him.

Explorer Admiral Richard E. Byrd on the experience of harmony

"I paused to listen to the silence. My breath, crystallized as it passed my cheeks, drifted on a breeze gentler than a whisper. The wind vane pointed toward the South Pole...The day was dying the night was being born but with great peace. Here were the imponderable processes and forces of the cosmos, harmonious and soundless. Harmony, that was it! That is what came out of the silence—a gentle rhythm, the strain of a perfect chord, the music of the spheres, perhaps. It was enough to catch that rhythm, momentarily to be myself a part of it. In that instant I could feel no doubt of man's oneness with the universe. The conviction came that that rhythm was too orderly, too harmonious, too perfect to be a product of blind chance that, therefore, there must be purpose in the whole and that man was part of that whole and not an accidental offshoot. It was a feeling that transcended reason; that went to the heart of a man's despair and found it groundless...For those who seek it, there is inexhaustible evidence of an all-pervading intelligence. Man is not alone."[17]

CHAPTER 4

I LOVE BEAUTY AND ART, THEREFORE GOD EXISTS

"Every experience of beauty points to infinity."[1]

HANS URS VON BALTHASAR (1905–1988)

While visiting an art museum a few years ago, I noticed that one wall had a modern, found-art sculpture behind glass, while an adjacent partition had a fire extinguisher behind glass. For the life of me, I couldn't understand why one was considered art and the other was not.

What is art—and why do millions flock to art museums annually, even though many of us don't understand much of what we see? Could there be a correspondence between the sudden rise in museum attendance and the sharp decline in church attendance?[2] Might it be that as we have turned our backs on God, our souls nonetheless crave transcendence, so we unconsciously settle for fleeting moments of sublime awe?

Though atheists and theists might differ about the answers to these questions, we have this in common: we love art and are often carried away by it. I have to confess that even though I'm a Christian, some of my most transcendent moments have occurred in museums rather than churches.

I remember sitting in the Accademia Gallery in Florence, Italy, spellbound by the finished perfection of Michelangelo's *David*, while at the same time feeling psychologically arrested by his roughly unfinished sculptures leading into the gallery, the less famous *Captives*. Likewise, I remember my astonishment the first time I beheld his *Pietà* in person, which only grew when I later entered the Sistine Chapel. (Can you guess who my favorite artist is?) Additionally, I have been privileged to visit many splendid art museums around the world, including the Louvre, the Prado, the Vatican, and the British Museum. No matter which country I visit, there seems to be a universal appreciation of art expressed in statues, paintings, calligraphy, and so on.

But why is art so moving, so evocative? Why do tourists not only visit museums but also buy pieces (mere replicas!) to display in their homes and offices? Why do people from different nations and continents consider the same pieces of art as beautiful? What is it about art that transcends culture?

Here is the central fact, the clue that we are investigating in this chapter: everyone—regardless of theological perspective—loves beauty in its myriad variety and fantastically diverse forms. Is there anyone on planet Earth who hasn't been touched by a beautiful sunrise or sunset, or by a moving piece of music? Is there anyone who doesn't have a favorite food or find some scents pleasant but others odious? We are all aesthetes; it's as if we all have an inborn appetite for beauty that cannot be denied.

But can it be explained? Is beauty merely in the eye of the beholder? Is "good art" a relative matter, a political statement, or a philosophical problem? And why is beauty so hard to define, yet we know it when we see it?

I'm seeing beauty right now as I write, in fact. From our family room window I look out on an exquisite vista: in our yard are several towering heritage oaks, native to northern California, each fifty to sixty feet tall and maybe over a hundred years old. It is difficult for me to describe how majestic, how magnificent, how beautiful these trees are. They take my breath away; I am at a loss for words.

Why are they so beautiful? As I look closely, I realize they are alike yet unique; balanced yet lacking symmetry. Each limb is similar in form but solitary in particulars. In fact, there would be no way to write a computer program that could perfectly draw any of these individual trees, just as no computer program could write a book. No—as every single word must be individually entered for a book to be typeset, so too every single branch, leaf, and piece of bark would have to be painstakingly rendered to produce an accurate drawing or painting of our trees.

Just beyond these trees I see our neighbor's pond, the beavers' home slightly off-center in the pond's middle, the cattails growing in sporadic places near the shore, and three stately trees growing on the far bank. This combination of trees, pond, and animal habitat together are, in my eye, a visual tour de force, a stunningly beautiful sight.

Let's take a moment to focus on just one aspect: the three trees. The trees stand off by themselves, silent sentinels manning their year-round post. They are survivors, like you and me; they have been through tough times and carry the scars of battles fought. Even from hundreds of feet away, at the base of one of the trees I can see where the beavers battled to take it down. I'm very happy they were unsuccessful; the scene just wouldn't be as pretty with two trees as it is with three.

Why is that? Why do landscape designers prefer trees, bushes, and rocks in odd groupings, rather than even? Why do interior designers also prefer sets of threes instead of twos? Is there some platonic reality to art forms, some metaphysical rule that says groups of three are more beautiful than groups of two? Why do sets of three show up in paintings by European masters, in sculptures in Hindu temples in Cambodia, and even in rice-paper Japanese calligraphy? Doesn't this suggest there are some transcultural constants that constitute beauty, or is this just an oddity of nature?

Think about this from the there-is-no-God perspective: if all reality is the result of accidental, purposeless evolution and the senseless march of time and entropy, then what is the experience of beauty? Is it just an electrical-organic moment within our brains and nothing more (which means we are fooling ourselves in art museums)? Or is it merely an evolutionary adaptation that makes us more likely to survive (this is the catch-all into which materialists retreat, their own god-of-the-gaps)? Is art nothing more than a historical record of human tastes? Are we naïve to value some landscapes, some paintings, and some sculptures as truly beautiful? In short, is beauty just an example of relativity, that things have different values to different people?

Are jokes about relativity permitted in a book about God?

"A snail was mugged by two turtles. When the police asked him what happened, he said, "I don't know. It all happened so fast."[3]

Or is our aesthetic intuition hinting at something profoundly important? When we view artwork that moves us with its beauty, maybe our hearts are revealing to us what our minds can't understand on their own. And we haven't even considered other realms of beauty: tactile, olfactory, auditory, gustatory, and even intellectual beauty. Einstein, for instance, believed some mathematical theories were more beautiful than others. Was he right or was he self-deceived?

We've all heard the riddle: if a tree falls in the forest and no one is there to hear it, does it make a sound? The question I would like to pose is this: if a tree grows in a forest and no one is there to see it, is it beautiful? My answer is yes, because the tree did not change form before we rounded the bend and were able to see it. It was and is beautiful in itself; beauty is a quality of the tree, regardless of whether anyone ever sees it (the same can be said of sunsets, ocean vistas, waterfalls, and so on).

This thought experiment suggests that beauty actually exists as a quality of being; it is much more than a mere judgment in the eye of the beholder. Because of this, I believe the transcultural appreciation of art and the human ability to apprehend beauty point to the existence of a supranatural, metaphysical aspect to reality. The existence of art is a clue to the existence of transcendentals, a shaft of glory that ultimately points to the existence of God.

For atheists confined within the materialist worldview, however, it is difficult to explain the existence of beauty and transcultural aesthetic values.[4] This is not to say that atheists cannot deeply appreciate and enjoy art; they certainly can and do.[5] This is also not to suggest that theists appreciate art or enjoy it more than atheists can—in fact, many theists, sadly, appreciate art less because of a false piety that avoids secular art as worldly.

My point is that both believers and nonbelievers have the ability to enjoy art, but only one group has reasons to believe in the actual existence of beauty, whereas the other group sees beauty as an arbitrary judgment imposed on a thing by another thing. This has led in our day to a rejection of art as *an expression of the beautiful,* which, in turn, is why contemporary art is trending toward the bizarre, shocking, and even crude. Divorced from historical values of harmony, balance, and beauty, much of what passes for art today is merely a vehicle for protest, a way to make a political or social statement.

The masters of art knew better. For them, art wasn't merely a medium to get their message across—it was a way to express *beauty.* Whether done with the precision of Leonardo or the bold palette of Van Gogh, whether using light and shadow like Rembrandt or Monet, art proclaims the existence of something called beauty, splendor, and good-form. In Hebrew, the word for "good" is *tov,*[6] which can convey the idea of beauty. God's assessment after each day of creation, "It was good (*tov*)," could also be translated, "God saw that it was *beautiful.*"

Thus, beauty is neither a mere social construct nor merely culture-bound. Instead, beauty is a reality *created by God.* People and objects are beautiful because the Lord "has made everything beautiful in its time."[7] The stars and heavens are beautiful,[8] people are beautiful,[9] and even land can be beautiful.[10] Indeed, all beautiful things are reflections of God who, in his very essence, is beautiful.[11] Every tree in every forest is seen and appreciated—by God.

Try this the next time you are looking at a beautiful sunset, holding a beautiful baby, or listening to a beautiful symphony: try convincing yourself there is nothing intrinsically beautiful there and your perception of beauty is ultimately just a projection of your own preferences. Or God exists. You can't have both. This is why those who love beauty and art may find that their aesthetic intuitions prompt them to lean toward belief in God rather than away.

What a surprise, for art lovers around the world, to discover that God is the ultimate artist and that he has left his mark—his signature, so to speak—in every one of his creations. As painters commonly sign their works in a bottom corner, so too God signed his works—in every brushstroke of beauty.

Two philosophers discuss beauty, materialism, and God

"Beauty is fundamentally useless; it is its own end and its own reward, and it eludes attempts to explain it in utilitarian terms. Materialists often argue that responses to beauty are evolutionarily adaptive, helping to attract mates or improve empathy, and thus increasing the likelihood of passing on one's genes. This is bunk. It is reductive to an extreme, and these explanations don't hold up to the actual experience of great art, music, literature, or natural beauty."[12]

—HOLLY ORDWAY

"Creation [is the] mirror of God's infinite beauty...The beautiful is unquestionably a transcendental orientation of the mind and the will, because the desire it evokes can never be exhausted by any finite object; it is an ultimate value that allows one to make judgments of relative value."[13]

—DAVID BENTLEY HART

CHAPTER 5

SPORTS FANATICS CAN'T HELP THEMSELVES, THEREFORE GOD EXISTS

"I think God was a Packers fan tonight."[1]

AARON RODGERS (1983–)

Sports fans are, well, *fanatics*. They really go overboard in cheering for their favorite team. In fact, they often appear more devoted than religious people. Can you imagine grown men cheering in church after baptisms as they do in stadiums after touchdowns? Or young adults painting letters on their chests to spell their church's name? Why are sports fans so passionate about mere games?

Prime examples of this (in my corner of the world) are Oakland Raiders fans. Maybe it's because their logo resembles the skull and crossbones, but some Raiders fans look as if they are attending a Halloween party rather than a pro football game.

And Raiders fans sometimes get violent. I know this for a fact because of the last Raiders game I attended in 1997. The exciting game ended, much to the dismay of Raiders loyalists, when Kansas City Chiefs quarterback Elvis Grbac threw a thirty-three-yard touchdown pass to Andre Rison with only three seconds remaining for a 28–27 victory. The stands went wild—with anger. I remember seeing several fistfights between opposing fans in the stands, as well as large, metal garbage cans thrown from an upper deck down at Chiefs fans below.

I attended the game with a friend who unwisely had worn a crimson sweatshirt (a San Francisco 49ers color—the arch enemies of Raiders). As he and I tried to exit the stadium and get in line for our bus to the parking lot, several profane slurs and gestures came our way just because of the color of his sweatshirt. I finally said, "John, I would rather walk the streets of Oakland to our car than risk our lives on that bus!"

That was about twenty years ago, but the arenas have become even more dangerous since then. Fans even have severely harmed—or murdered—other fans over trivial team rivalries. In 2003, a Dodgers fan shot and killed a Giants fan, and in 2011 a Giants fan was left with a permanent brain injury after he was attacked by two Dodgers fans, also at Dodger Stadium.

What is it about sports? (And what is it about Dodgers fans?)

Are sporting events just entertainment venues, as evolutionary biologists claim, that offer a source of community and identity? Or maybe sports are leftover vestiges of our warring and hunting behaviors of the past? Thus, for the vast majority of people, are sports simple, harmless pastimes today, and the fans who take matters to violent extremes are just nutcases that can be ignored?

Well, I can't ignore what I saw that evening in Oakland, California, because many, many people let their frustration boil over into violence. What could explain such behavior over a mere game?

Maybe the problem is that sports have never been just games. Historians agree that organized sports originated as *religious* events, competitions that were held either to gain favor from or to influence the gods. In ancient Greece, the first Olympics were organized to honor the gods (especially Zeus), and the athletes competed as a service to the gods, a form of worship.[2] In pre-Columbian North America, natives also participated in religious games. The first Europeans noticed, for instance, the Huron natives of Ontario playing a stick-and-ball game that they dubbed "lacrosse." Like other tribes' games, they "were a ritualized means of pleasing the gods, securing fertility, conjuring rain, prolonging life, expelling demons, and curing illnesses."[3]

Organized sports, then, arose as religious rituals that produced religious results—and still seem to function in modern society as quasi-religious expressions.

Take rituals, for instance, which are at the core of religious experience. The word *religion* may reflect ritualism since *religion* may be derived, etymologically, from "reading again" (in Latin, *re* meant "again," and *legere* meant "to read") and from the Latin for "to bend again" (such as bend down in worship). In other words, religious rituals involve lots of readings and bowing, done over and over again.

I recently observed this at a marriage ceremony performed completely in Latin. The seven ministrants (priests, deacons, and acolytes) performed a complicated choreography of rituals—for an hour and a half!—that made *Dancing with the Stars* look simple. It was major league ritual.

Sports also are replete with various rituals, many of them overtly religious. These including crossing oneself when at bat, gesturing to heaven after a win, or even praying in the end zone after a touchdown. Athletes are also known to be exceptionally superstitious about their rituals both on and off the field, and are cautious to avoid anything that might "jinx" a game.

Some people might discount the rituals of sports, though, as mere window dressings. Rituals are a part of the game but not the heart, just as rituals in religion are not ends in themselves but means toward the end of worshipping and serving God.[4] If that is the case, there are many other, deeper similarities between sports and religions that can be enumerated.[5] Here are a just a few notable ones:

- *The value of teamwork*. Religions encourage the importance of community involvement as well as warn about the dangers of aloofness and selfishness. Sports do the same. We all long to be a part of a team, a family.
- *The development of character*. Character is composed of many qualities that are not innate but are nurtured, usually through hard work, dedication, and under the supervision of seasoned mentors. Coaches serve as mentors in sports; priests and ministers do so in religions.
- *The worship of heroic figures*. Religions teach that reverence is appropriate and that God is to be honored for his superlative qualities. In sports, champions are mistakenly

idolized as bigger-than-life heroes—which is impossible to live up to.

- *An opiate that dulls pain.* As Marx noted (he was correct in noticing this aspect about religion, but incorrect in attributing all religion to this one factor), a religious focus can dull the pain one might experience from the hardships of ordinary, daily life. Sports can also divert attention and thus mitigate discomfort.
- *The need to celebrate.* Could a great tailgate party also be a foretaste of the banquets and feasts to come in heaven?
- *The desire to win.* Life, religions claim, is a contest between good and evil. This is why, even in sports, it's not enough to just play. We all are driven to be winners because, spiritually speaking, eternal life is at stake.
- *The need for redemption.* No one wins all the time.
- *Rules.* The Ten Commandments and other instructions in the Bible give structure and boundaries to people, as sports rules do for players. Just as God created the rules that bind relationships and the laws of physics that govern stars and planets, so too rules are an essential part of sports—and they cannot be negotiated upon or changed during play.
- *The insatiability of hope.* There's always next year—or the next life.

Also notable are the many references in the Bible to sports, especially by the apostle Paul. He talks of the Christian life as "running the race,"[6] struggling against opponents,[7] and undergoing "strict training,"[8] all for the purpose of straining "toward the goal to win the prize"[9] known as "the victor's crown"[10] that will last forever.[11]

Even more, the ineffable aspects of sports may point to something beyond themselves. Could it be that the community experienced in sports, the satisfaction of achievement, the beauty of experiencing excellence, the joy of victory—all these can be seen as preview glimpses of eternal paradise?

Could there be more to our fanatic devotion to sports than meets the materialistic eye? After all, sporting is big business today. *Forbes* magazine pegged the annual revenue of sports as $60.5 billion in 2014—in North America alone[12]—and $145.34 billion globally,[13] so sports mania is clearly a transcultural phenomenon. Most sports fans aren't rich, so why do they spend so much on sporting tickets and team attire, which they wear with pride like high school letter jackets? Who are these people who show such devotion to mere athletic teams?

The answer is that they are *fans*—in the literal sense of the word. *Fan* is a derivative of *fanaticus*, a Latin term referring to one "possessed by a deity" (sometimes etymologies are almost too good to be true). The very word *fan* suggests that God possesses our passions; he has "set eternity into the human heart."[14] Sports may not be a religion, but it certainly is a serviceable substitute for it.

So, in the end, fans really can't help themselves. They are hard-wired to worship, destined to be fans possessed by a loving God and to share eternity with him in the most fantastic place imaginable (Randy Alcorn even suggests there will be sports in heaven[15]). Theologian and Notre Dame football fan Robert Novak writes in *The Joy of Sports*, "Eternity, theologians say, is not extended time but altogether different, a different sphere of being, all-gathered-up simultaneity, presence, now. Those who have experienced contemplation—in prayer, play, the theatre, painting, holding one's own infant in one's arms and, yes, in sports—have already tasted it. We will know, at least, what to look for when we die."[16]

Atheists may balk at this suggestion, and all of this could be ascribed, I suppose, as mere coincidence from within a nontheistic worldview. Or, we can see a clue lurking behind the coincidences, a glimpse of greater glory. Maybe the Greeks, who thought Zeus was watching their Olympian games, were on to something.

Does God watch football games, then? Of course he does, since, if he exists, on a trivial level he watches everything. But does God *like* to watch sports games? I think so. God may not be a Packers fan, as Aaron Rodgers quipped, but as Novak concluded,

God is a sports fan. Certainly He is, if He likes to see humans straining to their utmost to be the best He made them, making moments of unperishable beauty. Sports have to be among His glories. I am often reminded of Him, not least by deeds of excellence and beauty.[17]

A theologian reflects on sports as a clue to something greater

"Life is meant to be lived fully, stretching past the limits of the world to that which is transcendent. Even a culture inclined to sit on the couch yearns for something more, and sports offers that. As a vicarious substitute for the great adventure of life, it becomes something sad. As a prelude, a motivation, a means to that greater realm, sports, like music or art, can raise our eyes beyond the horizon, even as an Alabama running back's eyes are always downfield, focused beyond the goal line. The striving of sports can bring a touch of the sublime, as the Crimson Tide experienced on Monday night, and of suffering, as was the case for the Irish. Both are essential to a complete life."

—RAYMOND J. DE SOUZA[18]

CHAPTER 6

HAPPINESS IS A MORAL RESPONSIBILITY, THEREFORE GOD EXISTS

"'Well,' said Pooh, 'what I like best,' and then he had to stop and think. Because although Eating Honey was a very good thing to do, there was a moment just before you began to eat it which was better than when you were, but he didn't know what it was called."[1]

A.A. MILNE (1886–1918)

A few decades ago when parents were asked, "What do you want for your child's future?" the common answer was, "I want my child to become a person of integrity." However, a monumental shift has occurred recently. Almost all parents now say, "I want my child to be happy."

Surprisingly, we have returned to the position of the Greek philosopher Aristotle who said, "Happiness is the meaning and the purpose of life, the whole aim and end of human existence."[2] For instance, when couples go through divorce, a common rationale is, "I just wasn't happy in our marriage. I have a right to be happy, don't I?" It seems as if the thrilling words of the Declaration of Independence have become our raison d'être:

> We hold these truths to be self-evident, that all men are created equal, that they are endowed by their Creator with certain unalienable Rights, that among these are Life, Liberty and the pursuit of Happiness.[3]

Yet happiness is an elusive goal, and two hundred years of pursuit doesn't seem to have produced a happier culture. As Thoreau famously said, "The mass of men lead lives of quiet desperation."[4] Indeed, it seems as if the more we pursue happiness, the less we seem to reach it. As the "longshoreman philosopher" Eric Hoffer said, "The search for happiness is one of the chief sources of unhappiness."[5] In a similar vein, physicist and author C.P. Snow wrote, "The pursuit of happiness is a most ridiculous phrase; if you pursue happiness you'll never find it."[6]

So can we find happiness—or raise children with that ability? Since both theists and nontheists pursue happiness so passionately, we all have learned similar lessons along the way. At the risk of oversimplifying matters, there seem to be three insights over which there is little dispute—and a fourth of my own that nontheists may disagree with.

First, happiness is a choice. As Abraham Lincoln said, "Most people are about as happy as they make up their minds to be."[7] Attitude makes an enormous difference in the amount of happiness or unhappiness one experiences. Even the choice of one's posture can affect one's level of contentment. Charles Schultz expressed this idea through his comic hero Charlie Brown:

> This is my "depressed stance." When you're depressed, it makes a lot of difference how you stand. The worst thing you can do is straighten up and hold your head high because then you'll start to feel better. If you're going to get any joy out of being depressed, you've got to stand like this.[8]

So if you want to be happy, first make the choice to be happy. Then walk and behave as if you are happy. Though you might not rise to levels of inexpressible joy, your happiness quotient may go up a few notches.

Second, happiness is not found in pleasure, power, or possessions, and neither is it reached through fame or fortune. Think of Howard Hughes at the end of his life: the richest man in the world but also the most miserable and pathetic. The Beatles sang, "Money can't buy love," but also showed by their lives that it can't buy happiness either.

Actually, the reality is worse than "money can't buy happiness." Money can actually destroy happiness. If money could bring happiness, then lottery winners should be mega-happy; in fact, the opposite is usually true. Many lottery winners curse the day of their "fortune," since the aftermath brought nothing but heartache. William "Bud" Post won the Pennsylvania lottery in 1988 but now says, "I wish it never happened. It was totally a nightmare." Post lost all the $16.2 million he won and now lives on his Social Security benefits. Evelyn Adams won the New Jersey lottery *twice* (in 1985 and 1986 for a total of $5.4 million). She later reflected, "Winning the lottery isn't always what it's cracked up to be...Everybody wanted my money. Everybody had their hand out." She also lost it all and now lives in a trailer. Willie Hurt of Lansing, Michigan, won $3.1 million in 1989, which he promptly spent on a divorce and crack cocaine. Two years later he was bankrupt and charged with murder. And the stories go on and on, as lines to buy lottery tickets get longer and longer.

So where do we find happiness, if not in money, fame, or power?

Third, happiness is predominantly a relational experience. Of course there are those who, like Albert Einstein, found happiness in solitude. He said, "A table, a chair, a bowl of fruit and a violin; what else does a man need to be happy?"[9] But even Einstein was married twice and had extramarital affairs, so being alone was obviously not sufficient for him.

For most humans, though, our happiest moments and memories are experienced with, not apart from, others. As Lord Byron said, "To have joy one must share it. Happiness was born a twin."[10] Furthermore, many luminaries have concluded that happiness is a result of a life focused on others. Eleanor Roosevelt said, "Since you get more joy out of giving joy to others, you should put a good deal of thought into the happiness that you are able to give."[11]

But even that is transitory. Happiness is a fleeting experience, here one moment and gone the next. Why is this so? Why do we long for lasting happiness, even though we experience time and again that it doesn't last?

From within a naturalistic framework, there is no reason why humans should be so confoundedly unhappy or why our moments of happiness should be so few and fleeting. Look at our pets: they certainly seem content, even happy as they wag their tails. It would seem that as a more advanced species, along with our superior mental abilities we also would have more advanced levels of contentment. But this is not the case. What is it about humanity that corrodes our contentment?

As Winnie the Pooh intuited (in the quote that began this chapter), even the taste of happiness itself can be a bit of a letdown. There is a sense that the anticipation of the "sweet" is better than the flavor itself. This is why the anticipation of a vacation is often better than the actual trip, and the excitement about having sex can be better than the act.

Pooh, what you were trying to describe is the key to happiness: it is called *longing*, the awareness that an event itself is not as pleasurable as the anticipation of that event. C.S. Lewis labeled this *Sehnsucht*, a German word that signifies a longing for, a craving or intense missing, a deep desire for lasting joy. He wrote:

> [*Sehnsucht*] is...an unsatisfied desire which is itself more desirable than any other satisfaction. I call it Joy, which is here a technical term and must be sharply distinguished both from happiness and from Pleasure. Joy (in my sense) has indeed one characteristic, and one only, in common with them; the fact that anyone who has experienced it will want it again.[12]

For Lewis, occasional experiences of joy-moments were so profound and moving that these became both the theme and the search of his life: he longed not only for more joys and lasting joy, but also for an explanation for his longings.

Lewis found all these when he became a Christian, even titling his autobiography *Surprised by Joy*. He realized that happiness is not just a transitory, chemical interaction in one's brain, but instead is a heavenly reality because it is grounded in the reality of God—for God himself is a God of joy. God's very being is one of unending happiness, and we humans, created in God's image, are designed to share in that unending joy. As the Old Testament summarizes, "The joy of the LORD is your strength."[13]

This ushers in the fourth insight about happiness, which I confess is not held in common between theists and atheists, like the prior three: Happiness is meant to last. Yet this does not occur on the earth because we live as mortals in a contingent world. We want lasting joy, but here can never find it. So our earthly joys are previews, foretastes, of the happiness to come.

There are only two alternatives. Either our longing for lasting happiness is a false longing, or there exists a land toward which we are oriented but only glimpse occasionally. Either our desire for permanent peace and joy is a juvenile fantasy, or it is evidence that we are more than mere material animals. Edgar Allan Poe called this "the desire of the moth for the star. It is no mere appreciation of the Beauty before us, but a wild effort to reach the Beauty above."[14]

Either Pooh was wrong or Pooh was right. For myself, I think Pooh was a pretty good philosopher, much better than many of us who have the degrees yet lack his common sense. Even though I have been disappointed a million times, I still love and keep looking for lasting happiness and joy, which is for me a pretty good reason to believe that God exists.

Fascinating converts from atheism to theism: Dr. John Suppe

John Suppe, professor of geosciences at Princeton, was raised in a church-going home but chose not to be confirmed as a young teen, as he simply puts it, "because I did not believe." Then, while in high school, he read Bertrand Russell's essay "Why I am Not a Christian" and became, in his own words, "for a fleeting moment an atheist, but I soon decided that atheism took as much faith as belief in God. I went off to college as an agnostic. [After that] I had no contact with Christianity."[15]

Years later there was still a gnawing sense of emptiness in Suppe's life, even though he had married, become a tenured professor at Princeton, and described himself as "successful and happy." He likened it to picking peaches: "The delight of aroma and flavor does not last. The peach is as perishable as we are...And so I lived, days adding up to years and years to decades in [a] two-dimensional world...

sensing but not articulating my dissatisfaction with this combination of success, happiness, and an absence of meaning and purpose. My unarticulated problem was that the combination of delight, beauty, and lack of meaning didn't ring true. I hungered for something more to life, and my hunger made me sense that there might be something to eat.

"When I get hungry, I start rattling around the kitchen, looking for something to eat. Similarly, my unarticulated hunger for something more to life eventually caused me to take breaks from work on Sunday mornings to walk across campus to the Princeton University Chapel...watching but not participating...something unidentifiable was satisfying my hunger and kept me coming back. I had no idea whether this stuff was true or false, and I wasn't convinced that the people I met at the chapel knew either.

"One Sunday a chaplain...said something to the effect that, 'You students have made it to the college of your choice, a top university... But you have a kindergarten knowledge of Christianity.'" This rang true in Suppe's own mind and launched the scientist on a research quest, reading book after book about Christianity. "What dawned on me was a possibility...that a loving Creator might want to communicate with a part of creation. My sudden impression was that if this were true, it would be the most important fact of human existence." In time, Suppe learned that God had in fact done so, in Jesus of Nazareth, and he prayed a simple prayer, "Jesus, I don't know if you even exist, but I'll try you out. I'll give you control of my life and you reveal yourself to me." God answered that prayer and, over time, Suppe says of the existence of God, "I have been convinced by experience."[16] That's quite a statement of faith based on evidence, coming as it does from a science professor at Princeton.

CHAPTER 7

SEX CAN BE OUT OF THIS WORLD, THEREFORE GOD EXISTS

"Every man who knocks on the door of a brothel is looking for God."[1]

G.K. CHESTERTON (1874–1936)

The title of the news release caught my attention, especially since I knew from other news stories that Charlie Sheen had been caught in yet another sex scandal:

"Charlie Sheen's Search for God"

The article, written by Father Raymond J. de Souza, suggests the search for sexual fulfillment and intensity may be, at heart, a misdirected spiritual longing. Reflecting on the words of G.K. Chesterton (quoted above), Fr. de Souza quips that if Chesterton is right, then Sheen "has been looking for God with prodigious intensity."[2] He then goes on to note the ironic contrast of the destruction of the man Sheen by the very actions that enliven his onscreen character:

> [Sheen] plays a character who only differs from Sheen's real life in degree, not in kind. It is a peculiar cultural moment that requires a Chesterton to properly express. Sheen has been brought to the brink of destruction by behaviour more or less celebrated by the character he plays on TV. A nation awaits him to return from rehab so that he can better pretend to be the man on camera—who he is trying to stop being in real life. Sheen's show is called *Two and a Half Men*. His urgent task now is to learn in midlife what it means to be a man. Just one will do.[3]

Of course, Sheen is just one example of the many celebrities, movie stars, and politicians who have been caught in sex scandals. We must also add to that list the many Christian leaders who have likewise fallen. And finally, we also must not forget the numerous and inexcusable criminal cases of sexual abuse perpetrated by members of the clergy.

Here is a fact of existence that both theists and atheists can agree upon: our culture—possibly all cultures—is bombarded with sexuality. But we are neither the first nor will we be the last to be so barraged. The earliest and most primitive cultures were filled with sexual icons (thus their idols with pronounced penises, hips, or breasts), and even today our culture is saturated with sexual images and themes. Future archaeologists won't have to look far to conclude that a primary characteristic of our culture was an obsession with sex.

A walk through any mall in America will reveal this, placarded on billboards of barely dressed models in sexually suggestive poses. For the life of me, I can't understand how a poster with an unclad model can successfully sell clothing, which, by its very nature, clads people. But so it is. Sex sells watches, cars, fast food, and, well, almost anything. Or consider TV and movies. Children and teens can now watch in their homes, via the Internet and cable TV channels, sexual content that a few years ago was available only on the seedy side of town in adult theaters (what a misnomer!). We've come a long way, baby—all downhill.

What is it about sex? Why do normally rational, sane, and even smart people do incredibly dumb things when sex is involved (think of a certain U.S. President and his intern, for example). Why are we twenty-first-century humans so sexually driven? And for those who have easy access to sex, why are their sexual appetites so unquenchable?

The very insatiability is, in my opinion, a first step to a possible answer. As Dennis Prager wrote in *Happiness Is a Serious Problem*, both men and women are insatiable when it comes to intimacy.[4] To paraphrase Prager, men are insatiable for sexual intimacy, whereas women are insatiable for emotional intimacy. This insight has helped me tremendously in my marriage. Recently, my wife and I spent a wonderful day together talking, laughing, and sharing from both mind and heart. Later at home, I was tired and ready for sleep, but she wanted to talk again. I thought, *Wow! Her need for emotional intimacy is truly insatiable.*

Perhaps this is why men are more likely to be involved in sexual scandals and women in emotional affairs.

From where does our insatiable need for intimacy come? Evolutionary biologists claim it is merely a leftover vestige of an evolutionary urge toward maximizing the number and quality of one's offspring. While this may explain, from an evolutionary perspective, the origin of the sexual drive, does it even come close to explaining why humans today are so completely dominated by and obsessed with sex (especially when the need to exponentially reproduce is now counterproductive in an overcrowded world)? I think not, in agreement with the Chesterton quote from a century ago that opened this chapter. De Sousa concurs, and quotes Pope Benedict XVI, who in his book *Light of the World*, has this to say about "the terrible scourge of drugs and the sex trade":

> You see, man strives for eternal joy; he would like pleasure in the extreme, would like what is eternal. But when there is no God, it is not granted to him and it cannot be. Then he himself must now create something that is fictitious, a false eternity.[5]

There it is. We humans desire intimacy and love that will endure and last, but instead we find here on earth intimacy that is only temporary and fragmented. Father de Souza explains:

> Man's heart desires that which endures, but when he denies himself enduring things, he turns instead to more intense experiences of passing things. It is a "fictitious, false eternity" but man demands eternity, whether authentic or counterfeit. The heart of man desires true love, something good that will last. If he gives up on that, or hardens his heart against that possibility, he teaches himself to settle for counterfeit love and makes do with superficial things that pass away. Not every man ends up at the brothel door, but every man knows the steps in that direction.[6]

What humans essentially are looking for, in their obsession with sex, is intimacy that will last, a oneness with another that will not disappoint. From an evolutionary viewpoint, there is no reason why our culture has grown more obsessed with sex. It should be the opposite. But from a theistic viewpoint, humans are hardwired for intimacy because we are designed for ultimate and eternal intimacy with God.

As a youngster reading the first Bible given to me, a King James Version, I thought the quaint terminology used to describe sex was to mask a Victorian embarrassment over sexual matters. Soon after Adam and Eve were created, the Bible says, "And Adam knew Eve his wife; and she conceived, and bare Cain."[7] I considered the New International Version a much improved translation: "Adam made love to his wife Eve, and she became pregnant and gave birth to Cain."[8] I later learned, however, that the Hebrew word *yadah* is in fact the general word meaning "to know," which I suppose is the origin of the phrase *carnal knowledge*. In addition, it is also the same word the psalmist used in describing human knowledge of God: "Be still and know that I am God."[9]

Now that I have begun what I fondly call "the back nine of life" (I'm over fifty years old), I see that *know* is actually a profound word sexually. A husband and wife don't merely "have sex." They "make love." And true love, as all lovers grasp, requires an intimacy of knowledge. Over the years, spouses come to know each other intimately in a beautiful balance of physical and emotional familiarity, a delicate dance that produces a deep sense of oneness. This is why sex therapists often claim that the best sex happens after couples are married for thirty or more years, and even that religious couples report higher levels of sexual satisfaction than nonreligious or nonmarried couples.[10]

I think the writer of Genesis recognized something deeply insightful about marital sexuality. Sex in the context of a healthy marriage helps two separate individuals approach the ideal of "oneness" more completely than any other earthly experience. The Genesis author writes, "That is why a man leaves his father and mother and is united to his wife, and they become one flesh."[11] Married couples know this is more than a momentary union of body parts, but a call toward a goal, a *teleos*, that the couple will seek to become in the years ahead. Two distinct persons can, over time in the marital union, achieve a deep sense of oneness. In addition to other avenues, they do this through sex, in which they learn to be "naked and not ashamed."[12] As Ben Witherington explains in a review of Rob Bell's book *Sex God*:

> nakedness of body should only be shared with one whom you share nakedness of soul. Being naked means peeling back the layers and letting down the defenses of body and soul—those two things should be done together, in harmony. If you share your body but not your soul, it's like having and holding and sharing the wineskins but not the wine.[13]

And this oneness is created within humans, as the Bible says, as a reflection of the oneness in God himself, for we are created, male and female, in the very image of God.[14] And there is more. The union of a husband and wife is a picture of the future union between those in heaven and God. This is why, in the Bible, the church is often called the Bride of Christ. Heaven will be the ultimate experience of intimacy, perfect and unmarred by sin, full of joy and eternal.

But there is an intervening problem. According to Christian theology, humans were created and designed for this oneness with one another and with God, but sin has destroyed the ability to achieve this. As a result, we have been "banished from the Garden of Eden"[15] and inhabit a world of desolate aloneness and isolation. All of us are like Cain, "restless wanderers"[16] in an unfriendly world. Here, too, is a place of commonality between theists and atheists. We all feel the sense of existential loneliness, the chasm that we cannot completely bridge even with those we love. Existentialist philosophy basically advises: loneliness is the reality, just deal with it. Yet there is another option. Perhaps we are not intended to be alone and alienated; maybe we were not made to be singular, isolated individuals. Could it be that our very desire for deep passion is evidence of an inborn potential for eternal, passionate, satisfying relationships—and especially one with God?

For the Christian, this is why total intimacy on earth is an approachable but unsatisfiable longing, only to be finally and perfectly satisfied in heaven. Great emotional/physical sex really is, therefore, a little bit of heaven on earth. It is a preview of heaven—not that heaven will be a giant orgy, but that the intimate oneness that spouses can experience in sex is an analogy to the intimate oneness everyone in heaven will feel with their Creator, and as a derivative also with one another. To put it plainly, heaven will be better than sex.

In our sexually supercharged world, this alone might make some people reconsider their philosophical positions and, because they love sex, choose to believe, therefore, that God exists. We love sex, which means we are really going to love ultimate intimacy in heaven.

Fascinating conversions from atheism to theism: Norma McCorvey

Norma McCorvey, aka Jane Roe of the *Roe v. Wade* Supreme Court decision that legalized abortion, found herself divorced, homeless, and pregnant as a twenty-one-year-old in 1969. She met with two young Dallas lawyers, Linda Coffee and Sarah Weddington, who were seeking a young, poor, white woman to represent in order to force the state of Texas to legalize abortion. She signed the one-page affidavit without reading it, met with her lawyers only once again, and never testified or attended any of the court proceedings.

In fact, she never had the abortion (her baby was born and given up for adoption long before the 1973 Supreme Court decision). For the next twenty years McCorvey was involved in promoting abortion and working at abortion clinics—until she was befriended by a little girl whose parents were protesters against a clinic. The seven-year-old girl, Emily Mackey, had almost been aborted herself, and she showered love, hugs, and friendship on McCorvey. As a result of her new friendships with Emily, minister Flip Benham, and other loving Christians, McCorvey abandoned her atheistic stance (which she held from age eleven until forty-eight) and became a Christian.[17] The epitome of the sexual revolution revolted against it—and turned to God.

PART TWO

YEARNINGS FOR A BETTER WORLD

Why is it that we hunger and thirst for a better, more just world?

We humans are innate moralists. Kids on playgrounds yell at one another, "It's not fair!" Teenagers get angry over hurt feelings and grumble, "She shouldn't have said that to me." And adults, well, we're the worst. We say, "Don't force your morals on me!" without realizing that that command expresses a moral position.

Even the rallying cry, "You can't legislate morality," seems oblivious to the fact that all laws reflect some moral position. Take mundane traffic laws. A speed limit in a school zone is a moral judgment that the lives of children are more important than one's right to speed in that time and place. Really, when we think about it, the truth is closer to "You can't legislate anything but morality."

So where did we humans get this deeply felt moral impulse?

Part 2's essays explore various moral impulses, such as the desires to protect the environment and to prevent cruelty to animals. In each case, there is a whisper in the wind, a "sense of the sacred,"[1] as Marilynne Robinson puts it, that hints at a Source behind our innate moral compass (and even a miscalibrated compass, though it no longer points to true north, nonetheless feels a pull in that direction).

When we feel a strong moral impulse to intervene in a situation (especially transculturally), or experience an inner yearning that something just is or isn't right, might these be evidences of God, hints of the supernatural whispering to us from our hearts, trying to inform our heads? It is to this question that Part 2 of our thirty-one-day journey is devoted.

CHAPTER 8

HUMAN TRAFFICKING IS A VILE EVIL THAT MUST BE STOPPED, THEREFORE GOD EXISTS

"The only thing necessary for the triumph of evil is for good men to do nothing."[1]

EDMUND BURKE (1729–1797)

A coffee shop near our town is organized as a nonprofit business so it can give its earnings to help defeat human trafficking. A thrift store nearby does the same. So does a clothing boutique. There is also a safe house in a neighboring town that exists only to serve girls rescued from human trafficking. And here's the kicker: workers in the coffee shop, stores, and safe house are almost all volunteers. People today—especially young adults—so deeply desire to end human trafficking that they volunteer their time to help defeat this appalling moral wrong.

Did I mention that the volunteers are both atheists and theists? Whether believers in God or nonbelievers, we have this in common: we are appalled by acts of evil in our world. No—we are more than appalled. We *hate* evil and those that perpetrate evil. We hate that free Africans were kidnapped, transported, and forced into slavery in the United States, Britain, and elsewhere. We hate that Native Americans were displaced and slowly exterminated. And we hate human trafficking today: little children who are sold into sex slavery in Thailand and Cambodia, and adults who are forced into economic slavery in India and Africa.

Hate is a strong word; it expresses a deep sense of moral outrage.

The same is true with the word *evil.* When an act or person is described as evil, we are saying more than "that person made a poor choice" or "that was a bad decision."

But think about this for a minute: how can we claim some actions are evil and always wrong? As Nobel Prize-winner Anatole France wrote, "Nature, in her indifference, makes no distinction between good and evil."[2] Because of that, how can we say, "I not only dislike what you are doing, but I hate it so much that I will fight you to stop, and I will trump your right of personal freedom to keep you from committing what I see as a heinous crime"?

This is the conundrum: if I demand that others ought not to force their morality on me, then how can I force my morality on someone else, such as a pimp in Las Vegas or a pedophile in Cambodia? Thoughtful people need to ask the question: what are "morals" anyway, and by what right does anyone enforce morals transculturally?

A common answer to this question, from the atheist perspective, is that morals are *cultural* inventions[3] that enable stability within a society. Each society develops its own mores according to its own situation and tastes, but these mores are always *local,* never universal. Since there is no God and all of reality is the result of accidental processes, then there are no universal or timeless moral laws. A specific culture might decide only monogamy is moral, another may approve of polygamy; one may approve of infanticide, another adamantly disapprove it; one is anti-same-sex marriage, another is pro. And the list goes on and on. This results in the prevailing ethic of our day: what's right for me may not be right for you, which is to say that what's moral in one culture may be immoral somewhere else.

However, this is a two-edged sword. If morals are temporary, cultural inventions begat by evolution, then they are binding only within the society in which they evolved. We may impose them on individuals within our society, but we cannot impose them on those in other societies. The cry of the individualist—"You have no right to impose your morality on me!"—applies with even deeper logic to societies. If morals and laws are cultural inventions, nothing more and nothing less, then they *cannot be imposed or enforced transculturally.*

This is the inevitable position of those who claim that morality is just a product of evolution. From the atheist position, morality must be seen like all evolutionary developments, always evolving within specific people groups as cultural facts. Moralities are evolutionary products like traditions: there is no way to judge traditions from one culture to be better than those from another. Therefore, morals carry no transcultural imperative.

But there is a substantial problem here: what then prompts and justifies one culture to step in and condemn a different culture? Who are we to say the sexual slavery of children in Southeast Asia is evil? That the forced immolation of wives upon the death of their husbands in India (a tradition called *seti*) should have been stopped? That slavery in America was evil, as was apartheid in South Africa?

If you agree that these evils were and always are wrong, you may want to rethink the central evidence of this chapter: some morals apply not only to cultures—they even apply universally (even to extraterrestrials, if they exist).[4] There are some actions that are so evil that no culture should be allowed to do them, no matter how separate, isolated, antiquated, or even alien. Some things are just wrong. Period.

This position leads inexorably to the conclusion that some universal moral laws, in fact, do exist. But where do such moral laws come from? Much ink has been spilled recently attempting to explain morality from within an atheistic worldview, but the results, in my opinion, are unsatisfying and insubstantial, like trying to build a house on an unstable foundation. Why is this? Over a century ago, the Russian writer Fyodor Dostoyevsky explained why atheist attempts to explain transcultural morals are bound to fall short: "If there is no God, then everything is permissible."[5]

If you don't believe in God, yet you believe it is moral (even heroic) for Westerners to go into Cambodia or India and rescue little children from sexual slavery, then, in order to be rationally justified, you must explain why your moral laws trump the laws of those in other cultures. This means your moral view must explain the existence of apparently universal moral laws. For nontheists, such explanations are difficult to support. However, the existence of transcultural moral laws are easily explainable within a theistic worldview: they reflect the character of a perfectly moral God, who has created humans in his image.

In short, if you believe something is universally impermissible, then some objective, transcultural source of morality must exist—which sounds a lot like God.[6] Specifically, if you believe that human trafficking is always wrong, I challenge you to consider whether your deep beliefs on this moral issue are best explained from within a theist worldview and not from an atheist one. Our deep intuition that human trafficking is always wrong leans us, I believe, toward belief in God.

Fascinating converts from atheism to theism: William J. Murray

William J. Murray, the son of America's most famous atheist, Madeline Murray O'Hair, was the fourteen-year-old plaintiff of record in the 1963 Supreme Court decision that banned prayer from public schools. After a life made miserable by his abusive mother, the hypocrisies of the atheists and socialists he knew, and by his own self-deceptions, Murray disassociated with American Atheists at thirty years old, and three years later became a Christian. In his memoir he recounts the day he realized God exists: "One day while driving home from work the truth struck me. I thought, There has to be a God because there certainly is a devil. I have met him, talked to him, and touched him. He is the personification of evil. He is Tom Evans, my mother [Madeline Murray O'Hair], and others like them I have known."[7]

The awareness of evil led Murray to the awareness of a real God.

CHAPTER 9

CRUELTY TO ANIMALS IS DETESTABLE, THEREFORE GOD EXISTS

"If you have men who will exclude any of God's creatures from the shelter of compassion and pity, you will have men who will deal likewise with their fellow men."[1]

FRANCIS OF ASSISI (1181–1226)

As a teenager in the early 1970s, I vividly remember watching a TV show about a modern day, real-life Lone Ranger as he bravely rescued the hurting and helpless from the bigger and stronger bad guys. But this Lone Ranger was different from the masked man in the early days of TV: this new hero traveled the seas, rode on boats, and his native language was French. His name was Jacques Cousteau, and he was rescuing whales and other marine life from the corporate villains who were hunting and fishing them to extinction. His adventures burst onto the international scene in the 1978 TV series *The Underwater Odyssey of Commander Cousteau.*

And thus began, in popular media, an immensely successful secular crusade for the ethical treatment of animals. This topic was not even on the social rights agenda fifty years ago (witness that clothing adorned with real animal furs was still popular), yet today this moral position is firmly entrenched as a result of what can be described as a worldwide revolution in how animals are treated.

Ask almost anyone in America or Europe and they will agree that it is morally wrong to treat animals cruelly. Yet few seem to notice that this is remarkably inconsistent with what actually happens to animals in the wild. To put it bluntly, Mother Nature does not treat animals ethically. There are species of spiders, for instance, that immobilize their prey by injecting a poison during the bite, and then proceed to feed on the prey while it is still alive. There are parents that consume their offspring or cannibalize their mates. There are also animals that cause unnecessary suffering to other animals.

While on a photography safari in the Mara Mari Game Preserve in Kenya, my youngest son and I witnessed the annual migration of the wildebeests. At one river crossing, a huge crocodile suddenly rose from the water, grasped a hapless wildebeest in its teeth, and slowly dragged it underwater. Our guide said the crocs bury them alive in the river bottom and return later to eat after the water and nature have tenderized the meat to the croc's satisfaction. Awful. The FDA definitely would not approve of such culinary practices. Yet nature is awful, in the negative sense of the word. As the poet Alfred Lord Tennyson said, nature is "red in tooth and claw."

Yet if there is no God, then humans are mere animals. We may be more advanced in our evolutionary journey, but we are animals nonetheless. So what makes it wrong for our animal species to treat other animal species cruelly, whereas it is not wrong for other species to do so to one another? Plus, will the rules that apply to humans soon be applied to other animals as well (for instance, in Spain "human rights" have recently been extended to apply to great apes[2])? Will human rights eventually be given to crocodiles and wildebeests? Rodents and insects?

Former President Barack Obama discovered the ethical treatment of insects was no joking matter when he swatted an annoying housefly during a 2009 TV interview. Talk show hosts raved about his lightning-fast reflexes, but People for the Ethical Treatment of Animals (PETA) called it an "execution"[3] and called on the president to be more compassionate toward "the least sympathetic animals." Most amazing to me in this whole nonsensical incident was the explanation from PETA: "He isn't the Buddha, he's a human being, and human beings have a long way to go before they think before they act." Huh? What? I certainly hope the president thinks before he acts in other areas of his life and duty. More to the point of this chapter, the PETA comment clearly asserts the moral position that Obama was *wrong* in his fly capital punishment. Believe me, PETI (People for the Ethical Treatment of

Insects) is not far away. Soon many will be unable to state why insects and humans should be treated differently because, from a materialist worldview, both are animals equally worthy of ethical treatment.

It gets even more confusing when we note that what began as a drive for the *ethical* treatment of animals has evolved into the *equal* treatment of animals. If we all are mere animals, then humans are no more worthy of protection and preference than any other species. In the infamous words of serial killer Ted Bundy: "Why is it more wrong to kill a human animal than any other animal?"[4] His statement is chilling, but consistent within a naturalistic worldview.

I remember once hearing the president of PETA interviewed on a radio talk show. Host Dennis Prager asked her a simple moral question, "If you were driving a car down a narrow alley, and a little girl and a dog both jumped suddenly into your path and you could not avoid both, which would you choose to hit?"[5] She refused to answer the question because in her view there is no way to judge that a human girl is more valuable than a dog.

What shall we say about this? I am repulsed by her conclusion, but I respect her consistency. Without God, there is no way to say human life is intrinsically more valuable than animal life. However, most adults—probably even most atheists—would instinctively choose to spare the child's life over the dog's. But why? Is this a case of mere species' prejudice (known as speciesism)? Or do our moral instincts here reveal a deep ethical awareness that human life is, in fact, more valuable than animal or insect life?

That's the gist of the matter: are human life and animal life equal in value? If there is no God, we humans are clearly just members of the animal kingdom and thus ought to be as diligent in protecting every living being's life as we are in protecting our own lives. We all must become vegetarians and must all—unlike our insect-murdering president—protect every insect life as well. No more In-N-Out burgers or Chick-fil-A nuggets. No more flyswatters, insecticide, or termite exterminations. Maybe we shouldn't kill viruses or bacteria that invade our bodies, for within a nontheist worldview don't they also have an equal right to exist?

Warning to animal lovers:
keeping pets is now seen as cruelty to animals

Gary L. Francione and Anna Charlton, professors of law at Rutgers, champion in their book *Animal Rights: The Abolitionist Approach* that pet ownership is immoral. In their view, "A morally just world would have no pets, no aquaria, no zoos. No fields of sheep, no barns of cows. That's true animal rights...Non-human animals have a moral right not to be used exclusively as human resources, irrespective of whether the treatment is 'humane', and even if humans would enjoy desirable consequences if they treated non-humans exclusively as replaceable resources."[6]

But if God exists as theists believe, we are able to affirm both that cruelty to animals is wrong and that human and animal life are not of equal value. This is such an important point that it is stated right on page one of the Bible. In chapter one of Genesis, humans are created along with other animals, but we are different from all other creatures in that we are created "in the image of God."[7]

Plus, the Bible does not condone cruelty to animals. In fact, the ancient Hebrews were one of the first civilizations to possess laws to protect animals from cruelty and abuse. The Jewish Scriptures taught that even animals deserved a Sabbath rest from labor,[8] it was right to care for the needs of animals,[9] and it was wicked to treat them with cruelty.[10]

There are two conclusions we can make.

Option 1: if we believe God does not exist, there is no sufficient basis to judge human life as more valuable than other animal life. Therefore, a little girl is not intrinsically more valuable than a dog, a fish, or an insect. Plus, since we all are animals, no more and no less, is there really any compelling reason to treat animals (or humans) ethically?

Pause and think about this for a moment, especially if you are a secularist who cares about the ethical treatment of animals. *Why* do you care so deeply about this? How can you demand that humans treat animals ethically but not demand the same of all animals? Could it be that your deep concern for the ethical treatment of animals is proof that there are some moral rights and wrongs that are not only transcultural but transspecies? Maybe your instinct against cruelty to animals points to the existence of an objective morality, a moral law that humans neither created nor can change.

Option 2: if we believe God exists, there indeed is a rational source for the judgment that humans are intrinsically more valuable than other animals, while there is also a rationale behind the call to treat animals ethically.

The conclusions of this chapter may be startling for many nontheists, who always have assumed that naturalism and the ethical treatment of animals go hand in hand. They do not. But the ethical treatment of animals (not equal treatment) is perfectly compatible within theism.

Therefore, if we believe human life is more valuable than animal or insect life, and if we also believe that cruelty to animals is wrong, these beliefs may be surprising clues that point to the existence of God.

Did environmental crusader Jacques Cousteau believe in God?

Though not an overtly religious man, Cousteau was a Christian theist who respected other religions, believing they each taught values that supported protecting the environment. In spite of rumors to the contrary, Cousteau did not convert to Islam, and he was buried in a Roman Catholic funeral in 1997. In his posthumously published *The Human, the Orchid, and the Octopus*, Cousteau clearly revealed his belief in theism: "The ideals of the scriptures have remained compelling through a sweep of millennia that buried most other masterpieces. Those ideals clearly include environmental protection… The glory of nature provides evidence that God exists; those who show no respect for nature show no respect for God. 'They are without excuse because when they knew God, they glorified Him not as God,' wrote Saint Paul. 'Professing themselves to be wise, they became fools…For the invisible things of Him from the creation of the world are clearly seen.'"[11]

CHAPTER 10

I'M EMBARRASSED BY THE BAD BEHAVIOR OF BELIEVERS, THEREFORE GOD EXISTS

"Organized Christianity has probably done more to retard the ideals that were its founder's than any other agency in the world."[1]

RICHARD LE GALLIENNE (1866–1947)

On the night of June 7, 1893, a young lawyer was thrown off a train at Pietermaritzburg railway station in South Africa because he refused to remove himself to the third-class compartment. This bona fide, first-class lawyer had been educated in Britain and admitted to the Bar of England and Wales. But the lawyer was from India and though he held a first-class ticket, he was forced by a white Christian porter to leave the whites-only compartment. To this point in his young life, the lawyer had been mild-mannered, timid, and politically disengaged. This blatantly racist event awoke his moral conscience and galvanized him toward a life devoted to ending the injustice of racism. Later he wrote of this event: "My active non-violence began from that date."[2]

The young lawyer's name was Mohandas Karamchand Gandhi, and that singular event not only turned him toward a life dedicated to civil rights, but it also turned him away—understandably—from Christianity.

Unbeknownst to that racist porter in South Africa, Gandhi had studied several world religions while a student in England and had been considering becoming a Christian. He was especially drawn to Jesus and the Sermon on the Mount, which inspired him for the rest of his life. He later recalled,

> The Sermon on the Mount went straight to my heart... the verses, "But I say to you, resist not evil: but whosoever

> strikes you on the right cheek, turn to him the other also. And if any man take away your coat, let him have your cloak as well," delighted me beyond measure.[3]

Gandhi was also very moved by the cross of Christ. During a brief visit at the Vatican, he happened to see a rough crucifix. Gandhi later wrote:

> Chance threw Rome in my way. And I was able to see something of that great and ancient city...and what would not I have given to bow my head before the living image at the Vatican of Christ crucified. It was not without a wrench that I could tear myself away from that scene of living tragedy. I saw there at once that nations like individuals could only be made through the agony of the cross and in no other way. Joy comes not out of infliction of pain on others, but out of pain voluntarily borne by oneself.[4]

As the American missionary Stanley Jones noted about Gandhi's experience, "Never in human history has so much light been shed on the cross as has been shed through this one man—and that man not even a Christian."[5] Gandhi had a deep appreciation for Christ and a deep grasp of the heart of Christianity, yet he refused to become a Christian. Why was that?

To put it bluntly, *the best argument for atheism is the God-awful behavior of believers.*

As Gandhi himself put it, "If it weren't for Christians, I'd be a Christian."[6] Of course, Gandhi isn't the only person who has been put off by the unchristian actions of Christians. Consider the words of these prominent world figures of the past:

> *Celsus* (AD 178): "Christians, needless to say, utterly detest one another; they slander each other constantly with the vilest forms of abuse, and cannot come to any sort of agreement in their teaching. Each sect brands its own, fills the head of its own with deceitful nonsense."[7]

> *Benjamin Franklin*: "I wish [Christianity] were more productive of good works...I mean real good works...not holy

> day keeping, sermon-hearing...or making long prayers, filled with flatteries and compliments despised by wise men, and much less capable of pleasing the Deity."[8]
>
> *Thomas Jefferson*: "I do not find in orthodox Christianity one redeeming feature."[9]
>
> *Napoleon Bonaparte*: "I am surrounded by priests who repeat incessantly that their kingdom is not of this world, and yet they lay their hands on everything they can get."[10]

Personally, my favorite quote about the unattractiveness of Christianity is from British journalist Katherine Whitehorn, who wrote in *The Observer*, "Why do born-again people so often make you wish they'd never been born the first time?"[11]

Are jokes about hypocrisy permitted in a book about God?

Armed robbers burst into a bank, line up customers and staff against the wall, and begin to take their wallets, watches, and jewelry. Two of the bank's accountants are among those waiting to be robbed. The first accountant suddenly thrusts something in the hand of the other. The second accountant whispers, "What is this?" The first accountant whispers back, "I'm a Christian. It's the fifty bucks I owe you."[12]

Of course, those on the atheist side also have their ardent believers whose actions or statements can be embarrassing at times. Christopher Hitchens's crude comments are one example (his biography of Mother Teresa was titled *The Missionary Position*), as are Richard Dawkins's sexist, arrogant, pro-pedophilia, and even cruel comments (to expectant parents of Down syndrome babies: "Abort and try again").[13]

Occasionally, I am tempted to think that I might know the people Whitehorn was complaining about—maybe hypocrites like Jimmy Swaggart or odious zealots like the Westboro Baptist Church leaders. But then it hits me between the eyes—maybe someone else had thought the same about *me*, and was repulsed at how non-Christlike

I was. I admit it. I am so far from Jesus-like that it boggles my mind, and my failures to live up to the standard set by Jesus deeply embarrass me. After all, I'm a pastor, for God's sake. If anyone should be good at this Jesus thing, it's me. I'm even *paid* to be like Jesus. But no matter how hard I try, I can't do it. I fail over and over. The bar is just too high.

That analogy is apt for me because I know a little bit about high bars since I was a pole-vaulter in high school. I had a modicum of success, even qualifying during my senior year for the California state track meet. But I was out of my league there: opening height was just four inches under my personal record. I spent the majority of the meet sitting in the stands, watching the really good vaulters who were skying (that's what we called it) two or three feet above my best.

You might wonder, was I discouraged at their success and my lack thereof? No, I was impressed and challenged. I knew that if I worked hard enough, I too could go that high. But there were limits to my optimism. I knew I would never be able to reach the heights of world-class pole-vaulters—the world record is over twenty feet high! That bar is higher than I can ever imagine achieving, even at my very best.

But Jesus, to persist with my pole-vaulting analogy, set the moral bar even higher for us humans. Speaking analogously, we might suppose that Gandhi cleared the moral equivalent of maybe twenty-two feet. And others? Well, these are only wild guesses, but maybe Nelson Mandela cleared a moral bar twenty-three feet high, Martin Luther King Jr. cleared twenty-four, and Mother Teresa cleared twenty-five? But even these moral champions pale in comparison to Jesus, because to equal him morally would compare to vaulting over a bar one hundred, five hundred, or even a thousand feet high. The bar is impossibly high.[14]

So what should we do: discredit theism as untenable because we can't measure up to Christ? I think not, for three reasons. First, in Jesus we have an admirable model we can strive to emulate, a bar we can shoot toward. In pole-vault practice, sometimes we would set the crossbar absurdly high—maybe four or five feet above our best. Then we would try during a vault to stretch up and touch it with the tips of our toes. Even failing to touch a ridiculously high bar helped us improve our form. Conversely, it would have been a waste to practice over and over without a bar; we would have remained sloppy and chaotic vaulters. In fact, the word *vaulter* would no longer even apply, since there would have been nothing over which we were aiming. So Jesus serves as a model of morality that transcends time and culture. Even the Dalai Lama said that Jesus was a "great, great master…don't even compare me to him."[15]

Second, we shouldn't abandon theism over the failures of Christians because this is exactly what Jesus predicted. Jesus knew that his followers would not clear the bar of perfection; in fact, he predicted his own disciples would abandon and betray him.[16] He knew their failures would open their eyes to their need for him.

Here's the surprise for both theists and nontheists: our embarrassing failures to live up to Jesus' standards can open our eyes today also; they can reveal the existence of moral standards deep in our psyche. The key question is this: if the godless behavior of believers bothers you, why is that the case? If there is no God and thus no universal and timeless moral standards, why should it bother you how other people live their lives, including how they live their lives collectively? In a godless universe, people are free to set their own moral bars wherever they please—or take them completely down if they so choose. Isn't that their business, and isn't it our job to be tolerant and accept their way as an *equally valid* choice?

How others live their lives morally shouldn't bother us—*but it does*, which is the big clue this essay is trying to reveal. The very fact that we are morally bothered is a signpost pointing away from materialism and toward theism.

In this regard, theists and atheists can relate: we both deeply sense that we have failed to live up to proper standards in some area of life. For Bertrand Russell, it was his shortcomings as a father that brought him remorse.[17] For Christopher Hitchens, his lack of willingness to agree to care for his brother Peter's children in the event that Peter and his wife should die left him "uncomfortably unnuttered."[18] Bad behaviors are to be expected on both sides of the aisle, but why behaviors are labeled "bad" can be explained only on one.

So though I am still embarrassed by the bad behavior of believers in God, in no way does this cause me to doubt the existence of God. Instead, it nudges me even more toward theism, since my embarrassment reveals a deep, transcultural moral compass within me.

Fascinating converts from atheism to theism: Alasdair MacIntyre

Alasdair MacIntyre might be called the foremost moral philosopher of the twentieth century. Born in Scotland in 1929, he began teaching at Manchester University in 1951, having embraced Marxism and its concomitant materialist worldview. In time, his attraction to Marxism waned and his adoption of teleological ethics drew him to Thomism (named after the Catholic theologian St. Thomas).

One year after his most influential work was published, *After Virtue* (1981), MacIntyre shocked the philosophical world by his conversion to Catholic Christianity. As Stanley Hauerwas summed up, "He learned that his attempt to provide an account of the human good in social terms was inadequate without a metaphysical grounding. 'It is only because human beings have an end toward which they are directed by reason of their specific nature,' he writes, 'that practices, traditions, and the like are able to function as they do.'"[19]

CHAPTER 11

PROTECTING OUR ENVIRONMENT IS A MORAL ISSUE, THEREFORE GOD EXISTS

"What's the use of a fine house if you haven't got a tolerable planet to put it on?"[1]

HENRY DAVID THOREAU (1817–1862)

In December 1997, Butterfly Hill (née Julia Lorraine Hill) learned that loggers were about to cut down a grove of giant redwood trees in Humboldt County, California. To the logging company, the trees were just commodities to be harvested and sold, much like wheat, salt, or oil. But to Hill, the trees were living beings who deserved to be protected.

At great risk to her own life, Hill climbed one of the trees (named Luna) and began an elevated sit-in to save the tree. Living on a six-by-six-foot platform, she persevered through freezing rain, 40 mph winds, loneliness, and harassment. What began as a weeklong commitment to sit in the tree extended for over two years. After Hill was aloft for an incredible 738 days, the logging company capitulated and agreed to protect all trees within a three-acre area around Luna. Environmentalists celebrated this victory nationwide, Hill became a hero in the green community, and environmental consciousness became further embedded in popular American culture.

Plus, environmentalism is cool today, as can be seen in the benefit rock concerts starring such celebrities as Sting, Elton John, Bruce Springsteen, and Lady Gaga. Actor Robert Redford even equated the importance of environmentalism with national defense: "I think the environment should be put in the category of our national security.

Defense of our resources is just as important as defense abroad. Otherwise what is there to defend?"[2]

Some celebrities get carried away with their activism. Jennifer Aniston claimed to take only three minute showers, including brushing her teeth, in order to conserve water. Sheryl Crow famously suggested a limitation on how much toilet paper one should use: "I propose a limitation be put on how many squares of toilet paper can be used in any one sitting...I think we are an industrious enough people that we can make it work with only one square per restroom visit, except, of course, on those pesky occasions where two to three could be required"[3] (Gasp! Now that's what I call commitment). Being an environmentalist is obviously an in thing to do today.

Let me get more precise: in most people's minds, protecting the environment is not just the in thing to do, it is the *right* thing to do. People consider it morally right to protect natural landscapes, such as the Grand Canyon, the Florida Everglades, and the Alaskan wilderness. And even nonactivists would cringe in horror if one of our giant sequoias (almost three hundred feet tall) were cut down for firewood or if one of our national parks were sold for development. Why this sudden devotion to Mother Nature?

First, protecting our environment is indeed smart because we depend on our earth for sustenance and survival. In the words of the anthropologist Margaret Mead, "We won't have a society if we destroy the environment."[4] Or as John Muir (considered by many to be the father of American environmentalism) said, "God has cared for these trees, saved them from drought, disease, avalanches, and a thousand tempests and floods. But he cannot save them from fools."[5] So there we have it: one is a fool if one is not an environmentalist; it's just the wise thing to do.

But "environmentalism is smart" does not really capture the moral passion and intensity within a portion of the environmentalist movement—*secular environmentalists*—who often carry out their mission with an evangelistic fervor that easily matches that of the TV evangelists they despise; they demonize and condemn their opponents with a judgmentalism that drips with the moral superiority they find offensive in religious folks. Secular people who care deeply about the environment believe their cause is the ethical and just—not merely smart—position.

But this brings us back to the conundrum of ethics within a godless worldview. If God does not exist and therefore all morals are cultural inventions that apply only locally, then who is to say that one environmental position is morally superior to another? How can the governments of the West call on China to reduce greenhouse emissions?

To take this a step further, think about the movie *Avatar*, in which director James Cameron clearly presented a moral argument that transplanetary killing is wrong. In *Avatar*, the killing of the alien mother tree is seen as a morally wrong act because the tree is a *living being*, and as such has a right to existence like any other living being. Here we have the same issue we dealt with in a previous chapter, our concern for animals, carried logically forward. Plant life—even on other worlds—is still life, even if not sentient. Therefore, killing it is morally wrong.

After all, if there is no God, no design, and no divine imperatives, no inherent worth or way to assess value, then how can we humans claim that only animal life is valuable? Who is to say that a human is more important than a tree or a flower? If one claims that plants can be harvested or eaten because their seeds can be used to create new plants, is not the same true with animals—and even humans?

Many people today are vegetarians or vegans based on the moral position that it is wrong to kill animals simply because one needs a food source. But if killing an animal is morally wrong, then why is it not morally wrong to kill a living plant? As someone has said, "I am the earth. You are the earth. The earth is dying. You and I are murderers." If all living entities are equally valuable, then how can one species take the life of another? If plant life is as valuable as human life, then vegetarianism is not enough—we should not be harvesting vegetables for consumption either. How can it be proper for humans to consume a plant for food when it is a living being?

Furthermore, how can we cut down any tree—not just an old-growth tree—and use it for lumber for our homes, paper on which to publish our environmental books, or posters on which to print our

Earth Day banners? If there is no God and all living beings have an equally valid right to existence, then is it moral for an atheist to write on paper, live in a log cabin, or take antibiotics? If all living things have an equally legitimate right to exist, then survival may prove to be difficult, if not impossible, for secular environmentalists.

For theists, though, our environmental sensibility is valid but is not inviolate. All of creation is good because God designed it and declared it to be so. The heavens and the earth are good; the plants and birds and fish are good; animals and humans are good. As my teenagers used to say, "It's all good." But that doesn't entail that it is all of equal worth.

The Bible presents a differentiation of value based on God's own design: human life is intrinsically more valuable than animal life, insect life, and plant life. Though God is the creator of all, humans are instructed to eat from plant life and animal life, with certain restrictions.[6] Humans are also instructed to care for and manage the environment, not abuse it. In the first chapter of Genesis, humans are commanded by God to "rule over"[7] every living thing (which means manage, not dominate), and in the second chapter humans are put in the Garden of Eden to "work it and take care of it."[8] Thus, theists are called to champion environmentalism, just not naturalism.

So from a theistic perspective should we protect and manage our environment? Yes, it is our God-given responsibility and duty to do so. Can we still eat our vegetables without a guilty conscience? Yes, with a thankful heart—to God, not to the vegetables. For theists, both the moral impulse toward environmentalism and the belief that human life is more valuable than animal or plant life are compatible when founded in God's design. But from an atheist position, there is no ultimate rationale behind our desire to protect the environment, and the arguments to do so may drive us to avoid consuming not only animal products but also plant products.

Maybe this will give secular earth-lovers and tree-huggers pause (noble people that they are) and cause them to listen to their hearts. If they deeply hold the position that valuing all living things is the right and moral thing to do, maybe they will grasp that their position makes more sense within a theistic rather than an atheistic worldview. Maybe the deep conviction that ecology is the right thing to do will serve as almost a sensory whiff of God's presence in his world of garden delights.

The Christian faith of the father of environmentalism: John Muir

Activist, naturalist, and author John Muir might be called the father of environmentalism. He was also a lifelong Christian. His father Daniel encouraged him to read the Bible every day, so much so that Muir claims to have eventually memorized the entire New Testament and three-quarters of the Old Testament. Muir loved the glory of God as revealed in both the Bible and in the book of nature.

Though sometimes wrongly characterized as a mystic or even as a Buddhist, Muir remained, to the end of this life, a simple Christian who reveled in creation as the beautiful handiwork of an awesome and personal God. As he wrote to Janet Douglas Moors in February 1887, "Aye, my lassie, it is a blessed thing to go free in the light of this beautiful world, to see God playing upon everything, as a man would play upon an instrument, His fingers upon the lightning and torrent, on every wave of wind and sky, and every living thing, making all together sing and shine in sweet accord, the one love-harmony of the universe."[9]

CHAPTER 12

I DESPISE NEEDLESS VIOLENCE AND CRUELTY, THEREFORE GOD EXISTS

"I do not see why man should not be just as cruel as nature."[1]

ADOLF HITLER (1889–1945)

Atheistic authors such as Christopher Hitchens, Sam Harris, and Richard Dawkins make a big deal—and rightly so—about the atrocities committed under religious banners.[2] They argue that the horrible violence done in the name of God is a good reason to disbelieve in the existence of God.

It may surprise you to hear this, but I agree with them wholeheartedly (or should I say, *brokenheartedly*?).

I vividly remember sitting in my high school English class, sinking lower into my seat, trying somehow to disappear. As we read Arthur Miller's play *The Crucible*,[3] I was aghast and ashamed: aghast at what Christians had done in the name of their religion, and ashamed of being a Christian myself (guilt by association). It was hard for me to fathom that church leaders had treated other human beings so cruelly. I was sure it was an aberration, a hideous exception. But I soon learned the Salem witch trials were just the tip of the iceberg. Our teacher reveled in quickly enumerating other carnage committed by Christians: the Crusades, the Spanish Inquisitions, and slavery in Christian America. His point was crystal clear to our young minds: the needless violence and cruelty done by religious people proves that religions are a sham.

Later, I realized his argument was even stronger because his list was too short by far. I added the genocide of Native Americans in nineteenth-century America, the barbaric treatment of Central American natives by the fifteenth-century Spanish explorers, the Irish wars between Protestants and Catholics. Sadly, the list goes on and on.

When I mention my revulsion for these atrocities to my atheist friends, I find an instant agreement between us. We all abhor what was done in the Crusades and the Inquisitions, and we hate these atrocities at a deep, visceral level. I almost get nauseated when I dwell on the tortures and inhuman treatment that was perpetrated. So here is another place where atheists and theists can stand in agreement, another belief that we have in common.

For many atheists, though, this is more than common ground—it is an argument in favor of atheism. Many times I have heard nonbelievers cite the Crusades, Inquisitions and religious wars as reasons why they choose not to believe in God. At first glance, this seems to be a very persuasive reason to disbelieve.

Sometimes it is stated this way, "More people have been killed because of religion than because of anything else." Conversely, the point is made like this: "The world would be a much more peaceful place without religion." John Lennon certainly believed this, as can be heard in the first three stanzas of his popular song "Imagine."[4] When the song hit the airwaves in 1971, most people thought it was a protest against the Vietnam War. It was easy to imagine that everyone could live in peace if there were no countries and thus no wars. But Lennon's real beef was with religion, which is clear because he mentioned religious beliefs several times in the song, yet never once specifically referred to war.

Lennon believed that if there were no religions there would be less killing and more peace. Sadly, the facts of the last century suggest the opposite is true: there is more killing when religion is absent. Rudolph J. Rummel, professor of political science at the University of Hawaii, has researched extensively what he terms "democide,"[5] which is defined as "genocide and government mass murder." Rummel's conclusion is not just surprising, it is mind-blowing: in the last century, 169,202,000 people were killed by genocide, politicide, and mass murder, excluding the war dead. Of that total, over 107,000,000 were killed by blatantly atheistic regimes, such as the Soviet Union and Communist China. When the secular governments that strongly discouraged the free practice of religion are added, such as Nazi Germany, the total killed by anti-religion regimes in the twentieth century rises to 147,346,000. Incredibly, over 87 percent of those killed in the last one hundred years have been by nonreligious regimes. And these, Professor Rummel stressed, are conservative numbers.

But what about the Crusades, the Inquisitions, and the witch trials? Their numbers widely diverge, based on the assumption that many more deaths occurred than were recorded. Estimates of the deaths caused by the Crusades vary from under 100,000 to almost 9 million, while the Inquisitions and witch trials caused from 60,000 to 100,000 more.[6] So even the worst-case scenario posits less than 10 million deaths caused by this medieval troika of atrocities, and that over a period of over half a millennium. Of course, these numbers represent tremendous tragedies, since even the murder of just one innocent person is a heinous crime. But the total number pales in comparison to the over 141 million persons murdered by atheistic and antireligious governments (not including the other 23 million military war deaths) in the twentieth century alone.

If it bothers you deeply that 6 million Jews were systematically murdered by Hitler's minions (over 46 million Europeans and 13 million others worldwide died as a result of World War II), that Stalin killed over 20 million of his own people (including starving 14.5 million to death, and killing at least 5 million in the Gulag), and that Mao Tse-tung's policies led to the deaths of 40 to 70 million people, you must admit that atheism was a far more dangerous ideology and a vastly more destructive force in the twentieth century than was theism.

Could this be another force that would cause honest people to lean in the direction of theism? I believe so, especially when we factor in that Christian violence is contrary to Jesus' intent, whereas communist violence is integral to Marx's intent.[7]

Why were over 141 million people murdered by state regimes in the twentieth century? The dead cry out for an explanation. Maybe we should listen to someone who witnessed and experienced the worst atrocities firsthand, the Nobel Prize winner Aleksandr Solzhenitsyn (1918–2008):

> Over a half century ago, while I was still a child, I recall hearing a number of old people offer the following explanation for the great disasters that had befallen Russia: "Men have forgotten God; that's why all this has happened." Since then I have spent well-nigh 50 years working on the history of our revolution; in the process I have read hundreds of books, collected hundreds of personal testimonies, and have already contributed eight volumes of my own toward the effort of clearing away the rubble left by that upheaval. But if I were asked today to formulate as concisely as possible the main cause of the ruinous revolution that swallowed up some 60 million of our people, I could not put it more accurately than to repeat: "Men have forgotten God; that's why all this has happened."[8]

Now, some readers might cry foul saying it is unfair to compare numbers from centuries ago to the last century. Here are two responses to this objection:

1. When critics, such as my high school English teacher, rail against murder done in the name of God, it is surprising that they fail to be likewise moved by the vastly greater number of democides committed in their own century by nonreligious people. What is the source of their myopic vision? After all, the number of persons killed in religious genocides in the twentieth century is so low that the comparison is skewed even further against atheism. One estimate is that less than 2 percent of all democide in the twentieth century was due to religion, which of course means that 98 percent was *not* religious in nature. One would think that the atrocities committed in their own lifetimes would register more with them than those committed centuries before.

2. Is it appropriate today to even criticize other cultures that commit democide? As the feminist scholar Catharine MacKinnon has said, "Can postmodernism hold the perpetrators of genocide accountable?"[9] This is indeed a difficult question. Postmodernists, suspicious as they are of meta-narratives, tend to hold that all moral positions are merely social constructs that change due to time, place, and power relations.

If this is the case, then how can one culture pass judgment on another, or people from one century look down morally upon another?

But don't let all the numbers in this essay mislead you. My point is not to develop some calculus in order to prove that nonreligious people kill more people than do religious ones, because such arguments tend to minimize those caused by one's own side and maximize those caused by the other. Simply put, the whole of human history has been a pretty murderous affair. We humans are a deadly lot—regardless of our religion or lack thereof.

Instead, my question is: if all these murders bother you—as they do me—how can we explain this from within our worldviews?

If naturalistic evolution is true, it seems as if the evidence of history shows that fatal violence is as hardwired into humanity as any other observable trait—and it is increasing of late rather than the opposite. Violence looks like an inescapable feature of those who have been shaped by the survival of the fittest. Furthermore, there don't seem to be many reasons to believe that humans will become less violent in the future. So after millions of years of experience with death, democide, and the reality of survivalist human violence, it appears that the longing for peace may only be a utopian dream unsupported by the historical facts of the last several centuries.

From a Christian worldview, however, human violence is sadly but easily explained. We humans are fallen creatures, twisted by sin from our original design and incapable of living peaceful lives based on unselfishness and love. Most of us can't even get along with the spouse of our own choosing (thus divorce) or with those in our own religious communities (thus church splits and the multiplication of denominations). We long for peace and the cessation of conflict, but are unable to achieve this in our personal relationships, much less on a national or global level.

I wonder if John Lennon would have rewritten his lyrics had he been shown the enormous amounts of violence done by both the religion and no-religion crowds? To be sure, it would have involved a massive paradigm shift for Lennon to embrace Christianity. As he famously said in 1966:

> Christianity will go. It will vanish and shrink. I needn't argue with that; I'm right and I will be proved right. We're more popular than Jesus now; I don't know which will go first—rock 'n' roll or Christianity. Jesus was all right but his disciples were thick and ordinary. It's them twisting it that ruins it for me.[10]

Well, what ruins atheism for me is the indisputable evidence of 141 million senseless murders in the last one hundred years. The sheer enormity of the number reveals this is no aberration or exception. We all, atheists and theists alike, have blood on our hands, historically speaking—yet we still long for a world without violence. Our desire for an end to human violence, in spite of our clear tendency toward it, is a reason to believe in the existence of moral truths that are not grounded in experience. Thus, I believe that our abhorrence of human violence is a clear nudge—no, a shove—that might cause caring souls to lean even further toward theism.

CHAPTER 13

I DEEPLY VALUE FREE SPEECH AND SELF-EXPRESSION, THEREFORE GOD EXISTS

"Free speech is the whole thing, the whole ball game. Free speech is life itself."[1]

SALMAN RUSHDIE (1947–)

My kids can hardly fathom it, but I had long hair once.

In the countercultural heydays of the early 1970s, we teenagers thought young men with long, unstyled hair were cool, as were bell-bottom jeans and tie-dyed shirts. In the lingo of the day, the look was "groovy." Today, when I look back at those old photos, we just look goofy. (Warning to young generations: no matter how much you like today's styles, choose moderation. Then, in forty years you will seem only moderately goofy, rather than totally so.)

In retrospect, I can see now that what we really wanted was not fashion but self-expression. We believed strongly in personal rights, especially the rights of free speech and individualism. Of course, in our quest to express our individualism we all looked alike—and the joke today really is on us. This is true for every generation: in trying to be unique, we become trite. (Remember when riding Harley-Davidsons and sporting tattoos were traits of rough bikers? If Harley riders pass you on the freeway today, they are more likely to be retirees than gang members. Tattoos and leathers are no longer symbols of rebellion.)

Do theists and atheists tend to follow the same trends and styles? It appears to me that we do, so this is yet another example of common ground. We both strongly intuit that self-expression is a self-evident human right. This is because self-expression is really just a variation of the right of free speech. This right is so essential that it is protected by the First Amendment of our U.S. Constitution:

> Congress shall make no law respecting an establishment of religion, or prohibiting the free exercise thereof; or abridging the freedom of speech, or of the press; or the right of the people peaceably to assemble, and to petition the Government for a redress of grievances.

But when is free speech a protected right, and when is it a violation of others' rights?

A few years ago, this issue made headlines in the United States as the Supreme Court took up the case of *Snyder v. Phelps*. Albert Snyder is the father of Marine Lance Corporal Mathew A. Snyder, who died of a noncombat-related vehicle accident in Iraq on March 3, 2006 (Matthew was twenty years old at the time of his passing). Albert attempted to bury his son with dignity in a funeral service in Westminster, Maryland, on March 10 of the same year.

Sadly for the family and friends of fallen soldier Snyder, the Westboro Baptist Church from Topeka, Kansas, chose his memorial service as an opportunity to protest the military's "Don't ask, don't tell" rule regarding homosexuality. The few church members held signs reading "God hates fags" and "America is doomed." Albert Snyder later said,

> They turned this funeral into a media circus and they wanted to hurt my family. They wanted their message heard and they didn't care who they stepped over. My son should have been buried with dignity, not with a bunch of clowns outside.[2]

The small Kansas church was formed in 1955, and achieved local notoriety in 1991 when Pastor Fred Phelps led an antigay protest a few blocks from their church property. The negative media attention did more to spread his message than all of his previous efforts combined, and Phelps realized that protests were a constitutionally protected way to raise the visibility of his message. As a result, he began protesting at abortion sites, other church properties, rock concerts, and even football games. The greatest media attention, though, came with the funeral protests. Albert Snyder sued the church for publishing defamatory information and for invasion of privacy, but on March 2, 2011, in an 8-1 decision, the Supreme Court voted against Snyder, stating that even "outrageous" picketing is still protected by the First Amendment.

As a Christian and a pastor, I find Westboro Baptist's strategy and behaviors despicable, appalling, and even evil; the church is an embarrassment to all who call themselves followers of Christ.

Be that as it may, I also support the Supreme Court's decision. As George Washington said, "If the freedom of speech is taken away, then dumb and silent we may be led, like sheep to the slaughter."[3] I also agree with the quote that is often (falsely) attributed to Voltaire: "I disapprove of what you say, but I will defend to the death your right to say it."[4]

For those who cherish and uphold the rights of free speech and freedom of expression, I need to point out these human rights were self-evident only from within a theistic worldview. The members of the Constitutional Congress knew this, as Jefferson clearly expressed:

> We hold these truths to be self-evident, that all men are created equal, that they are endowed by their Creator with certain unalienable Rights, that among these are Life, Liberty and the pursuit of Happiness.[5]

However, within a naturalistic worldview it would seem that the strong have the right to silence the weak should they choose to do so. Indeed, Vladimir Ilyich Lenin certainly believed he had the right to take away freedom of the press and of speech in his communist revolution in Russia. He said, "When one makes a Revolution, one cannot mark time; one must always go forward—or go back. He who now talks about the freedom of the press goes backward, and halts our headlong course toward Socialism."[6]

Atheism showed its true position on the rights to free speech and free press in the Soviet Union: from a materialist perspective (remember that Marxism is based on *dialectical materialism*), there are no such things as natural rights or God-given rights. The only right is the power of the strong to impress its will on the weak; as a result, there is no compelling rationale for universal free speech rights. Thus, today we are left, in our secular public arena that dismisses both theism and communism, with a notion of democracy as a "vague and empty affirmation of equality and individual and collective autonomy."[7]

It is ironic to me that atheists now call themselves "freethinkers," since there is no rationale for an inalienable right to free thinking or expression from within an evolutionary viewpoint. Instead, freedom of thought is merely a contingent value that is maintained because it confers a temporary benefit. But who is to say whether freedom of thought will be valued in the future?

On the other hand, the framers of the U.S. Constitution purposefully embedded the notion of human rights within the framework of theism. The American heritage of human rights came not from the soil of atheistic Enlightenment but from the fertile ground of theistic Christianity. James Madison also knew this: freedom of thought was a God-given birthright, a "natural and absolute right."[8] Think about it: if there are no moral absolutes, then freedom of thought cannot be an absolute right either. And if freedom of thought is not an absolute moral endowment—an example of God's moral law—how can we protect free speech, press, religion, or even self-expression as moral rights?

If you value free speech and thought, and if you believe, along with Washington and Rushdie, that they are absolutely essential to flourishing human life and culture, then you may want to thank God for implanting an intuition within our souls that such freedoms exist. For without God, there is no basis to believe in these liberties.

Of course, to pray and thank God you may first have to accept the conclusion that God exists. I think the two are connected: if you love the rights to free speech and free expression, it is hard to justify those rights without believing that God exists. In addition, if you believe God exists, free speech and other related freedoms are eminently reasonable as God-given and God-based, and never should be taken away from any human being.

Fascinating converts from atheism to theism: Leah Libresco

Leah Libresco, former atheist blogger and writer for the *Huffington Post*, was raised in Long Island by nonbelieving parents. In order to better understand the reasons for belief that she was hearing from Christian friends in college—*so she could defeat them*—Libresco began reading books by C.S. Lewis, G.K. Chesterton, and others. Reading *Mere Christianity* affirmed Libresco's belief in the existence of Moral Law. So she then read atheist Sam Harris's *The Moral Landscape* in search of a way to support morals from within atheism, but found it to be a "total disappointment." Alasdair MacIntyre's *After Virtue*, though, provided just the foundation for ethics she needed, and she was happy that, as she reported to her boyfriend, she had "found a non-Christian writer who could stand for my side. And then my boyfriend told me that MacIntyre later converted to Catholicism, because he didn't think his system worked without it. And I was kinda [upset] at him for letting the [atheist] side down.

"The big question I was worried atheism wasn't going to handle was how I had access to moral law. If eyes respond to light, ears to sound, etc., what is it that conscience responds to? I didn't think the answer was 'nothing in particular' or 'cultural norms, which are themselves arbitrary' or something like that. I'd been a moral realist for a long time, thinking of it as being something like math: transcendent, true, beautiful…[Then] my Lutheran friend told me to stop summarizing the answers I'd discarded and to try to think about what the answer might be…And that's when I blurted out, 'I don't know, I guess Morality just loves me or something.'" A short time later, Libresco converted from atheism to Christianity.[9]

CHAPTER 14

I BELIEVE IN THE JUSTICE OF SEEKING JUSTICE, THEREFORE GOD EXISTS

"I believe the only time when we can call for intervention is when there is an ongoing genocide."[1]

BIANCA JAGGER (1945–)

In the summer of 1977, I traveled to Europe and was invited to tour Auschwitz, the infamous concentration camp located in southern Poland. Though I had been taught about World War II and the atrocities of the Nazi regime, I was completely unprepared for what I was about to see.

Gallery after gallery was filled with pictures of concentration camp victims. Children starved to death as "scientific" experiments. Men and women standing on snow covered ground, their emaciated bodies wearing nothing but paper-thin inmate uniforms. Hundreds and hundreds of skeletally thin, naked corpses grotesquely twisted together in mass graves.

Then we were ushered into the display rooms: large, long rooms filled with the items "saved" from the victims before they were cremated. One room was full of prostheses and crutches, and I couldn't help but envision these helpless human beings, limping and even hopping to the gas chambers after losing their supports. Yet another room was full of eyeglasses, probably the last piece of property owned by each victim, and a smaller room was full of dentures.

One very large room stands out in my mind even forty years later: it was filled with huge mounds of burlap bags, which at first glance seemed to be filled with some sort of stuffing, some of it spilling out the side of the bags. And then the awful truth hit me: the bags contained women's hair, saved for use as padding in beds, cushions, and pillows (imagine the nightmares of hapless consumers, not aware their heads were resting on pillows stuffed with human hair). I became silent and numb, unable to comprehend the enormity of evil I was witnessing.

Soon after, we were led to the crematoriums, huge ovens that burned continuously for about thirty months, consuming in their hellish fires the lives of 1.1 million souls. Our tour guide informed us that before the war ended, nearby townspeople complained about the horrific smell coming from the camp, as well as about the fine ash that settled on their homes and gardens.

Yet nothing was done to stop these machines of mass murder, so powerful was the influence of one man, Adolf Hitler. In one of the most well-educated and scientifically progressive cultures in the twentieth century, one monstrous, immoral, destructive person exploited a whole nation's darker impulses. What he did was so wrong—so utterly, completely, unquestionably evil—that he had to be stopped at all costs. Even Dietrich Bonhoeffer, the celebrated German theologian and pastor, abandoned his pacifistic stance and became involved in a plot to kill Hitler, which resulted in Bonhoeffer's execution in 1945.

What would cause one of the greatest theologians of the twentieth century to discard his deeply held pacifism? Nothing except the overwhelming enormity of evil he faced. Some actions are so clearly and utterly vile that it is impossible to view them as anything else than absolutely wrong. Consequently, they deserve to be stopped by all necessary force available.

After the war ended and the atrocities came to light, the world united in condemnation of Hitler and his evil empire. This alone is a remarkable fact. When in all of human history have people in every nation agreed to this extent about anything, and especially about a moral matter? Most people today, with the exception of a few kooks and neo-Nazis, agree that the treatment of the Jews by Hitler and his minions was *absolutely wrong*. And we could add to our list of agreements that what Stalin did in the Gulags, what Pol Pot did in Cambodia, and what Idi Amin did in Africa were also absolutely wrong.

Here's one of the central questions in this book: if there is no God and there are no moral absolutes, then how can one person say to another, "What you are doing is wrong, so awfully wrong, that I will fight you and even kill you if necessary to get you to stop"? If we are going to fight worldwide for justice, where did we get our notion of justice in the first place?

Atheist and Cambridge scholar C.S. Lewis realized there was a massive problem here. He, like many survivors of World War I, was traumatized by the horrors of war. Moreover, many atheists—including Lewis—disbelieved in the existence of God precisely because there was so much cruelty and evil in the world, which is to say there were so many things wrong. Surprisingly, Lewis came to see this in reverse and realized it revealed a key weakness within his materialistic worldview. The reality of things that were clearly, morally wrong led Lewis to grasp that God indeed must exist. He wrote:

> My argument against God was that the universe seemed so cruel and unjust. But how had I got this idea of *just* and *unjust*? A man does not call a line crooked unless he has some idea of a straight line. What was I comparing this universe with when I called it unjust? If the whole show was bad and senseless from A to Z, so to speak, why did I, who was supposed to be part of the show, find myself in violent reaction against it?
>
> [T]hus in the very act of trying to prove that God did not exist—in other words, that the whole of reality was senseless—I found I was forced to assume that one part of reality—namely my idea of justice—was full of sense. Consequently, atheism turns out to be too simple. If the whole universe has no meaning, we should never have found out that it has no meaning: just as, if there were no light in the universe and therefore no creatures with eyes, we should never know it was dark. *Dark* would be without meaning.[2]

There are two important concepts to grasp here. First, if atheism is true, then we really have no solid basis upon which to trust our own rationality. But we do trust our own rationality, which is another convincing piece of evidence pointing to the conclusion that God exists (I will discuss this further in chapter 20).

Second, if there is no God, how can we be so sure that what Hitler did was wrong? Upon what rational foundation did we condemn the Nazis for what they did in World War II?

The difficulty of our position was illuminated in the war-crimes trial of Adolf Eichmann, which took place in Israel in 1961–1962. In his defense Eichmann said, "Why me? Everybody killed the Jews."[3] As Dennis Prager explained, this was equivalent to Eichmann saying, "You don't understand; in my society, killing Jews was the good and right thing to do."

Furthermore, Eichmann claimed that he was only carrying out orders and thus was not responsible. The court decided otherwise. Eichmann was found guilty of crimes against humanity, was sentenced to death, and was hanged on June 1, 1962. As Simon Wiesenthal wrote in *Justice, Not Vengeance*, "The world now understands the concept of 'desk murderer.' We know that one doesn't need to be fanatical, sadistic, or mentally ill to murder millions; that it is enough to be a loyal follower eager to do one's duty."[4]

So, the Eichmann saga is evidence that one culture can, in fact, decide that what a person in a different culture chose to do was absolutely wrong. Furthermore, it is evidence that transcultural morals exist. Even Bianca Jagger realized that one couldn't be a consistent noninterventionist across cultures (see her quote at the front of this chapter). If Jagger could figure this out, I am confident that others have the capacity to do so as well.

But let us focus here and consider deeply the fact, or shall I say the piece of evidence, that caused C.S. Lewis to begin to abandon his dogmatic atheism.

Both atheists and theists hold that some actions are absolutely wrong and unjust (namely, the actions perpetrated in the Nazi concentration camps). But how can we trust that our sense of justice is right if in fact the whole universe is meaningless, without purpose, and amoral? For Lewis there was only one rational conclusion: our deeply held morals are real. Therefore, not only are there universal natural laws (such as the laws of gravity and thermodynamics), but there are also universal moral laws that proclaim certain actions to be always wrong (such as sexual abuse of children and racial extermination). Otherwise, our deepest beliefs about morality may someday prove to be antiquated and replaced by a new moral scheme.

But no, that is not possible. I cannot conceive of a possible world in which what Hitler did was right or in which the atrocities committed at Auschwitz were not wrong. Some actions are absolutely wrong and will never be right in any possible society.

Thus, I believe our intuitive sense of justice—as well as our visceral hatred of injustice—points to the existence of a transcendent moral law, and therefore a transcendent moral lawgiver. This explains why atheists like Dawkins, Hitchens, and Harris are so vehemently upset at the injustices they perceive have been done by theists. They are *right to be so upset*, and their vehemence reveals a deep, tacit awareness of *justice*: that some things are always terribly wrong. (Alvin Plantinga calls this the *theistic argument from evil.*[5])

This is an enigma for atheists: why do they feel so strongly drawn to the cause of justice, yet also realize that atheism provides very little upon which that belief can be firmly supported? A strong sense of transcultural justice simply makes meager sense in an absolutely atheistic and amoral universe.

In short, the fact that we all identify and vilify evil is strong evidence, it seems to me, that should lean us in the direction of theism.

Fascinating converts from atheism to theism: John Rist

John Rist, professor of classics emeritus at the University of Toronto, is an expert on classic Greek philosophy and is most known for books he has written about Plato, Aristotle, Epicurus, Plotinus, and many other classic philosophers. Though raised in the Anglican Church in Britain, like many of his peers Rist abandoned belief in God during his school years. He wrote, "Humanism was what mattered, and Christianity looked increasingly alien, obscurantist, and hypocritical." Then, during his two years in the military, "religion had virtually disappeared. I was in the habit of saying that Christianity had got only one thing right: the doctrine of original sin."[6]

It was his impulse toward justice that brought Rist back to theism. "It seemed to me that if a sense of and a desire for justice were to be anything more than an indulging of a feeling that I did not like certain kinds of behavior—that there is nothing intrinsically wrong, for example, in anything Hitler had done—then there must exist something like a Platonic Form, for we surely did not merely agree or contract that genocide should be avoided. Yet if there is something like a Platonic Form of Justice, it must, as Plotinus held, exist in a mind—which was assuredly not my (or our) mind...The question facing me was, If there is a Justice which governs [moral issues], where is the Platonic Mind? Ought I perhaps to believe in some sort of God after all? Was it inconsistent not to do so?"[7]

Eventually, the pieces of the theological puzzle fell into place after intense study by Rist on topics such as free will, man's capacity for evil, the reliability of the Bible, and the likelihood of divine revelation. In time, the nonbeliever became "a convinced theist" at about forty years of age.[8]

PART THREE

SHAFTS OF GLORY

Late one night I stepped onto our front porch and looked up at the stars. Since we live in the country, the night sky was undiminished by ambient light from nearby cities and the stars shined with a ferocious intensity—as if they were straining to speak to me.

There was Orion in perfect clarity, his sword dangling from his famous belt and his shoulders tipped at the jaunty angle of a confident gladiator, eternally fearless—telling me that I also had good reasons to be unafraid. Also in the sky appeared the ever-faithful Big Dipper, its bowl pointing unfailingly to the North Star—reminding me, again, that there are some things I can always count on. The night also happened to be during the annual Pleiades meteor showers, which entertained me at the rate of about one meteor per minute—showing that life is a spectacular adventure.

Why do the stars seem to have a story to tell, not only to me today but also to humans even before recorded history? Why does it seem like there is more to the night sky than mere nature? Why do stars seem to be more than mere balls of gas (as the flatulent warthog Pumbaa so hilariously put it in the movie *Lion King*), more than a beautiful yet meaningless light show that plays without ceasing?

To me, the stars shine *shafts of glory* into our world, hints of order within the cosmos that further hint at an Orderer behind it all. Forgive me for sounding redundant, but to me the heavens seem so... *heavenly*.

Carl Sagan, the ardent atheist and science educator, famously said in the opening of the TV series *Cosmos*, "The cosmos is all that is or ever was or ever will be"[1] (which was, certainly, a philosophical rather than scientific statement). Sagan loved the word *cosmos*, whereas he despised the word *creation* because it implied a Creator. Physicist Hugh Ross once recounted to me the story of a fellow physicist who, at a White House meeting of scientists, innocently mentioned the word *creation* in a proposal. Sagan reacted instantly, objecting to the word because of its divine implications.

Yet those of us who have studied Greek know that *cosmos* implies design; in ancient Greek, *kosmos* meant "order" or "arrangement." This is why beauticians are also known as "cosmetologists" : they bring order and pleasing arrangement to women's hair and makeup. I wonder what Sagan would have said if asked, "Doesn't *cosmos* imply an arranger just as much as *creation* implies a creator?" To me it clearly does. The orderliness of our universe is a shaft of glory.

> The heavens declare the glory of God;
> the skies proclaim the work of his hands.
> Day after day they pour forth speech;
> night after night they reveal knowledge.
> They have no speech, they use no words;
> no sound is heard from them.
> Yet their voice goes out into all the earth,
> their words to the ends of the world.[2]

As this ancient song recounts, people have long agreed—throughout the world and understandable in every language (which alone is remarkable)—that God speaks through his creation, and his creation speaks of him. As all ancients knew, nature itself is a signpost that points toward theism rather than atheism. That may sound surprising to those weaned on the secular scientism of our day, but several scientists that we will meet in the following chapters believe it to be true.

Thus, the topics in Part 3 look at scientific matters, as well as science itself. We consider the existence of real things that serve as hard evidence either for or against the existence of God: existence itself, the universe, languages, and mathematics. Plus we investigate the reasons we can trust the scientific method and our own reasoning ability, and we look at the truth about truth. You might call this *science week* in our thirty-one-day journey.

CHAPTER 15

I'M AMAZED AT THE EXISTENCE OF EXISTENCE, THEREFORE GOD EXISTS

"The explanation of one thing is another thing."[1]

BERTRAND RUSSELL (1872–1970)

Martin Heidegger, one of the intellectual giants of the twentieth century, claimed that the fundamental problem of philosophy was "Why does the universe exist?"[2]

Indeed, why is there something rather than nothing? Why does the cosmos exist in all its staggering enormity, complexity, and beauty? This question has occupied the greatest minds in science, philosophy, and religion, including the celebrated mathematician and theoretical physicist Stephen Hawking. He asked, "What is it that breathes fire into the equations and makes a universe for them to describe?...Why does the universe go to all the bother of existing?"[3]

Hawking himself is an incredible man, almost completely paralyzed due to a motor neuron disease, yet his mind remains brilliantly alive and able. Along with his associate Sir Roger Penrose, Hawking is credited with proving the existence of gravitational singularities and Hawking Radiation. But he is not one to just remain in the ivory tower. Due to his belief that science should also be taught to the masses, Hawking became a bestselling author in 1988 with the publication of *A Brief History of Time*, which has sold over ten million copies worldwide. In that book, Hawking concludes:

> However, if we discover a complete theory, it should in time be understandable by everyone, not just by a few

> scientists. Then we shall all, philosophers, scientists and just ordinary people, be able to take part in the discussion of the question of why it is that we and the universe exist. If we find the answer to that, it would be the ultimate triumph of human reason—for then we should know the mind of God.[4]

Another famous Hawking reference to God is his disagreement with Einstein: "So Einstein was wrong when he said, 'God does not play dice.' Consideration of black holes suggests, not only that God does play dice, but that he sometimes confuses us by throwing them where they can't be seen."[5] (From a 1994 debate with Penrose at Cambridge.) He also once said, "The whole history of science has been the gradual realization that events do not happen in an arbitrary manner, but that they reflect a certain underlying order, which may or may not be divinely inspired."[6]

Although Hawking uses language that suggests he believes in God, such is not the case. In his recent book, *The Grand Design*, coauthored with Cal Tech physicist Leonard Mlodinow, Hawking claimed there is no need for God in the creation of the universe:

> As recent advances in cosmology suggest, the laws of gravity and quantum theory allow universes to appear spontaneously from nothing. Spontaneous creation is the reason there is something rather than nothing, why the universe exists, why we exist. It is not necessary to invoke God to light the blue touch paper and set the universe going.[7]

As one might expect, this set off a frenzy of positive reviews and comments from those who lean away from theism. For instance, the title of a 2010 *Wall Street Journal* review captured the over-the-top enthusiasm of atheists for Hawking's new theory: "Why God Did Not Create the Universe: There is a sound scientific explanation for the making of our world—no gods required."[8] The *London Times* was even more succinct, one day earlier, in the title of its page-one article: "Hawking: God Did Not Create Universe."[9] As one can see, these journalists not only departed from Hawking's speculation that God was "not necessary" for creation, but they also arrived at the negative fact-like pronouncement "God did *not* create" the universe (italics added). This is an unwarranted conclusion. After all, there is quite a difference between claiming that it was not necessary for me to write this book and the claim that I did not write it.

Rather than jump to such unwarranted conclusions, let's return to Hawking and ask: what does he base this conclusion upon? The key word in the quotation from *The Grand Design* is "universes." Yes, one little *s* makes all the difference. You see, Hawking's bold claim is based on the multiverse theory (M-theory): that our universe is only one of untold billions or trillions or whatever-illions of universes that exist. Until recently, scientists believed we inhabited one universe, made up of hundreds of billions of galaxies, which in turn were comprised of hundreds of billions of stars and solar systems, of which ours is just one. But now there is speculation that the universe itself is just one of many.

M-theory was first proposed in 1995 by the physicist Edward Witten as an attempt to unify what were then the five competing string theories into one coherent whole. The result, Hawking explains, is the conclusion that reality may be comprised of eleven dimensions of space-time, which each contains strings and branes (originally called membranes), and are compacted into the four space-time dimensions we observe.

What are common folk to make of this proposal, since most of us lack the mathematics and theoretical physics expertise to even understand the equations? A helpful perspective is to consider how one notable expert in Hawking's own field critiques this model.

The expert is Hawking's research partner, the aforementioned Penrose. In an interview after *The Grand Design* was published, Penrose called Hawking's theory of the universe "hardly science" and "not even a theory." Penrose explained, "It's not an uncommon thing in popular descriptions of science to latch onto an idea, particularly things to do with string theory, which have absolutely no support from observation. They are just nice ideas." In Penrose's opinion, string theories are "very far from any testability. They are hardly science." Concerning M-theory, Penrose said: "It's a collection of ideas, hopes, aspirations.

The book is a bit misleading. It gives you this impression of a theory that is going to explain everything; it's nothing of the sort. It's not even a theory."[10]

Strangely, this is just the sort of thing that atheists commonly attack theists for: holding to beliefs that are neither testable nor based on observations. To date there is not one shred of evidence—much less significant evidence—upon which the multiverse claim is based. None. Nada. Zip. So why do nonbelieving scientists not only welcome this theory but also fervently herald it from the rooftops? The answer is the apparent fine-tuning of the universe, which will be the subject of the next chapter. In essence, the universe is so fine-tuned for life that it appears to be *designed.*

Well, such a conclusion is anathema to materialists because it strongly suggests the existence of a designer. The odds are just too astronomically low for our universe to have just happened accidentally, which entails the probabilistic conclusion that it was created. To counter this, materialists suggest that our universe is only one of a huge number of universes, which would allow enough chances for our universe eventually to pop into being.

Hawking and other theoretical physicists have attached themselves to this purely theoretical notion of a multiverse in order to claim there is no need for a divine designer. However, this merely backs up the issue to a set of prior questions: how and why did the multiverse come into existence? If there is no need for a creator of our universe because such an entity (our universe) was bound to emerge given the laws of physics and the enormity of the multiverse, then how did a multiverse arise?

Hawking's multiverse solution to the problem of existence is based on his belief, quoted above, that "the laws of gravity and quantum theory allow universes to appear spontaneously." Above all, Hawking believes in the existence of the laws of physics. But this belief is contrary to materialism. Setting aside the important question whether pure laws could ever bring matter into existence, we can simply ask whether it is acceptable to claim the laws of science exist undetermined and yet themselves "determine" everything else? As naturalist philosopher

Milton K. Munitz explained in *The Mystery of Existence*, "We could not obtain an explanation for the existence of the world by including that which is to serve as the explanation, as part of that which is to be explained."[11] Or as Descartes put this over three hundred years ago, "*ex nihilo nihil fit*" (nothing comes from nothing).[12]

Bottom line, we must ask the question, *contra* Hawking: does it make any more sense to claim the laws of physics have always existed than it does to claim God exists? Interestingly, other scientists think not.

For instance, Vera Kistiakowsky, MIT physicist and past president of the Association of Women in Science, has written: "The exquisite order displayed by our scientific understanding of the physical world calls for the divine."[13] Or to again quote the avowedly humanist, non-religious Penrose: "I would say the universe has a purpose. It's not there just somehow by chance."[14]

So the answer to the question, "Why is there something rather than nothing?" seems to point toward a *source* for both the existence of the universe and the laws displayed therein. For me, the universe's existence is an awe-inspiring reality, as are the existence of the laws of science. Yet neither of these seems to be an adequate cause for existence of all matter, nor do they seem to be capable of self-causation. Rather than posit farfetched ideas such as contingent multiverses, it seems less of a stretch to posit a noncontingent Being who created all this beauty and wonder. Thus, I believe the existence of the universe and its laws lean us toward the belief that God exists.

Two philosophers discuss the existence of God

"We cannot be more certain of the existence of anything, than the existence of a being absolutely infinite or perfect—that is, of God."[15]

—BENEDICT DE SPINOZA

"God does not 'exist' in the sense that some finite object like a tree, an individual mind, or perhaps a god exists, but is himself the very power of unconditioned being from and in which anything that does exist has its dependent and imparted being...To think of God in our categories of existence 'would be to reduce God to the level of the finite'...God, in short, is not a being but is at once 'beyond being' (in the sense that he transcends the totality of existing things) and also absolute 'Being itself' (in the sense that he is the source and ground of all things)."[16]

—DAVID BENTLEY HART

CHAPTER 16

I'M STAGGERED BY THE GLORY OF OUR UNIVERSE, THEREFORE GOD EXISTS

"There is for me powerful evidence that there is something going on behind it all...it seems as though somebody has fine-tuned nature's numbers to make the Universe...The impression of design is overwhelming."[1]

PAUL DAVIES (1946–)

Paul Davies, a physicist and prolific author of popular science books, aims at explaining astrophysics to the masses. His scientific research originally focused primarily on quantum field theory in curved space-time, but he seems to have a particular interest in the philosophical and even theological implications of cutting-edge science. This can be seen in several of his book titles, such as *God and the New Physics* (1983), *The Cosmic Blueprint* (1987), and *The Goldilocks Enigma* (2007). In *The Mind of God* (1992) Davies made two sweeping conclusions: there is something special about the universe and there is something special about us. He even concluded the book with the sentence, "We are truly meant to be here."[2]

What would lead the nonreligious Davies to make such an astonishing statement? Just this: scientists have discovered that the universe is remarkably fine-tuned. The very laws of physics and biology seem tailor-made to enable material reality as we know it and even human life to exist. Scientists have been able to accurately measure over a dozen constants (such as the electromagnetic force constant, the gravitational constant, and the speed of light) and dozens of other parameters (such as the ratio of electron to proton mass and the mass density of the universe), and have concluded their values must fall within exceedingly constricted limits. One scientist lists over ninety such constants and parameters.[3] Geneticist Francis Collins wrote in his book *The Language of God*:

> When you look from the perspective of a scientist at the universe, it looks as if it knew we were coming. There are 15 constants...that have precise values. If any one of those constants was off by even one part in a million, or in some cases, by one part in a million million, the universe could not have actually come to the point where we see it. Matter would not have been able to coalesce, there would have been no galaxy, stars, planets or people.[4]

The incredible odds against just one such parameter—the ratio of protons to electrons—are an accuracy rate of 1 part in 10^{37}, according to astrophysicist Hugh Ross.[5] Such a small number is hard to grasp except by analogy, thus Ross suggests we imagine the earth covered with dimes to a height of 239,000 miles (the distance to the moon!). The odds of a blindfolded person choosing the one dime that was painted red and randomly mixed in with the others are 1 in 10^{37}. In addition, the ratio of the electromagnetic force[6] relative to gravity is precise to 1 part in 10^{40}, the cosmological constant is precise[7] to 1 part in 10^{53}, and the accuracy of the original phase-space volume as 1 part in 10 billion multiplied by itself 123 times. Roger Penrose remarked that it would be impossible to even write down that number in full since it would require more zeroes than the number of elementary particles in the entire universe.[8]

Leading scientists agree—the apparent fine-tuning of the universe is compelling evidence that points to the existence of a supernatural designer, capable of creating the universe with both grandeur and specificity. Arno Penzias, a Nobel Prize winner in physics, wrote:

> Astronomy leads us to a unique event, a universe which was created out of nothing, one with the very delicate balance needed to provide exactly the conditions required to permit life, and one which has an underlying (one might say 'supernatural') plan.[9]

Edward Harrison, who was a cosmologist and fellow of both the Royal Astronomical Society and the American Physical Society, said:

> Here is the cosmological proof of the existence of God—the design argument of Paley—updated and refurbished. The fine tuning of the universe provides prima facie evidence of deistic design. Take your choice: blind chance that requires multitudes of universes or design that requires only one...Many scientists, when they admit their views, incline toward the teleological or design argument.[10]

George Greenstein, Dillon Professor of Astronomy at Amherst, wrote:

> As we survey all the evidence, the thought insistently arises that some supernatural agency—or rather, Agency—must be involved. Is it possible that suddenly, without intending to, we have stumbled upon scientific proof of the existence of a supreme being? Was it God who stepped in and so providentially crafted the universe for our benefit?[11]

The most humorous explanation, though, came from astrophysicist and self-described agnostic Robert Jastrow, the founding director of NASA's Goddard Institute for Space Studies from 1961 to 1981:

> For the scientist who has lived by his faith in the power of reason, the story ends like a bad dream. He has scaled the mountains of ignorance; he is about to conquer the highest peak; as he pulls himself over the final rock, he is greeted by a band of theologians who have been sitting there for centuries.[12]

So it seems clear to many scientists that the precise fine-tuning of the universe, so precise that it boggles the imagination, implies the existence of a fine-tuner, which is another word for God. Robert Griffiths, winner of the Heinemann prize in mathematical physics, quipped, "If we need an atheist for a debate, I go to the philosophy department. The physics department isn't much use."[13]

However, not every scientist agrees with this conclusion. Astrophysicists John Barrow and Frank Tipler illustrate, in their book *The*

Anthropic Cosmological Principle[14] (which is a fancy name for the fine-tuning problem), how farfetched some attempts are to explain away the necessity of a fine-tuner. They suggest that rather than holding to a version of WAP (weak anthropic principle), SAP (strong anthropic principle), or even PAP (participatory anthropic principle), they favor FAP (final anthropic principle), which suggests evolution will continue until the universe reaches the Omega Point and will acquire the properties of omnipotence, omnipresence, and omniscience, and thus the ability to create in the past. Thus, the universe is slowly evolving into God,[15] who will then go back in time to create the universe that will in turn create him. My favorite response to this argument is from the science critic Martin Gardner:

> What should we make of this quartet of WAP, SAP, PAP, and FAP? In my not so humble opinion I think the last principle is best called CRAP, the Completely Ridiculous Anthropic Principle.[16]

Really now, does anyone seriously believe that a naturally produced entity or being could reach back in time and create the very matter and laws governing matter that would in time create that entity/being? This appears to be a recursive problem to the extreme—and an example of the lengths to which materialists will go to keep an uncaused Cause out of the picture.

Yet even Paul Davies, the author with whom we began this chapter, is now inclining toward a back-in-time scenario. As a committed naturalist, he is averse to accept the conclusion that a God, outside space and time, created the laws of science. Thus, he is now pursuing the idea that because quantum particles are not bound by time, they might reach back to the very beginning of the universe and influence the development of the laws of physics. In this way, the universe might have created its own laws,[17] recursively in time.

But I must ask, what takes more faith—to believe in the existence of a supernatural designer or to believe that unintelligent, undirected quantum particles might be able to somehow traverse time and influence the development of the very laws that govern their behavior, and that these laws somehow could be retroactively fine-tuned to such an infinitesimal degree? Surely Ockham's razor[18] would tip us toward the former rather than the latter, if one is not predisposed against theism.

As for me, the extreme fine-tuning of the universe is a fact that cannot be wished away by quantum science wish fulfillment. If we instead base our inductive conclusions on the science of probability as well as upon Ockham's razor, it seems to me the fine-tuning of the universe would lean us away from the existence of multiverses—which *no one* claims to have *ever* experienced—and toward the existence of God, which millions of humans for thousands of years have claimed to have experienced.

Fascinating converts from atheism to theism: Richard Smalley

Known worldwide as the "Father of Nanotechnology," Richard Smalley was also the Nobel Prize winner in chemistry (1996) and was called by *Time* magazine a "rock star" in technology for his many breakthroughs in nanotechnology research. He was reared as a Darwinist by his mother and remained a religious skeptic for most of his life. However, just a few years before cancer took his life at age sixty-three, Smalley became first a theist and then later a committed Christian. In his words, "Recently I have gone back to church regularly with a new focus to understand as best I can what it is that makes Christianity so vital and powerful in the lives of billions of people today...Although I suspect I will never fully understand, I now think the answer is very simple: *it's true.* God did create the universe about 13.7 billion years ago, and of necessity has involved himself with his creation ever since. The purpose of this universe is something that only God can know for sure, but it is increasingly clear to modern science that the universe was exquisitely fine-tuned to enable human life...The burden of proof is on those who don't believe that 'Genesis' was right, and there was a creation, and that the Creator is still involved."[19]

CHAPTER 17

THE MARVEL OF LANGUAGE CAN'T BE PUT INTO WORDS, THEREFORE GOD EXISTS

"Knowledge is power. Information is liberating."[1]

KOFI ANNAN (1938–)

Have you ever heard of the Navajo Code Talkers? These World War II heroes were movingly depicted in the 2002 film *Windtalkers,*[2] starring Nicholas Cage and Christian Slater. Cage and Slater played Marine sergeants who were tasked with protecting two Navajo soldiers, eventually (spoiler warning!) sacrificing their lives in the process. Though the storyline is fictional, the Navajo Code Talkers are a factual piece of history.

Code Talkers were bilingual soldiers who were able to send radio messages that were *undecipherable* by the enemy. Native American languages are highly complex, with difficult syntax and tonal aspects, so much so that even speakers of close dialects cannot understand each other. The first Code Talkers, in World War I, were Cherokee and Choctaw. In World War II, Code Talkers included Comanche, Meskwaki, Basque, and Navajo speakers. Adolf Hitler knew of the use of Code Talkers in World War I and even sent a team of linguists to learn Native American languages before the beginning of World War II. However, the languages proved too difficult and diverse to master, so that effort was abandoned.

In 1942, World War I veteran Phillip Johnston, who was raised by missionary parents on a Navajo reservation, suggested to military officials that Navajo was an excellent language to serve as a code. The military then recruited twenty-nine Navajos who served in the Pacific theater. They developed code words in Navajo to specify military items, such as *tortoise* to signify a tank, *potato* a hand-grenade, and *ink-sticks* as pens (some of these terms are still used in military slang today). The Navajo Code Talkers were highly efficient and error-free in their messaging. After the battle for Iwo Jima, Major Howard Connor stated, "Were it not for the Navajos, the Marines would never have taken Iwo Jima."[3]

The Code Talkers were successful because languages cannot be deciphered, only taught. Therefore, Navajo served as an excellent code because languages convey information in highly structured, specific, and complex ways—which can never be created by algorithms or computer programs. Random, infinite processes can never produce significant information.

Another example of this is the book you are reading. Books are great examples of *specified complexity*[4] and, I admit, sort of an addiction for me. (I relate with Erasmus's wry confession: "When I get a little money I buy books; if any is left I buy food and clothes.") There simply is no way that a computer could be programmed to write a book; instead, every word, space, and punctuation mark has to be painstakingly rendered by an autonomous author. And though we may disagree vehemently with the political or philosophical positions of an author, we nonetheless immediately grasp that the book was crafted by a person, not cranked out by a machine. In a similar manner, a painting or a musical score is full of highly complex, specific information that no computer could ever reproduce except as a result of line-for-line or pixel-by-pixel instructions. As Isaac Newton, the early eighteenth-century pioneer of modern science said, "Blind metaphysical necessity, which is certainly the same always and everywhere, could produce no variety of things."[5]

Yet this is just what naturalism requires: blind necessity to produce everything. So how do today's naturalists get around Newton's statement when it comes to the existence of information? The solution is time—tons of time—and the maxim that given enough time, anything can happen.

This maxim is often expressed, tongue in cheek, as the "infinite monkey theorem," which proposes that an infinite number of monkeys, given an infinite number of typewriters and years, could produce the works of Shakespeare. In popular culture, these fictitious monkeys even appeared in an episode of *The Simpsons* in which Homer was shown a room filled with a thousand monkeys and typewriters and was told, "Soon they will have written the greatest novel known to man!"

The infinite monkey theorem is usually attributed to Thomas Huxley, a nineteenth-century early adapter of Darwin's theory of evolution, and it is sometimes used to illustrate the mathematics of chance. However, a real-life experiment with monkeys, well, threw their proverbial wrench into the theorem. Researchers at Plymouth University in England put a working computer into an enclosure with six monkeys—Sulawesi crested macaques, to be exact—for one month. The result: Researchers concluded that when the monkeys did touch the keyboard, their literary output was far from random. In one month the monkeys pushed the S key most often and *A*, *J*, *L*, and *M* only occasionally. In fact, the monkeys rarely "typed" at all; when interested in the computer they mostly beat it with stones and, *ahem*, used it as a toilet. The monkeys created no random words during the experiment.[6]

Of course, Huxley's theorem probably never envisioned real monkeys; they were only symbols for what we might call perfectly random typing machines. Thus, today's computer experts have attempted to replicate the intention of the monkey theorem virtually. One example of apparent success was trumpeted in a CNN headline, "Digital Monkeys with Typewriters Recreate Shakespeare."

"This is the first time a work of Shakespeare has actually been randomly reproduced," software engineer Jesse Anderson said. "Furthermore, this is the largest work ever randomly reproduced. It is one small step for a monkey, one giant leap for virtual primates everywhere." However, a closer reading of the article reveals fatal flaws in this virtual attempt to illustrate Huxley's theorem. The CNN article explained that Anderson programed the software to recognize "when a chunk of text matches a word used in Shakespeare's catalogue," and then further instructed it to "cross off" that word from a database of Shakespeare's plays and poems. Then, as all the words in a specific play or poem were located, that work was considered to be "completed."[7]

Surely this is virtual cheating on multiple levels: First, no book is considered a complete replica unless all its words are assembled in the exact order in which they were originally written (otherwise, a dictionary would also be a completed volume of Hamlet). Second, how would nature know to cross off certain sets of letters as words, much less significant words? Third, and most crucially, the experiment succeeded only because Anderson preprogrammed the database of Shakespearian works, which is surely adding a huge informational element that naturalism disallows.

This may come as a surprise to many nontheists who have bought, hook, line, and sinker the notion that given enough time anything will happen, but the maxim—when used as an example of how information could have been randomly developed on planet earth—is false. This is because the infinite monkey theorem works only with an infinite number of monkeys or an infinite amount of time, which in any real world are impossibilities. Since the odds against randomly typing the text of the Bard's *Hamlet* has been calculated as $4.4 \times 10^{360,783}$ (a number far greater than the number of protons in the universe), the likelihood that significant amounts of information—such as that contained in human DNA—were generated during the formation of life on earth is nil.[8] The error in thinking is that given the elapsed time in our universe, every highly unlikely event could have occurred as it may in an infinite time scenario. This may seem plausible to science fiction enthusiasts, but it is not true in real life or real physics in which only finite amounts of time and monkeys (real or virtual) can exist.

So if information cannot finitely be produced randomly or programmatically, what exactly is information? This is the crux of the issue. Information is not a material thing. Information is a meaningful pattern conveyed through highly ordered matter, but it is distinct from the matter since it could be equally conveyed through other mediums. The Navajos could transmit a message over radio, on the printed page, or via Morse code. In the same way, the name Shakespeare could be written in ink on a page, carved in stone, or composed of hundreds of tiny dots on a TV screen. The medium is not the message.

The conclusion to all this is stunning: reality is composed of at least two parts—matter and information. Thus, there are two distinct questions for those who desire to think about the origins of things: where did matter come from, and where did information come from? This second question is even more difficult to explain from a materialist, naturalistic perspective than the first (which we discussed in the previous chapter), since information is meta-natural, that is, nonphysical.

When one considers the human genome, the incredibly complex and highly specified genetic code in each cell of DNA, the mind boggles at the clear evidence of information. Francis Collins,[9] leader of the Human Genome Project that mapped our entire genetic code, explains the complexity of our DNA in terms of a text:

> This newly revealed text was 3 billion letters long, and written in a strange and cryptographic four-letter code...a live reading of that code at a rate of three letters per second would take thirty-one years, even if reading continued night and day.[10]

What is the likelihood that such a highly complex, information-bearing message would assemble by chance? The authors of the popular graduate textbook, *Biochemical Predestination*, thought such was the case. But after they conducted experiments to confirm their theory, one of the authors, Dean Kenyon, abandoned his own theory in a stunning reversal.[11] For Kenyon, the biochemical evidence revealed an information sequence that simply could not have developed through chance over a finite amount of time.

As philosopher Frederick Ferre said, "Every common biological organism is more intricately articulated, more astoundingly put together, than the most sublime literary composition...Despite all evasions, the ultimate agency of intelligence stares one in the face."[12]

Of course, the idea that an information generating, "ultimate agency of intelligence" is staring directly in one's face is an unwelcome notion for an atheist, not to mention unexplainable.

But the theist has no such problems. The Bible describes God as the source of not just matter but also information and order: "In the beginning was the Word, and the Word was with God, and the Word was

God."[13] In the original Greek of the New Testament, the noun *Word* is *logos*, which can be translated "reason," "account," or "rationale" (the English word *logic* is a derivative of *logos*). I suggest the verse could be translated, "In the beginning was *Information*..."[14] with the caveat that Information is a proper name for a Being, an ultimate, supreme Logos commonly called God.

A poet reflects on language and God

"God is the perfect poet."[15]

—ROBERT BROWNING

This is because the God of the Bible is also *personal*, seen in the phrase "God is love,"[16] and thus God is the source and model for love. In a parallel fashion, the personal God is also the *logos*, which means God is the source and model for information and rationality. God is love and logic combined in one unified, supreme Being.

Shakespeare intersects our flow of thought here again since he suggested the opposite: that love and logic seldom are found together. In *A Midsummer Night's Dream,* he wrote:

> Methinks, mistress, you should have little reason for that: and yet, to say the truth, reason and love keep little company together now-a-days; the more the pity that some honest neighbours will not make them friends.[17]

But here is the glorious claim of Christian theism: reason and love do eternally come together in God himself, who is—astoundingly—both love and *logos*. Furthermore, these attributes are incarnated in Jesus, who is proclaimed by believers and nonbelievers alike as both the greatest teacher and the greatest example of love of all time. Pure logic and love in one package! So Jesus proves, *contra* Shakespeare, that reason and love can keep company. They can best coexist in our world today through belief in a God who is both love and *logos*, and who calls his followers to live like Jesus and by those twin principles.

Let me try to sum up this chapter: the Navajos were successful Code Talkers because their language was little known and also extremely specific and complex (remember, Hitler's agents couldn't master it, though they tried). Another Navajo, on the receiving end, could easily hear a message and discern that it was not random sounds but a meaningful and intentional message. In the same way, all complex information sequences are products of design; complex information cannot be produced randomly or naturally within finite circumstances. If this is true, we are confronted with two massive questions: How can we explain the very existence of information? and Why is our universe so reasonable? As Einstein said, "The most incomprehensible thing about the universe is that it is comprehensible."[18]

Without God, it is hard to fathom why information exists since complex information sequences cannot be produced by accident. With God, it all falls into place. This is why, if you love information, books, languages, and maybe even movies about Navajo Code Talkers, then it makes sense to lean toward theism.

Fascinating converts from atheism to theism: A.N. Wilson

At thirty-eight years of age, A.N. Wilson had a dramatic "conversion experience" that resulted in twenty years of strident devotion—to atheism. He reveled in his associations with famous atheists Christopher Hitchens and Richard Dawkins, and that others considered him to be a prominent skeptic like them. Religion, for Wilson, "was a nonsense, together with the idea of a personal God, or a loving God in a suffering universe. Nonsense, nonsense, nonsense."

However, "Watching a whole cluster of friends, and my own mother, die over quite a short space of time convinced me that purely materialist 'explanations' for our mysterious human existence simply won't do—on an intellectual level. The phenomenon of language alone should give us pause...

"Do materialists really think that language just 'evolved,' like finches' beaks, or have they simply never thought about the matter rationally?

Where's the evidence? How could it come about that human beings all agreed that particular grunts carried particular connotations? How could it have come about that groups of anthropoid apes developed the amazing morphological complexity of a single sentence, let alone the whole grammatical mystery which has engaged Chomsky and others in our lifetime and linguists for time out of mind? No, the existence of language is one of the many phenomena—of which love and music are the two strongest—which suggest that human beings are very much more than collections of meat. They convince me that we are spiritual beings, and that the religion of the incarnation, asserting that God made humanity in His image, and continually restores humanity in His image, is simply true. As a working blueprint for life, as a template against which to measure experience, it fits.

"My departure from the Faith was like a conversion on the road to Damascus. My return was slow, hesitant, doubting. So it will always be; but I know I shall never make the same mistake again."[19]

CHAPTER 18

MATHEMATICS AND NUMBERS ARE NO MERE GAMES, THEREFORE GOD EXISTS

"God is a pure mathematician."

SIR JAMES JEANS, ASTRONOMER (1877–1946)

I remember my high school calculus class vividly: we students toiled over equations and formulas, all the while knowing that we never would need them in real life and probably would soon forget them. One day, a fellow student asked the inevitable question, "Why are we learning all this anyway? Most of us will never use this stuff after high school." Our teacher answered, "Mathematics is just one big game. That's all it is. I am here simply to teach you the rules of the game so you can play it if you want to."

At the time I thought his answer was a copout, a weary response developed over the years to pacify disinterested students. Almost forty years later, I now wonder if he really believed that (and how sad he would be to learn that this is the only thing I remember from his class). Maybe he knew that the real answer would lead into philosophy—and then inexorably into theology—danger zones that are best left alone in public schools.

Still, his answer was clearly wrong. Mathematics is just too effective to be just a game, too consequential to be classified as a mere form of entertainment. For example, math makes chemistry possible, which in turn empowers medicine. Math also enables physics, which governs everything from nanotechnology to the exploration of space. It makes our homes safe (structural engineering), our lights work (electrical engineering), and our cars and trains run (from which the term *engineering* originated).

But what is math? Aristotle said it was "the science of quantity," which worked well as a definition for almost two millennia. Today, however, even mathematicians cannot agree on a definition. Some say it is a science, for others it is an art form, and for still others simply a mental activity. Some see it as the necessary conclusions of logic, whereas others warn about the "myth of certainty" often ascribed to math.[1] Einstein, for instance, said, "as far as the laws of mathematics refer to reality, they are not certain; and as far as they are certain, they do not refer to reality."[2] Yet how do we explain, if Einstein is right, what Nobel Laureate Eugene P. Winger asserted in a famous article titled, "The Unreasonable Effectiveness of Mathematics in the Natural Sciences"? Winger wrote, "The enormous usefulness of mathematics in the natural sciences is something bordering on the mysterious, and... there is no rational explanation for it."[3]

If there is no rational explanation for math, then where did math come from? Is it a human invention or a discovery? That is, is math a useful gadget created within human minds or a supra-physical reality that existed before and beyond human minds? And to get even more basic, what are numbers anyway? Are they merely tools by which humans quantify and measure reality? That cannot be the case, for some numbers, such as π (which, apropos to this book's theme, is called a *transcendental* number), are neither quantifiable nor even knowable.

As chemist/philosopher Michael Polanyi pointed out, mathematics cannot be based on mere logic or on scientific induction alone.[4] If this is getting a bit too weirdly unscientific for you, get ready for this: it is the criterion of "beauty" that guides and sustains mathematics. Polanyi wrote, "It is on account of its intellectual beauty...that the mathematician feels compelled to accept mathematics as true," and thus "fundamental progress in mathematics, including conceptual reform, is found to be guided by a search for beauty."[5]

So science is based on mathematics, but math is based not only on our ability to reason (more on this in chapter 20), but also on our tacit knowledge, our feelings, and our ability to discern beauty. If this is the case, where do the laws of mathematics (not to mention the laws of physics) come from?

We have already heard from the materialist's position: there is no rational explanation. The theist's position is quite different. Augustine, for instance, "believed that numbers are unchangeable and have existed eternally in God's mind."[6] According to mathematicians James Bradley and Russell Howell,

> For Augustine, numbers were already present in God's mind at the time of creation. He goes on to argue that the reason we find mathematics so helpful in describing the physical world is that God used mathematics to provide patterns for his creation...How then are we able to access them? His answer is that, in creating humans, God built the capacity to deal with numbers into our minds. Thus God has given us a kind of "mathematical sixth sense."[7]

So the laws of mathematics come from God. As historian R.G. Collingwood sums up the matter: "The possibility of an applied mathematics is an expression, in terms of natural science, of the Christian belief that nature is the creation of an omnipotent God."[8] Or as the skeptical husband of author Kathleen Norris explained to her, "If there is a God, it's because the prime number theorem is true, and someone had to be organizing it."[9]

Interestingly, even atheist Steven Hawking seems to hint that numbers come from God, since he edited a book in 2005 titled *God Created the Integers*.[10] This is an adaptation of the statement by the mathematician Leopold Kronecker: "God made the integers; all else is the work of man."[11] (By the way, Kronecker converted to Christianity in the last year of his life.)

Here, it seems to me, we have come to the ground of what Hawking really believes in, which are the laws of mathematics and physics. As he himself explained in interviews, he uses the word *God* "as a shorthand for the laws of physics," and further clarified,

> The question is: is the way the universe began chosen by God for reasons we can't understand, or was it determined

> by a law of science? I believe the second. If you like, you can call the laws of science 'God', but it wouldn't be a personal God that you could meet, and ask questions.[12]

As a philosopher and a theologian, I have two quibbles with Hawking's statement. First, to be fair, Hawking should have completed the first sentence above as follows: "or was it determined by a law of science *for reasons we can't understand*?" After all, what's good for the goose is also good for the gander. Second, who is he to decide whether or not God is a being we could meet or talk to?

Aside from these small objections, my bigger issue is this: what if we could understand God's reasons for creating numbers? Could it be that numbers are an aspect of the very being of God? As we have noted in previous chapters, many aspects of creation are simply manifestations of the character—we might even say personality—of the Creator. God is moral, so his creation follows moral laws based on God's own being. God is beautiful, so his creation manifests that quality as well. And God is, above all, love, and therefore his highest creation also has the capacity to love.

In the Christian worldview, God is Trinity. This cannot be understood by simplistic analogies such as ice/water/steam. Instead, Trinity is the profound expression that the being of God is *love expressed in community*, within the three persons of the Godhead: Father, Son, and Holy Spirit. Reality at its deepest level—namely, God—is not impersonal and material. Instead, God is personal and loving. In the very core of God's being, love exists. Reality is relational.

And this, surprisingly, is also being discovered in the minute world of quantum physics. As Kathleen Norris delightfully notes,

> Although I have very little grasp of how science is done, I love to read about quarks, those subatomic particles that exist in threes. There is no such thing as one quark, but only three interdependent beings; I picture them dancing together at the heart of things, part of the subatomic glue that holds this world together...[This] is a good image for the Christian Trinity, I think.[13]

Frank Wilczek, winner of the 2004 Nobel Prize in physics, explains another aspect of quark-ness, "The color of a quark is not a single number, but a triple. More precisely, it encodes position in a three-dimensional property space...It is a fact [that is] so central, so beautiful, and so important."[14]

Could it be physical reality is based on quarks because it reflects the very being of God: his three-in-one-ness? And perhaps here we have found a solution to our key question in this essay: that numbers exist because God himself is numbered, three-in-one? Or might it be the case that reality is orderly because God is orderly within his very being: again, three-in-one? And maybe this even solves the aesthetic question, raised in chapter 4, why groups of three appear to be more beautiful than groups of two or four.

Within a theistic perspective, then, both the existence and the usefulness of mathematics are easily supported. So if you are left unsatisfied by the materialist perspective that there are no rational explanations for the origin of or the enormous usefulness of mathematics, then this is yet another surprising reason to lean toward theism.

Tolstoy on mathematics

"God and the soul are known by me in the same way I know infinity: not by means of definitions but in quite another way...Just as I know assuredly that there is an infinity of numbers so do I know that there is a God."[15]

—LEO TOLSTOY

CHAPTER 19

THE SCIENTIFIC METHOD IS FABULOUSLY EFFECTIVE, THEREFORE GOD EXISTS

"God does not play dice with the universe."[1]

ALBERT EINSTEIN (1879–1955)

Though atheists and theists disagree about many important issues, one thing they absolutely concur on is the value of the scientific method. But what, exactly, is the scientific method?[2] Is it a theory proven by science, or is it based on something else?

What no one questions is its fabulous effectiveness. It is the key to the astonishingly successful accomplishments of the natural sciences today—from the microscopic to macroscopic, the intracellular to interstellar. It is the scientific method that we have to thank for the wonders (and dangers) wrought in medicine, engineering, and technology. It has made life easier through inventions such as automobiles, refrigerators, and computers. We have decoded the human genome and have made progress in the war against disease. We can dive to the bottom of the ocean, fly above the clouds, and even travel to the moon. We can count the stars and tell how old the universe is. And, of course, we can extinguish the whole human race if we want to. The scientific method is a true and fearful wonder.

Are jokes about science permitted in a book about God?

Some tourists at the Museum of Natural History are marveling at the dinosaur bones. One of them asks the guard, "Can you tell me how old these bones are?"

The guard replies, "They're three million, four years, and six months old."

"That's an awfully exact number," says the tourist. "How do you know their age so precisely?"

The guard answers, "Well, the dinosaur bones were three million years old when I started working here, and that was four and a half years ago."[3]

But where did the scientific method come from? The answer may shock you.

According to renowned science historian Loren Eiseley, science is "an invented cultural institution, an institution not present in all societies, and not one that may be counted upon to arise from human instinct."[4] History bears this out, as Eiseley further notes, "several great civilizations have arisen and vanished without the benefit of scientific philosophy."[5] This is a staggering thought, especially to those of us who have grown up in technologically saturated first-world countries. Our privileged position often leads to the erroneous assumption that science would inevitably have evolved in all cultures.

But nothing could be further from the historical truth. Science and the scientific method arose in one and only one place: Western Civilization (Western Europe, to be precise). Why is this the case? Why did science not arise in India, a culture that spanned over five thousand years? Why not in Egyptian or Aztec culture, which each possessed significant astronomical abilities? Why not in China or Japan or Africa or a thousand other cultures, all filled with intelligent, observant, insightful people? What was so special about Western Europe?

The surprising answer is Judeo/Christian theology.

In most ancient societies, nature was viewed as capricious and erratic, as were the gods themselves. The gods of Olympus, for instance, were unruly and impulsive. One could never be quite sure what would happen next. And since the gods controlled the sun, moon, planets, stars, and the weather, these were erratic as well. The same was true in the animistic cultures of Egypt and Africa in which the gods *were* the elements, such as the sun, the waters, and the animals. As a result, for the most part, nature was not considered to be law-abiding or predictable.

In a similar vein, scientist and historian Joseph Needham explained why the Chinese never developed the scientific method:

> There was no confidence that the code of Nature's laws could be unveiled and read, because there was no assurance that a divine being, even more rational than ourselves, had ever formulated such a code capable of being read.[6]

That is exactly it. Science and the scientific method could arise only if the universe and world were orderly, predicable, and inherently rational. This is also a key conclusion in James Hannam's *The Genesis of Science: How the Christian Middle Ages Launched the Scientific Revolution*. Hannam is a graduate of both Oxford and Cambridge, from which he earned a PhD in the history of science. In *The Genesis of Science*, published in 2011, Hannam includes many examples of the contributions of medieval scholars to the development of science—based on their theological belief in the rationality of God. For instance, concerning William of Conches (1085–1154), Hannam writes:

> William of Conches also believed that God is loving and consistent rather than capricious and arbitrary. This meant that he could expect natural laws to remain the same forever...he had a reason for believing that nature is regular enough in its workings to be worth exploring in detail.[7]

The scientific method arose in the minds and investigations of medieval theologians and philosophers because they believed the world to be orderly, predicable, and inherently rational because God himself was so, he had created the world to be so, and because he had created human reason to be trustworthy. This is why early scientists were called "natural philosophers" and why Newton's scientific magnum opus was titled (when translated into English) *Mathematical Principles of Natural Philosophy*.

In other words, the scientific method is a philosophy that was born not in a laboratory or petri dish, but in the minds of proto-scientists who held four essential beliefs, which they had learned from the book of Genesis:

1. *Monotheism*: the universe was created and is ruled by one God.
2. *Law*: this God is a lawmaker and his universe obeys his laws.
3. *Order*: since God is an orderly creator, his laws are therefore orderly, reliable, and understandable.
4. *Imago Dei*: humans are created in the image of God and thus are also rational beings, that is, able to understand the orderliness of creation.

All four of these beliefs were revolutionary and are worthy of extensive discussion, but let's just focus on belief 2, that God is a lawmaker and his universe obeys his laws. Before the Hebrew revolution in theology, humans viewed nature as neither lawful nor rational, but instead saw nature as "mysterious and dangerous, at best inharmonious to man."[8] It was only the worldview-shattering thought that God is a lawgiver that ushered in a new perspective on our universe, namely that it is a law-abiding entity. As Nancy Pearcey and Charles Thaxton point out in *The Soul of Science*:

> The order of the reasoning here is important. The early scientists did not argue that the world was lawfully ordered, and *therefore* there must be a rational God. Instead, they argued that there was a rational God, and *therefore* the world must be lawfully ordered. They had greater confidence in the existence and character of God than in the lawfulness of nature.[9]

This may be a surprise to many readers. Note carefully: the notion of "laws of nature" was not derived by observation via the scientific method—they were derived from the faith doctrines that a specific religious community claimed to have received via special revelation from

God. In the words of Pearcey and Thaxton, the idea of God-given natural law that undergirds all of modern science "was not a fact of experience but an article of faith."[10]

This is also the conclusion of Hannam in *The Genesis of Science*:

> The starting point for all natural philosophy in the Middle Ages was that nature had been created by God. This made it a legitimate area of study because through nature man could learn about its creator. Medieval scholars thought that nature followed the rules that God had ordained for it. Because God was consistent and not capricious, these natural laws were constant and worth scrutinizing. However, these scholars rejected Aristotle's contention that the laws of nature were bound by necessity. God was not constrained by what Aristotle thought. The only way to find out which laws God had decided on was by the use of experience and observation.[11]

A few years ago I attended a debate about the existence of God that featured atheist Michael Newdow. I remember him stressing, "I am a medical doctor, a scientist. I believe in science and in evidence. Oh how I love that word—*evidence*." Instantly I thought, *Well, we both love science and evidence. But I doubt that Dr. Newdow has seen the evidence that science emerged from the womb of religious faith and is based on theological doctrines. What a surprise it might be for him to consider that!*

Sadly, I was not able to talk personally with Dr. Newdow. But I can ask you, dear reader: do you realize that the evidence points to a belief in an orderly and reliable God as the source of the scientific method? Furthermore, do you appreciate the fact that naturalism cannot supply a rational basis for scientific reasoning itself (this will be the focus of the next chapter)?

For theists, however, the value and validity of the scientific method is based upon—and therefore points to—the existence of a supernatural God who created the orderly and predictable universe we inhabit. If you believe in the scientific method, that's a good reason to lean toward theism.

Einstein's thoughts about order and God

"I'm not an atheist and I don't think I can call myself a pantheist. We are in the position of a little child entering a huge library filled with books in many languages. The child knows someone must have written those books. It does not know how. It does not understand the languages in which they are written. The child dimly suspects a mysterious order in the arrangements of the books, but doesn't know what it is. That, it seems to me, is the attitude of even the most intelligent human being toward God."[12]

—ALBERT EINSTEIN (1879–1955)

CHAPTER 20

I NEED REASONS TO TRUST MY OWN REASON, THEREFORE GOD EXISTS

"Poor human reason, when it trusts in itself, substitutes the strangest absurdities for the highest divine concepts."[1]

JOHN CHRYSOSTOM (C. 347–407)

As a PhD philosophy student at a secular university in the 1980s, I remember the incredulity of some students and professors when I mentioned that I was an ardent believer in God. One fellow student said to me, "I could never be a Christian, and especially not a Catholic. How can one believe that the pope should be trusted over one's own reason? It boggles my mind." (His statement was prompted by an encounter with the only Christian professor on our faculty—a Catholic monk.)

I responded, "Well, you have just revealed your ultimate source of certainty. I'm not a Catholic either, but it seems to me that you are in effect your own pope. You believe that your beliefs are right, even though you are repeatedly incorrect in daily life. Why is it more rational for one person to believe in him or herself rather than in a person drawing on the lessons and strengths of a two-thousand-year-old community?"

His response was shock. Before that moment, it had never crossed his mind that he was acting just like our Catholic philosophy professor. He replied, "Yes, I admit it. I am my own pope. It may not be any more rational, but I'm comfortable with my own ability to reason."

His confidence in his own rational abilities raises an important question: why are we so assured, especially philosophers who disagree on so many matters, of our ability to reason? Everywhere we look, people are confident of their rational ability, whether scientists or theologians, atheists or theists, elites or ordinary folk. In a strange twist of fate, my friend had much in common with the pronouncements of religious authorities, such as the founder of Buddhism, the Buddhist Dalai Lama, and the Hindu Mohandas Gandhi. Consider these comments:

> Believe nothing merely because you have been told it. Do not believe what your teacher tells you merely out of respect for the teacher. But whatsoever, after due examination and analysis, you find to be kind, conducive to the good, the benefit, the welfare of all beings—that doctrine believe and cling to, and take it as your guide.—Siddhartha Gautama[2]

> The ultimate authority must always rest with the individual's own reason and critical analysis.—Dalai Lama[3]

> I reject any religious doctrine that does not appeal to reason and is in conflict with morality.—Mohandas Gandhi[4]

Of course, belief in the ultimate power of human reason is not something unique to religious people. Few people were ever more confident of the power of reason than Thomas Jefferson who said,

> Fix reason firmly in her seat, and call to her tribunal every fact, every opinion. Question with boldness even the existence of a God; because, if there be one, he must more approve of the homage of reason, than that of blindfolded fear.[5]

But not all scientists, philosophers, poets, or even theists bow down before the altar of reason. The mathematician and scientist Blaise Pascal clearly believed in the limits of reason, as is reflected in his famous statement, "The heart has its reasons which reason knows nothing of."[6] The Italian existential philosopher Nicola Abbagnano, having survived the horrors of both World War I and World War II, also warned against the limits of reason: "Reason itself is fallible, and this fallibility must find a place in our logic."[7] My favorite critique of the idol of reason, though, was the reformer and theologian Martin Luther, who said, "Human reason is like a drunken man on horseback; set it up on one side, and it tumbles over on the other."[8]

So what is the answer? Should reason be trusted or not? In a fascinating twist, it is the evolutionary theorists who today are casting doubt on the veracity of reason.

How is this so? The school of evolutionary biology is attempting to mimic in cultural studies what has been so persuasive in the life sciences: to explain all phenomena as results of the natural selection process. For instance, though men were originally polyamorous (some still act as if they are), females found their offspring were better cared for when the male remained committed to protecting and providing for the children. Thus family commitment evolved, which later evolved into some rough form of polygamy, then bigamy, and then into the institution of marriage as is seen today—monogamy.

This schema also has been applied to religion in order to show that spiritual beliefs and experiences are the result of evolutionary adaptation, rather than the result of encounters with an actually existent God. Daniel Dennett, in the final work of his illustrious career, wrote *Breaking the Spell: Religion as a Natural Phenomenon*. There he explained that, in earlier ages, religious beliefs helped communities to gather and coalesce, thereby increasing the survival rate of more people. Thus, our religious sensibilities are merely genetic remnants of what once conferred evolutionary advantages, but now no longer do so.[9]

But here's the rub: if all human values and abilities are the results of evolutionary selection, then reason itself can't really be trusted. If naturalism is true, then all our morals and reasons are themselves contingent and valuable only in a pragmatic sense—in that they confer evolutionary advantages. They are not ultimately true or false, but only temporarily useful to propagate my line or species. Tim Keller's excellent explanation of this evolutionary cul-de-sac shows that evolutionary theorists, in explaining away cultural values, have robbed reason of all trustworthiness. Keller writes,

> In the last part of [Richard] Dawkins's *The God Delusion*, he admits that since we are the product of natural selection, we

> can't completely trust our own senses. After all, evolution is interested only in preserving adaptive behavior, not true belief...Evolution can only be trusted to give us cognitive faculties that help us live on, not to provide ones that give us an accurate and true picture of the world around us.[10]

Keller goes on to quote the atheist philosopher Thomas Nagel: "[Can we have any] continued confidence in reason as a source of the knowledge about the nonapparent character of the world? In itself, I believe an evolutionary story [of the human race] tells against such confidence."[11] In addition, it seems as if Darwin himself had concerns about this issue. Darwin wrote, "The horrid doubt always arises whether the convictions of a man's mind, which has been developed from the mind of the lower animals, are of any value or at all trustworthy."[12]

Dawkins also acknowledges, in the last part of *The God Delusion*, that since evolution only preserves adaptive advantages rather than true belief, we cannot completely trust our own senses.[13] This is an astonishing admission. If we cannot completely trust our own senses (and therefore our reason, which is based on sense evidences), then how can we completely trust evolutionary theory, since it too is a mere evolutionary product?

The philosopher Alvin Plantinga, considered by many to be the foremost Christian philosopher in America today, argues that naturalism is ultimately irrational.[14] He shows that if every belief and value we hold is caused by natural selection, there is no basis to completely trust belief in natural selection itself. Belief in naturalism is self-defeating. If we are mere evolutionary products, our mental sensibilities are not ultimately right or wrong but just better suited for survival.

Interestingly, this even puts the rationality of science in question. Allow me to again quote Pearcey and Thaxton:

> Once separated from the teaching of divine creation, science has no philosophical ground for its most basic assumption—the lawfulness of nature. "Since the time of Hume," Whitehead says, "fashionable scientific philosophy has been such as to deny the rationality of science." Hume

> demonstrated that pure empiricism gives no grounds for belief in even such fundamental principles as cause and effect. As a result, Whitehead concludes, scientists today maintain a "scientific faith" in the order of nature while lacking any rational basis for it.[15]

This is similar to the gist of the infamous "Argument from Reason," which was presented in C.S. Lewis's book *Miracles* (in a chapter titled "The Self-Contradiction of the Naturalist").[16] The argument became infamous after a debate between Lewis and philosopher G.E.M. Anscombe, which led Lewis to revise and rename the chapter, "The Cardinal Difficulty of Naturalism." (An updated, rigorous defense of Lewis's argument is presented in Victor Reppert's *C.S. Lewis's Dangerous Idea*[17] and in Alvin Plantinga's "Evolutionary Argument Against Naturalism."[18]) But the concept may go back even further, to both G.K. Chesterton and then, according to Chesterton, to Thomas Aquinas. Chesterton wrote in *Orthodoxy* (1908):

> The peril is that the human intellect is free to destroy itself... It is idle to talk always of the alternative of reason and faith. It is an act of faith to assert that our thoughts have any relation to reality at all. If you are merely a skeptic, you must sooner or later ask yourself the question, "Why should *anything* go right; even observation and deduction? Why should not good logic be as misleading as bad logic? They are both movements in the brain of a bewildered ape?"[19]

Here's the bottom line: all of us, both theists and atheists, trust human reason more than this; we trust our reason more than Darwinism warrants. Why is this? Maybe this is a clue, as Keller puts it, to the existence of a Higher Rationality who created the cosmos as a knowable entity, and then created humans with the capacity to reason, infer conclusions, and discover meaning.

The Bible actually uses language of this sort in describing God: "Dominion and awe belong to God; he establishes order in the heights of heaven."[20] God, according to the Bible, is the source of all order and reason. "Come now, let us reason together."[21] It follows that if God exists, then there is a reason why we trust reason. But if all of nature is a mindless, meaningless accident, there is no compelling reason to trust our own minds. So if you find that, in spite of your atheistic preferences, you trust the abilities of human beings to discover the truths of science and existence by means of human reason, then maybe that is a strong "reason" to lean in the direction of theism.

Fascinating converts from atheism to theism: Alister McGrath

Alister McGrath might be called an academic superachiever since he holds three different doctorates from Oxford: A PhD in molecular biophysics, a DD for theology,. and a DLitt for research into science and religion. He began his academic career at Oxford as a committed atheist, but converted to Christianity because to him "it seemed more intellectually robust." As he recalled in a 2013 interview, "I grew up as an aggressive atheist and I think there were a number of things that fuelled that. Firstly I was studying the Sciences at school and that seemed to me to demand that you were an atheist. And secondly when I was growing up it was the late 1960s and it was very fashionable to be a Marxist in those days. After all, what 16-year-old can resist fashions?

"I began to read books about the history and philosophy of Science [at Oxford], and began to realize that perhaps the sciences weren't quite as straightforward as I thought…I went to Wadham College in Oxford University to study chemistry but also began to be really challenged about what I thought about deeper things. Gradually I began to realize that atheism was a faith position—in other words something you believe, not something you can prove. And I began to realize that it wasn't even a very good faith position. Christianity was much more intellectually robust. And so I experienced an intellectual conversion. It wasn't shining bright lights or great emotional releases. It was just 'This is right, that's for me.'

"As a scientist it is very difficult to make sense of the world without bringing God in somewhere. You can say, 'Look, the world just happened. End of discussion!' But to me that is just brushing a deep question under the carpet. There is also a question of the very deep intuitions we have: there has to be more than this world we see, there has to be justice, there has to be something that keeps us going in life. It's not just one thing, it's the realization that if there were a God (and if this God is like the God that Christians believe in) then actually it gives you a way of looking at the world that makes far more sense than anything else."[22]

CHAPTER 21

TRUTH IS MORE REAL AND IMPORTANT THAN PREFERENCE, THEREFORE GOD EXISTS

"One word of truth outweighs the entire world."[1]

ALEXANDER SOLZHENITSYN (1918–2008)

The intelligent young man looked me straight in the eye and said, "Well, that may be true for you, but it's not true for me."

At the time, I was an adjunct philosophy teacher at a California State University, and it suddenly dawned upon me that his way of thinking had become commonplace. In shock, I realized that the philosophical world was changing beneath my own feet. In the mid-1980s, postmodernism was making its way into academic philosophy, though not yet by that name, and I slowly was learning to wrestle with this new, nameless opponent. I was confronted with the notion popularized by the Lebanese-American poet Kahlil Gibran, "Say not, 'I have found the truth,' but rather, 'I have found a truth,'"[2] which is to say there is no such thing as absolute truths. (Of course, no academic philosopher would ever quote Gibran, but they were nonetheless swimming in the same cultural stream.)

But I had been raised and weaned, in modernist America and academia, to believe there were such things as truths and falsities. It was true that the moon orbits the earth, the scientific method was effective, and that real truths that could be derived from reflection (like mathematics). In like manner, it was true that the earth was not flat, that the Holocaust really happened, and that child abuse is immoral.

But the seeds sown by analytic philosophy (the dominant school of philosophy in America and England in the twentieth century) came to fruition in the postmodernism of the latter quarter. The perspectivism of Nietzsche, the deconstructionism of Derrida, the power structures of Foucault, and the linguistic indeterminacy of Quine led to a loss of the notion of absolute truth within scholarly circles.

An example of this was the philosopher Richard Rorty, who has been celebrated as a champion of postmodernism. Postmodernism denies that anyone or any one culture has access to something called "the truth." For Rorty, language, truth claims, and even scientific methodologies are merely "contingent vocabularies" that are embraced or rejected due to social conventions and power relations. Statements of fact are not "mirrors of nature"[3] as the Enlightenment thinkers once thought. Instead, statements cannot really tell us the truth about nature but only the socially constructed conventions about our perspective on nature. As fellow postmodern philosopher Daniel Dennett put this in a 2006 TV interview with Bill Moyers (made famous on YouTube), "It's [one's worldview is] constructed all the way down."[4]

But think carefully with me about his statement. He clearly uttered what he considered to be a true statement, maybe even a metastatement that communicated real truth about all other statements. Yet if truth claims are constructed all the way down, should we not make the same judgment about Dennett's sentence? And if it too is constructed all the way down, then it need not be taken as an accurate statement about the world or reality. Therefore the statement is self-contradictory. The axe Dennett used to fell other philosophies ultimately brings down his own.

This happens often in philosophy, most notoriously to the Logical Positivism school of philosophy that enjoyed a short, immense popularity in the 1920s and 1930s. It held that a proposition was meaningful only if it were analytic (a tautology) or verifiable. However, the philosophers soon discovered that by that definition of meaningfulness, their definition itself was meaningless. Their position was self-refuting.

This is the problem with statements such as "No one can know the truth." If it is presented as true, then it is false. And if it is false, its converse is therefore true: the truth can be known.

So is truth knowable? Can it be expressed in language? Of course it is and of course it can, since we all live this way. As my philosophy professor was fond of saying, "All idealists become realists when they get on the freeway." We all abandon any philosophical doubts about whether objects are real and whether signs such as "Do not enter" or "Wrong way" are meaningful. We drive as if the signs on our roadways are absolutely meaningful and as if the existence of oncoming cars is an absolute certainty.

In the same way, I believe postmodernists become modernists on the freeway, in the dentist's chair, and in the home. Their spouses say, "Watch out for that drunk driver." They say to their dentist, "The pain is in my top left wisdom tooth." And they tell the plumber, "Help, there's a leak under our sink that needs to be fixed." In each case they convey real truths, not merely power-laden statements.

A similar thing happens in the realm of morality. A professor may teach that all ethics are situational and constructed "all the way down," but if her university should deny her tenure, watch out! She will probably respond with a high level of moral wrath, believing that an actual wrong has been perpetrated against her, even though she teaches such things do not exist.

But for final proof that truth exists, just ask a parent. All parents teach their children that some things are true and others false. It is true that 1 + 1 = 2, that birds fly and little kids cannot, and that Mommy and Daddy love them. We teach elementary kids to tell the truth and punish them when they do not. And belief in the existence of real truth persists through the teenage years: it is true that you missed your curfew last night, it is true that something happened to cause the dent in the car, and it is true that we still love you and always will, even if you don't always feel it.

As Francis Schaeffer used to say, there are such things as true truths.[5] Truths that endure. Truths that are supracultural and binding on all humans everywhere, such as the laws of physics and the laws of morality. As Shakespeare said in *Measure for Measure*, "Truth is truth, to the end of reckoning."[6]

This is why, in the final analysis, we all live as if certain truths are not mere preferences. "I dislike sex-trafficking" is not the same as

"Sex-trafficking is wrong." "I feel I deserve tenure" is not identical to "I have earned tenure." And some people's belief "I don't want God to exist," doesn't entail that "God doesn't exist."

I remember a middle-aged man who was adamant in his preference for atheism. "Not only do I not think that God exists," he said to me, "but I don't want him to exist." My response was simply, "Well, that won't make him go away. Your preferences won't determine the reality of God's existence."

For theists, the notion of enduring, objective truths is based on the idea of a God of truth who is objectively real and who conveys his truths to humans in accessible ways. This is why God said to the prophet Isaiah, "I, the LORD, speak the truth; I declare what is right."[7] It is also why Jesus claimed, "I am the way and the truth and the life."[8] In other words, God not only speaks truth, but he is Truth. Truth is his very nature and being. Thus, when we humans discover or find something that is truly true, we catch a hint of divine presence, a whiff of God's fragrance.

If you are an atheist, theism might actually sneak up on you through the backdoor of truth. Your belief in the truth of atheism may be the lightbulb that goes on to illuminate your deeper belief in the validity of truth claims—which is difficult to support within atheism.

This is the atheist conundrum. To claim there are no real truths is, in fact, to make a statement that claims to be true. To assert that truth statements are mere contingent constructions (houses of cards is the analogy that comes to my mind) is to undermine that very claim. The theist has no such problem, because truths about reality can really be known, since truth is founded in the existence of God and honesty is one of his key attributes.

In the end, there just are some things that we deeply know are true. And these are persuasive nudges, I believe, that move us to lean toward theism.

Is truth, if it exists, even knowable?

Great minds disagree on both the existence and knowability of truth. For instance, on the yes side, Winston Churchill said, "The truth is incontrovertible. Malice may attack it, ignorance may deride it, but, in the end, there it is."[9] In a similar vein, the Buddha is attributed to have said, "Three things cannot long be hidden: the sun, the moon, and the truth."[10]

On the no side, we have those who make pronouncements such as, "There are no facts, only interpretations" (Nietzsche)[11] and "The universe is transformation: life is opinion" (Marcus Aurelius).[12]

So I ask you, which side strikes you as more correct? Can people actually know real truths, or is everything we think we know to be true just our own particular slant on reality? It probably is no surprise to you that I side with the yes camp. I hold this position because this is simply how everyone lives life every day. It is true that as I write this essay I am sitting on a chair; it is true that the chair is in a friend's house in Oregon; and it is true that it is raining outside. None of these are mere interpretations or opinions. They are facts—knowable, true facts.

PART FOUR

THE MIRACLE THAT IS ME

All freshman philosophy students learn René Descartes's charming phrase, *Cogito ergo sum*, which initiated a Copernican revolution in the history of ideas. In fact, the story of philosophy is sometimes delineated by these three words, and thinking is seen as either Cartesian or pre-Cartesian, with Descartes himself as the turning point, the lynchpin in philosophical history. In Latin, *cogito* means "I think," *ergo* is "therefore," and *sum* is the first person, singular form of the verb "to be," hence "I am." Thus, the English translation happily follows the word order of the Latin: *I think, therefore I am.*

Of course, there are always those who find humor in unlikely places (for those who have studied philosophy and have been bored to tears, it may be the most unlikely place of all), so the following adaptations are a welcome relief, showing up often on novelty shop T-shirts:

I wear this T-shirt, therefore I am.

I shop, therefore I am.

I fly-fish, therefore I am.

Descartes's little phrase also is often truncated in academic circles to just the first word, *cogito,* a philosopher's shorthand for the complete phrase. But either way, the gist is the same: *It's all about me*.

Yes, the revolution in philosophy was that Descartes moved the locus of intellectual certainty from God to the individual thinker. In the Christian medieval world, before Descartes, thinking began with God, so the basis for truth and knowledge was the Bible, which claimed its source of truth was God himself. "Because God exists, we can know such and such," or "Because the Bible says this, we can know this or that." Scientific discoveries had to line up with the Bible rather than vice versa. But Descartes reversed that order. After Descartes, all knowledge starts with me: "*I* think." I am the arbiter of all knowledge. I am the center of my universe.

In addition, Descartes' revolution changed the human source of certainty: *the one reality I am most sure exists is myself.* But there is even more here: it is through the reality I call *me* that I know of all other realities.

Think about this for a moment: everything you know and experience—*everything!*—comes through the filter of you. There is nothing you know that has not been grasped through that which you call your *self* (which David Bentley Hart calls our "inaccessible first person subjectivity"[1]).

There are many real things that no one else knows but you. No one knows your inner ideas and doubts. Nor does anyone else know, as you do so intimately, your hopes and dreams, fears and emotions, or feelings about your own importance. No one knows the dialogue of thoughts you have with yourself within your head or of the worries that trouble your heart, and no MRI or brain scan could ever decipher what you are contemplating from the electrical firings in your brain. Internally and consciously, you are a universe unto yourself.

What a wonder we are—every human being! Even more, we are wonders filled with wonders—who have the capacity to wonder. To borrow a term from Billy Crystal, you not only look marvelous, you are marvelous.

Could these marvelous realities, known only to ourselves, be signposts that point to an even bigger Reality, an even more wondrous Self?

Do they contain a hidden message, subtle clues that point toward the existence of God? And since the self may be on shaky ground in naturalism (which we will see in the next seven chapters), then is everything we know on shaky ground within that worldview? Are these questions more reasons to lean in the direction of theism?

These are the issues we will ponder during the fourth part of our thirty-one-day journey.

CHAPTER 22

I WONDER ABOUT THE WONDER OF THE SELF, THEREFORE GOD EXISTS

"I am not an animal!"[1]

JOHN MERRICK[2] IN *THE ELEPHANT MAN*

Here's a little pop quiz: what do Kirk Douglas, Robert De Niro, John Hurt, Owen Wilson, Martin Lawrence, Jerry Seinfeld, and Sarah Michelle Gellar have in common? Answer: in productions as diverse as *Spartacus* and *Buffy the Vampire Slayer*, they all played a character who said, "I am not an animal!"

Why is it that we instinctively believe this? What is it that leads us to the intuitive, even visceral claim that we are not mere beasts? Darwinism, of course, claims the opposite, as do all naturalistic and materialist positions. According to evolutionary theory, humans are just one accidental species that arose by accident on an accidental planet in an ultimately accidental universe.[3] Had strict Darwinists been given roles in *The Elephant Man*, they would have had to say, "Sorry, John Merrick. You *are*, in fact, merely an animal."

But we don't—and can't—live that way. We don't view other humans as if they are unimportant, and we certainly don't regard people of other races as if they are mere animals. We don't treat infants like we do newborn animals, we don't treat handicapped humans as animals (more on this in chapter 28), and we don't deal with criminals (or politicians) like animals—though we may consider their behavior to be animalistic.

This notion that humans are not animals, indeed that we are of great value as individuals, is rooted in our American conscience. America, to the benefit of the entire world, was founded upon the concept that each human being has inherent worth and rights. As we mentioned earlier (Part 2), the preamble to our Declaration of Independence states:

> We hold these truths to be self-evident, that all men are created equal, that they are endowed by their Creator with certain unalienable Rights, that among these are Life, Liberty and the pursuit of Happiness.

So is our Declaration of Independence correct, or is it just wishful thinking? Are individual human beings unique and equal bearers of unalienable rights, and thus inherently valuable? This would mean that all six billion of us on this planet—six billion!—are each uniquely important. This is quite a statement. How could all six billion (and growing) individuals each be tremendously important? It boggles the mind if this is true (and it depresses the soul if it is not), but this mind-blowing truth is consistent with how all of us live. We all behave as if the people we know and love, and maybe even some enemies that we find hard to love, are immensely important.

This is especially true at home: we don't treat our kids as if they are merely accidental beings with no ultimate purpose, value, or importance. In fact, all across America, we teach our kids the opposite.

A heartwarming example of this occurred on the children's TV show *Sesame Street* in the early 1980s. Jesse Jackson (the civil rights leader) led a group of kids in a responsive chant, repeating over and over the phrase, "I am somebody." The kids repeated statements including: "I may be poor, but I am somebody," "I may be young, but I am somebody," "I may be on welfare, but I am somebody," "I am black, brown, white...but I am somebody." Check it out on the Internet—it really is a touching video clip.[4]

Why do we teach our children this? Why do we instill in each youngster the notion: "I am important"? Are we just pragmatists at heart, teaching our kids something that is not ultimately true but in the short run will make them feel good? Do we believe they will function better in life if they ignore for a time that they are just animals and instead naively develop positive self-esteem? Or is there something deeper, something richer, something real about themselves that we want them to grasp?

And it's not just our children that we firmly believe have inherent worth and value—it's anybody's children. Plus, we have the same tacit awareness about ourselves. Every one of us has a deep sense that "I'm somebody special," "I'm not a nobody," and "I am important." We certainly don't view our own lives as unimportant, and we get upset when someone devalues us or demeans us.

Again, clarity comes when we get on the freeway. Personally, I get very upset when another driver cuts me off or drives unsafe around our family car. Occasionally I even yell, "You idiot!" which makes my wife worry that I'll be the victim of road rage. But behind my outbursts of anger lie feelings of danger and injustice. How dare those other drivers treat us so unfairly and imperil our well-being. Don't they know who we are?

Well, the reckless drivers probably don't know who we are. To them we are just another group of nameless faces with no relationship or personal connections to them at all. What does it matter if they treat us poorly? If naturalism is true, and if we are all just accidental beings on this "pale blue dot," as Carl Sagan was fond of calling earth, then we actually are quite unimportant. We are just specks in a colossal universe that appear for a moment and then vanish without a trace, at least in the cosmic scheme of things.

From the Christian perspective, however, we are not insignificant, mere grains of sand along an infinite seashore. We essentially are incredibly important, a fact revealed in the basic existential questions asked by atheists and theists alike: "Who am I?" and "Why am I alive?" Even Derek Zoolander, in the comedy film *Zoolander*, asks, "I'm pretty sure there's a lot more to life than being really, really, ridiculously good looking. And I plan on finding out what that is."[5]

But these questions are difficult philosophically, because it is not clear what "I" refers to. As we will discuss in the next chapter, David Hume, the atheist Scottish philosopher of the eighteenth century, made a persuasive case that the existence of an enduring "self," what we each call "I," cannot be deduced from sense experiences. We each consider ourselves to be enduring, self-aware beings, but there is no logical way to connect the various sense and thought experiences we have, moment by moment, into a coherent concept of an enduring self. Shockingly, this entails that an enduring self-identity is difficult to explain from a materialist, naturalistic worldview. There is no ultimate, atheistic explanation for the "I" in "I am somebody."

This difficulty is so large that it led Berkeley philosopher John Searle to write:

> There is exactly one overriding question in contemporary philosophy...How do we fit in?...How can we square this self-conception of ourselves as mindful, meaning-creating, free, rational, etc., agents with a universe that consists entirely of mindless, meaningless, unfree, nonrational, brute physical particles?[6]

Yes, the materialist view of a universe totally made of "brute physical particles" is not compatible with what we all experience as a self. So you, dear reader, must look deep into the reality that no one can deny: the miracle that is you and the miracle that is me. Are you an "it" or an "I," or, as Martin Buber put this, an "it" or a "Thou"? A meaningless grain of sand in a colossal universe or an important individual who deserves to be treated by others with dignity?

In my opinion, the reality we look at in the mirror every day—the existence of a "self," the "I" that we see peering through our eyes—is clear evidence that the materialist view of reality is insufficient. Furthermore, our instant agreement with John Merrick's claim, "I am not an animal!" is a clear signpost that reveals we humans are more than just evolved animals.

In this chapter, we have discussed two facts that tip the scale in the direction of theism: the profound awareness that every person on planet Earth deserves to be treated with dignity and the deep belief that every one of us is a somebody. In each case, the awareness of "I am" seems to point toward a conclusion, like a dissonant note calling for resolution.

In a strange turn of events, we could say that Descartes had the *sum* in the wrong place in his famous formula, *Cogito, ergo sum*. The "I am" may serve better as the evidence, not the inference; the premise, not the conclusion. So from the "It's all about me" perspective, Descartes could have justifiably written: *I am, therefore God exists*.

Which is bad theology, albeit a surprisingly good reason to believe in God. Of course, bad theology is the expected result when one begins from a bad premise, such as "It's all about me." So I am not suggesting that *I am, therefore God exists* is good, Christian theology. I am merely pointing out that even from within a humanist worldview, the premise "I am somebody important" ends up leaning us toward theism.

Christian theology—as well as the fact of the matter, I believe—is the opposite of the Cartesian cul-de-sac. As I have suggested throughout this book, our essential human qualities are reflections of the very Being and characteristics of God. God is love, therefore we are loving beings since we are created in his image; God is just, therefore we value justice; God is beautiful, therefore we love beauty; and so forth. The message of these many chapters, taken together, is that *God is, therefore we exist*.

Kierkegaard on the mysteries of life

Where am I? Who am I?
How did I come to be here?
What is this thing called the world?
How did I come into the world?
Why was I not consulted?
And if I am compelled to take part in it,
Where is the director?
I want to see him.[7]

SOREN KIERKEGAARD

CHAPTER 23

I WONDER ABOUT THE WONDER OF FREE WILL, THEREFORE GOD EXISTS

"You say: I am not free. But I have raised and lowered my arm. Everyone understands that this illogical answer is an irrefutable proof of freedom."[1]

LEO TOLSTOY (1828–1910)

Paleontologists for decades were confused as to why, suddenly, the great dinosaurs became extinct. What would cause such wonderful beasts as the ferocious tyrannosaurus rex, the massive brontosaurus (now renamed apatosaurus), and the soaring pterodactyl to abruptly die? Neither evolutionary theory nor biology was able to give satisfactory explanations. But in the 1980s, the father-and-son team of Luis and Walter Alvarez suggested a surprising solution.

After discovering a layer of iridium in the thin geological strata that separates the time of the large dinosaurs from the time in which they were suddenly extinct, they noted that iridium is a rare element on earth but is abundant in meteorites. From this they conjectured that an immense asteroid crashed into the earth approximately sixty-five million years ago. This cataclysmic event led to instant and worldwide chaos and destruction: the enormous shift of mass led to a hefty wobble in the rotation of the earth; volcanoes simultaneously erupted worldwide, spewing tons of ash and toxins into the air; clouds obscured sunlight globally for months and possibly years; and tidal waves and tsunamis flooded large portions of land. And, of course, these catastrophic events led to the extinction of the dinosaurs.

Why do I bring this up? For this simple observation: I have never heard this meteor that wrought such devastation described as *evil*. Though this one entity caused more physical, planetary devastation than any other known event in the history of the earth, we intuit that the meteor was not a moral agent, and therefore the descriptor "evil" seems inappropriate.

In a similar vein, let's imagine that our solar system someday were to be suddenly wiped out by the supernova of a nearby star, and the whole human race were to become extinct in the blink of an eye. Would we call such an event "evil"? After all, in chapter 11 we concluded that mass extinctions of species or races are, in fact, immoral events. Remember *Avatar*?

Here we must refine the moral argument a step further: mass extinctions that are a result of natural causes, such as a supernova or a meteor, are not moral events. This is because morality and evil can be done only by cognitive beings with *intentionality*, that is, by beings with free will and moral capacity. We don't consider stars, meteors, or tsunamis capable of crimes, though their actions may produce huge amounts of misery.

Well, is it the ability to think and reason that constitutes a moral being? No, because nonhuman animals think and reason, though sometimes on rudimentary levels. We can't argue that fish that eat their young are immoral (child abuse!), that praying mantises that kill their mates after fertilization are evil (spousal abuse!), or that foreign predators that decimate native species are wicked. We can't convene a trial for one species of animals that treats another immorally, no matter how civilized the animals in the *Lion King* appeared.

On planet Earth, only *Homo sapiens* is considered a moral agent. This is because only human beings possess not just the requisite mental ability but also the free will necessary to make moral judgments. Without free will, there is no such thing as morality. If humans are not autonomous, capable of self-rule and self-government, then we are no more responsible for our actions than are meteors or supernovae.

But no one believes this—except the philosophers and brain researchers we will mention in the next chapter, who see the human brain as an organic computer. In such a computer, all results are the consequences of synaptic wiring and conditioning, chemicals interacting and electrons firing in a preordained and predictable manner. For those materialists working on the frontiers of either the philosophy of mind or the physiology of the brain, there is no soul so there can be no such thing as free will or choice. What appears to you and me as a choice is, in their view, the predetermined result of our unique physiology. To put it bluntly, for many materialist scientists and philosophers today (the technical name for them is *determinists*), there is no such thing as free will.

Leonardo da Vinci on the reality of the soul

"You think that the body is a wonderful work. In reality this is nothing compared to the soul that inhabits in that structure…It is the work of God."

"The works of God are appreciated best by other creators."[2]

However, no one lives this way. As I mentioned in the previous chapter, a beloved philosophy professor of mine liked to say, "All idealists become realists when they get on the freeway." Yes, when we get on the freeway, all notions of reality-as-illusion go out the window. In the same way, determinists become nondeterminists on the freeway. They make lane choices and speed decisions, decide on route changes, and get mad at others who make poor driving decisions. Drive with a determinist during rush hour and you will see what I mean. We all do this, determinist and nondeterminist alike: "What a dumb driver!" "Can you believe how he just cut me off?" "What a fool!"

We all behave in real life as nondeterminists, regardless of our philosophical positions, believing that people make real choices in life. Parents raise their children to make wise choices. Teachers grade students on their ability to learn and make correct choices on tests. Juries decide civil and criminal cases based on the choices they conclude the defendant made. Judges mete out sentences based on the severity of the criminal choices made by the convicted. We live in a real world full of choices, no matter what our views are philosophically.[3]

In my short stint in the philosophical corridors and classrooms of academia, I witnessed several debates about free will versus determinism. I humorously look back now and think: How odd! In their argumentations, the determinists were attempting to persuade the nondeterminists to change their positions. But that attempt itself is self-refuting. If I really believe my opponents have no free will, how can I convince them to change their minds?

Plus, in spite of the ruminations of philosophers and scientists, don't all of us tacitly know that we have free will, as Tolstoy claimed in the epigram that began this chapter. And aren't all of us aware that free will is the basis of law and society? After all, without free will there is no rationale for saying any action is criminal, for the criminal had no choice but to do what he did. In addition, free will is the basis of love, for love becomes mere instinct when free will is denied. These and many other examples could be enumerated of how free will is not ancillary to what makes us human. It is not optional equipment that could have been left out at the factory; free will is at the heart of what it means to be a person. Our very lives are built through the multitude of free-will decisions that we make over a lifetime. As Marley's ghost says in Charles Dickens's *A Christmas Carol*, "I wear the chain I forged in life...I made it link by link, and yard by yard; I girded it on of my own free will, and of my own free will I wore it."[4]

If the determinists are wrong, as I believe they are and as everyone *behaves* as if they are, then where does free will come from? Can free will arise out of materialism? No. Out of naturalism? No. Out of the physical sciences? No. Even quantum mechanics can't help here. Quantum mechanics is based on randomness, not free choices. As a result, the honest atheist answer to "How did free will arise?" is "We don't know." That's the atheistic conundrum: free will is extremely difficult to support within an atheistic worldview, but without free will there is no "view" left in one's worldview.

The most plausible solution to the existence of free will is the theistic one: there exists a transcendent, personal God who is free essentially; that is, it is the very essence of God to be free. And since God created humans in his image, we too are endowed with a transcendent *self*. This self, though based upon physical matter, is more than physical; it is spiritual, and thus its volitional hands are not tied by biology or chemistry.

The ability to make free choices necessitates what religious people call a *soul*, an aspect of each human that is supranatural. This is why God is usually described as a Supreme Being, supra- (or above) nature, supremely free and holy, and who freely chose to create humans in his image. We are free because we are like God, who is absolutely free. And because we are free we are free to love, to commit, and to be human. Most of all, we are free to love God in return, which may be the point of everything.

The fact that we are free demands an adequate explanation, which belief in God's existence amply provides. If one were to choose whether theism or atheism provides a more adequate explanation for the existence of human free will, the theist would win hands down. It is only the prejudice against theism that would choose, based on the available evidence, the atheistic answer. But even there we encounter that pesky word—*choose*—which is evidence of free will. It seems as if we cannot escape from this aspect of our being no matter how much some materialists desire to do so.

So what do you think—does God exist or does he not? If you sincerely believe you can think and make real choices, that you are free to follow the available evidence and make an informed decision about this or any question, I would argue that your free choice is significant evidence that once again impels us to lean toward theism.

Fascinating converts from atheism to theism: Philip Vander Elst

Philip Vander Elst is a British journalist who graduated from Oxford in 1973 with a degree in politics and philosophy, and also as a convinced atheist. "Growing up in a non-Christian family with intellectually gifted but unbelieving parents, I used to think that belief in God and the supernatural had been discredited by the advance of science, and was incompatible with liberty. Religious faith seemed to me to involve the blind worship of a cosmic dictator, and the abandonment of reason in favour of 'revelation.'"

His atheism was rattled, at age twenty-four, when he became attracted to a young woman who was a Christian and who later would become his wife. He wrote, "Shocked by the discovery that this highly intelligent and beautiful woman was 'one of them,' I determined to find out whether there was any good evidence for the existence of God and the truthfulness of Christianity, making it quite clear from the outset, however, that I was not prepared to become a believer just to cement our relationship!"

He agreed to read books by C.S. Lewis, whose intellect he respected. One of Lewis's arguments for God was what some call "the free will defense." Vander Elst learned from Lewis that "True love is a voluntary union of free individuals giving themselves to each other for their mutual delight and for the mutual enjoyment of life and all its blessings. Consequently, when God created the first human beings, He gave them the gift of free will...But the problem with free will is that it can be corrupted and misused...And that, sadly, is what has happened to the human race."[5]

Along with explanations for the problem of evil and the possibility of miracles, the free will defense convinced Vander Elst, and he converted from atheism to Christianity.

CHAPTER 24

I WONDER ABOUT THE WONDER OF DOUBT, THEREFORE GOD EXISTS

"Modest doubt is called the beacon of the wise."[1]

WILLIAM SHAKESPEARE (1564–1616)

You and I have doubts. Lots of them. Some of them are mundane: Did I turn off the burner on the stove? Did I pay my bill on time? Did I close the garage door? (I hate that last one, which sometimes forces me to turn around and drive home, just to calm my doubts. Arrgh.)

Other doubts are important: Did I just say something wrong and was misunderstood by my friend? Does she feel about me as strongly as I feel about her? Will my kids (for some: will my spouse) ever grow up? Doubts abound—we can't escape them.

In fact, René Descartes's famous *cogito ergo sum* also can be translated, "I doubt, therefore I am." He was searching for the one bedrock statement that could absolutely not be denied, the one foundational premise upon which a solid structure of knowledge could be built. As he tore away layer after layer of his thoughts and beliefs, as a cook might peel away layers of an onion, Descartes came to what he considered the unmistakable core. When he thought, and even when *he doubted that he was thinking*, he realized his very doubt was a real experience that could not be denied.

When I was a teenager in the 1970s, doubt was in. We doubted what the government claimed (Vietnam), we doubted what politicians said (Watergate), and we doubted that our parents knew best (a malady common to all adolescents). In colleges and universities we were taught to doubt everything and everyone. (Except, of course, the teacher's call to doubt everything and everyone. Do you see the self-referential problem there?) As a kid, I thought that someday I would grow up and learn more about life and the world, leading to fewer doubts. Amazingly, the opposite has been true. I have more doubts now than ever.

As a pastor in a church, I often have people ask me, "Rick, is there something wrong with me if I have doubts?" I usually respond, "No, but there is something wrong with you if you have no doubts." As Thoreau said, "Faith keeps many doubts in her pay. If I could not doubt, I should not believe."[2] Doubts are common to all humans; only robots have no doubts.

Which is exactly what many materialists are forced to believe each of us is: a robot. Our minds are such fascinating and brilliant organs that the only thing we can compare them to is a computer. Because of this, it is quite common within a naturalist worldview to assume that our minds are no more than organic computers.

But computers don't think—they merely process externally designed and instigated commands.[3] As a result, computers can't doubt. Thus, there will never in reality be a Hal as in *2001: A Space Odyssey*, or a C-3PO as in *Star Wars*, or a Sonny as in *I, Robot*. Never. People who believe there will be a day when computers can doubt have been duped by science fiction (just as they have been duped by the media into believing that IBM's Big Blue "played chess" against Gary Kasparov[4]).

There is absolutely no evidence that a computer can think or doubt; such an idea is an anthropomorphism, a projection of human abilities onto computers (which is striking, because atheists often criticize theists for anthropomorphisms toward God). This is because doubt requires not only thought and the ability to make authentic choices, but doubt requires consciousness and a sense of enduring self-identity. And though these are common experiences for all humans, they are enormously difficult for materialistic philosophers and scientists to explain.

As I mentioned in chapter 22, David Hume, the atheist Scottish philosopher of the eighteenth century, made an extremely strong case that even the existence of *an enduring self* cannot be proven scientifically or philosophically from a materialist base.[5] We each experience ourselves as enduring, self-aware beings, but there is no logical way to connect the various sense and thought experiences we have, moment by moment, into a coherent concept of an enduring self. Shockingly, neither consciousness nor our enduring self-identity is easily supportable from a materialist, naturalistic worldview.

So it is not just doubt that is hard to explain, it is also our concepts of self and consciousness. Computers don't doubt, they have no concept of self, and no meta-consciousness. It is exactly parallel to a book: both computers and books are highly programmed and designed, but neither has the capacity for independent thinking, much less self-knowledge or self-doubt. You may doubt this the first time you think about it, but doubt is an enormously difficult experience to explain from within an atheistic, materialist worldview.

For believers in God, though, the explanation is easy: we are material beings but also more than mere matter. God created us out of material matter (the "dust" of Genesis 2:7), but he also created each of us with a self-conscious soul (God "breathed" into us the "breath of life," also found in Genesis 2:7). Thus, we are chemical/physical beings who function based on organic processes, but we are more than processing machines. We are made of natural materials but are also supranatural; we are animals but more than mere animals; we are transcendent beings who think and question and doubt. We are made of dirt but also much more—the breath of the divine is in us as well.

Think about it, even try to doubt it, and then try to explain your doubt. If you do, I believe you will grasp that the best explanation for the existence of doubt is that we are self-conscious beings who also have free will, which both reflect the being and personhood of God. No doubt about it: the very existence of our doubts points us toward the existence of God.

Fascinating converts from agnosticism to theism: Kathleen Norris

Kathleen Norris enjoyed an urban, agnostic lifestyle as a poet and as the arts administrator of the Academy of American Poets in New York in the early 1970s. But after inheriting her family's farm in 1974, she and her husband moved to South Dakota where she experienced a gradual spiritual awakening.

"Perhaps my most important breakthrough with regard to belief came when I learned to be as consciously skeptical and questioning of my disbelief and my doubts as I was of my burgeoning faith." What she found surprised even her—pride and a "tyranny of the self" hidden in her agnosticism. "There is a certain pride in apostasy, which often manifests itself as a remarkable faith in oneself, as in 'I know what is right for me'...The possibility of error is never considered and one's feelings are always right...[this is] a disastrous self-absorption.

"The individual stands alone, a church of one, convinced that he or she is free of the tyranny of any creed or dogma...If I had to come up with a synonym for apostasy...it is simple vanity."[6]

CHAPTER 25

I WONDER ABOUT THE WONDER OF EMOTIONS, THEREFORE GOD EXISTS

"Love is the only reality and it is not a mere sentiment. It is the ultimate truth that lies at the heart of creation."[1]

RABINDRANATH TAGORE (1861–1941)

Edith was my first girlfriend—though I don't think she knew it. We were in the same first grade class in Williwah Elementary School in Anchorage, Alaska, and I don't remember ever speaking to her. All I have is an old class photo with her picture circled and "My Girlfriend" written under it.

In hindsight, I wonder: What stirred my preadolescent soul to even think about romance? What force drew my attention to her and singled her out as special?

The answer is, in one word, love, which is our irresistible, emotional impulse to tie our affections to specific people. And by love I certainly do not mean lust, for those glandular stirrings had not yet begun at that point in my boyhood.

And though apologists rarely mention emotional love as a reason to believe in the existence of God, I think it is an important reason because love is important. Affective love isn't just a trivial, transitory experience of second-level importance. Love is a big deal. As the saying goes, love makes the world go 'round. Author Leo Buscaglia said, "Love is life. And if you miss love, you miss life."[2] Or, to paraphrase the apostle Paul: three of the most important things in life are faith, hope, and love—but the one that matters the most is love.[3]

Why is this, when faith, hope, and love are not tangible, material realities? If life is mere matter, as naturalism supposes, then what is the essential nature of this vital trio? Are emotions just evolutionary adaptations that make us more likely to thrive in communities, and thus more likely to survive? Are they simply somatic impulses, organic responses to stimuli that we are fooled into thinking are important? And as such do they need to be corralled by our more reliable rationality? Bertrand Russell certainly thought so, for he said, "The degree of one's emotions varies inversely with one's knowledge of the facts."[4] (Wouldn't he have been a peach to be married to—which he was four times?)

No, lovers know the truth: emotions are neither merely advantageous adaptions nor irrational bodily urges—emotions are what life is all about. Love, joy, humor, anger, fear, gratitude, compassion—these are the very stuff that makes us human. As C.S. Lewis said, "Affection is responsible for nine-tenths of whatever solid and durable happiness there is in our lives."[5]

Plus, contra Russell, emotions are not empty of reasons. Shoshana Zuboff, psychologist and professor at Harvard Business School, helps us capture the tremendous value and *rationality* of feelings: "People have to stop thinking of their feelings as irrelevant and messy, and realize they are in fact highly differentiated, nuanced patterns of reaction, knowable sources of information…Attention is our most precious resource. Feelings are our body's version of the situation; everything we want to know about our situation is revealed in our feelings."[6] (As this statement reveals, Bertrand Russell's maxim on the relation between emotions and knowledge was simply wrong. Like many of his pronouncements, it was based on pure personal preference and not—surprise!—on any scientific footing at all.)

Zuboff's comment is supportive of the theory championed by psychologist Daniel Goleman in his 1995 bestseller, *Emotional Intelligence: Why It Can Matter More than IQ*.[7] Goleman wrote,

> Much evidence testifies that people who are emotionally adept—who know and manage their own feelings well, and who read and deal effectively with other people's feelings—are at an advantage in any domain of life, whether romance

> and intimate relationships or picking up the unspoken rules that govern success in organizational politics.[8]

So it's not just love that makes the world go 'round—it's all of the emotions. They are not just the spice of life; emotions are life itself. Emotions are incredible, irreplaceable components of human reality—vastly important contributors to our human quality of life.

But appreciating our emotions is not something that comes natural to many of us. We have been taught—especially in Christian circles—falsehoods such as that anger and hatred are always sins, and we know experientially that romantic passion can lead to poor choices. So we tend to be wary or, like Russell, dismissive of our emotions. Yet learning to acknowledge and embrace our negative emotions, such as anger, hatred, and even shame, are essential for our mental health.

An example of this appears in the novel *The Promise* by Chaim Potok. Michael Gordon is a boy who becomes mentally ill because he can't handle his anger toward his father. Commenting on Potok's novel, author Harold Kushner notes an interesting parallel with another character, Rabbi Kalman, whose wife was killed in the Holocaust. Kushner writes, "Just as Michael became sick because he couldn't handle his anger toward his father, Rabbi Kalman has become a tyrannical, unsympathetic person because he can't face up to his anger at his Father in Heaven."[9]

Along a similar line, Christian psychologist Dan Allender and Old Testament scholar Tremper Longman III write that Christians "have learned to distance themselves from anger, irrespective of whether it is righteous or unrighteous." What is needed is not to jettison all anger. Instead, we need to learn to distinguish between the two, and then avoid the bad while giving full expression to the good. In a phrase that shocked and delighted me, they wrote, "Christians are never angry enough."[10] This is why the Psalms are so full of emotion, including anger. There even is a whole category of Psalms known by scholars as the Imprecatory Psalms, which is a fancy way of saying Cursing Psalms.[11]

The point of all this is that our emotions are not unessential aspects of our humanness, like fashion items one may use to accessorize an outfit. Emotions are not tangential to human reality—they are central to it.

But how can we account for them? As I mentioned earlier, from a materialist viewpoint emotions are just advantageous adaptations or glandular impulses, which have no metaphysical or platonic reality beyond that.

Yet if emotions are merely adaptions that aid survival, from a naturalistic viewpoint they then may disappear when no longer needed. This is why many science fiction stories include advanced beings like Spock, who have evolved beyond the need for emotions. Yet as the Star Trek series continues to emphasize in its many iterations, emotions are *necessary* human attributes, and it is Spock who slowly learns to value emotions, rather than humans who slowly learn to dispense with them. Kirk is a good captain because of his emotions, not in spite of them. In the same way, Captain Picard is effective because he values his emotions—he even has a lieutenant commander, Deanna Troi, who serves as the ship's "counselor" because of her ability to sense emotions.

As even Gene Roddenberry realized, evolving beyond and dispensing with emotions cannot ever happen for humans, for they are not just tools that aid survival. Nor can emotions be mere bodily functions because, as we noted above, our emotions are not devoid of information. On the contrary, emotions are what life is all about. Love, joy, humor, anger, fear, gratitude, compassion—these are the very stuff that makes us human, the very essences of who we are.

Love summarizes what human existence is, even though it is difficult to put into words. I think this was put best by the Jewish theologian Martin Buber, who said, "The world is not comprehensible, but it is embraceable: through the embracing of one of its beings."[12]

So we humans might be called *embracing beings*. We cannot exist in solitude, just as three quarks cannot (see chapter 18). But unlike quarks, we are sentient, personal beings. Think about this: could it be that our embracing nature points to God—the ultimate Embracing Being—embracing from before and beyond time? And sharing both thoughts and emotions within that embrace? Aristotle famously called the Prime Mover "thought-thinking-thought," but the Christian God is a more balanced being who could be described as "emotion-thinking-emotions."[13]

Author Nikos Kazantzakis on the surprising emotional intensity of God

"My God and I are horsemen galloping in the burning sun or under drizzling rain.

Pale, starving, but unsubdued, we ride and converse.

'Leader!' I cry. He turns his face toward me, and I shudder to confront his anguish."

NIKOS KAZANTZAKIS[14]

The grand conclusion, therefore, is that emotions are real and have always been, from a theistic perspective, because they are aspects of God's own Embracing Being. As the apostle John wrote, "God is love."[15] Note carefully, he didn't write, "God loves," or "God is a God of love," as so often is asserted in pop-spirituality today. Love is not something God simply does; love is who God is. In the same way, love is not something that we humans just do; love is who we are. Love is who I am, so I am fully me only when I am embracing another—emotionally, physically, or spiritually. I am complete only when I am reflecting the image of God.

Therefore, love and emotions make profound sense when viewed from the Christian perspective, but are rather temporary or trivial when regarded from the nontheist point of view. So, if you feel that love is *supremely* important (even more important than survival), this is yet another reason to lean toward theism.

Fascinating converts from atheism to theism: Nicole Cliffe

Nicole Cliffe, a Canadian-American journalist best known for cofounding the feminist website *The Toast*, became a Christian after what she calls "a very pleasant adult life of firm atheism." A committed atheist since college, she "started out snarky and defensive about religion, but eventually came to think it was probably nice for people of faith to have faith. I held to that, even though the idea of a benign deity who created and loved us was obviously nonsense, and all that awaited us beyond the grave was joyful oblivion."

Then, during a difficult period in her life, she read a sentence online that rocked her world. In response to a question about total depravity, Dallas Willard, chair of the department of philosophy at the University of Southern California for many years, responded, "I believe that every human being is sufficiently depraved that when we get to heaven, no one will be able to say, 'I merited this.'"

Cliffe recalls, "A few minutes into reading the piece, I burst into tears. Later that day, I burst into tears again. And the next day. While brushing my teeth, while falling asleep, while in the shower, while feeding my kids, I would burst into tears." So she read some books about Christianity, and kept crying. She wrote, "It was getting out of hand. You just can't go around crying all the time."

Cliffe emailed a Christian friend to talk with her about Jesus. She wrote, "I spent the few days before our call feeling like an idiot, wondering what on earth I planned to ask her. Do you...like Jesus? What was Jesus' deal? Why did he ice that fig tree?

"About an hour before our call, I knew: I believed in God. Worse, I was a Christian."[16]

CHAPTER 26

I WONDER ABOUT THE WONDER OF COMPASSION, THEREFORE GOD EXISTS

"Love and compassion are necessities, not luxuries. Without them humanity cannot survive."[1]

THE FOURTEENTH DALAI LAMA (1950–)

The young non-Christian sat across the desk from me, a subtle smirk across his face. He was filled with the confidence of the untested, the hubris of a soldier who has never seen battle—and especially the bravado of one who never has had to put his theories into practice, such as believing in God while burying a good friend or believing in love while suffering a betrayal. Nothing bursts our youthful bubbles like reality.

He had gone to college and there decided to abandon his childhood belief in Christianity, which his professors had touted as old-fashioned, unenlightened, and unnecessary. He could believe in God but didn't need the Jesus stuff. All religions were essentially the same, they told him, since all roads lead to the top of the mountain. There was no need for heaven or hell, churches, or the Bible. God was love, and as the Beatles sang decades before, "All you need is love." How simple it all seemed in the classroom.

His parents were upset at his newfound religious beliefs, but were not equipped to argue with the new set of weapons he had gathered at the university—which they ruefully realized they had paid for. So they sent him to meet with me.

How I identified with this young man! I too went away to college and then graduate school, including PhD level studies in philosophy at a secular university. I too had been astounded by the worlds of thought that opened up to me, the marvelous books that stretched my thinking, and the profound writers who challenged my beliefs. But unlike this young man, these encounters left my faith stronger rather than weakened, more vital than before. As Nietzsche said, "*Was mich nicht umbringt, macht mich starker*" ("That which does not destroy me, makes me stronger").[2]

After we exchanged a few superficial pleasantries, I decided to jump to the heart of the matter. I asked him, "Your parents told me that you've decided you are no longer a Christian. I know and respect many brilliant people who also are not, and I find some of their arguments quite compelling. I'd like to hear your reasons. So let's get to the core issues: what do you believe, and why?"

He replied, "I believe in love, and I believe in a God of love. I don't think we need the Bible or churches or anything like that. We all know love is the right way to live. We just need to live it out. That's what I believe."

"What proof do you have that God is a God of love?" I asked. "After all, most religions in the history of mankind have not believed in a God of love."

"What do you mean? In my studies I learned that all religions teach the same thing—that God is love."

"Okay," I said, "name me one other prominent world religion, not based on Christianity, that historically has taught 'God is love' as a core doctrine."

Silence. More silence. Finally he said, "Well, I can't remember the facts at the moment, but I'm sure they exist."

I responded, "There really are only a few candidates. How about the Greeks? Was Zeus a God of love? How about Hinduism, a religion that's about four thousand years old? Or Judaism, Buddhism, or Islam?" Again silence from our young scholar.

"Since we aren't making much progress here," I said, "let's test your other belief instead. How do you know that 'We all know that love is the right way to live'? Did people in ancient societies believe that? Did the Greeks feel they were supposed to love the Persians? The Aztecs the other Central American tribes? The Comanches the Utes? Or how about more recently? Did the Japanese feel they were to love Koreans before World War II? Did the Nazis believe they were to love the Jews? Do the members of ISIS feel they are to love non-Muslims? The Russians the Poles?"

Again silence. I thought of the comment by writer Marilynne Robinson, "It is a truism that humanity is deficient in humanity."[3]

So I said to the young man, "Look, I'm not trying to embarrass you or trick you. I went to a couple of graduate schools and I heard the same things. But when I checked their theories against history, their facts didn't pan out.

"The truth is pretty simple: before Jesus, this world was a pretty mean place. Some religions taught love for family and countrymen, but the idea of loving one's enemies or loving foreigners as equals was unheard of. Nations fought nations incessantly, and tribes routinely murdered other tribes without second thought. Slavery was practiced almost everywhere in the world, and the disabled were treated horribly.

"And then one person, Jesus, suddenly changed the course of human history. He said we should love our enemies and forgive our debtors. He modeled that we were to love the sick, the poor, and even those with leprosy. And above all, he taught that love involves self-sacrifice, so much so that he allowed himself to be crucified to prove it.

"It took time, but because of his influence, over the past two thousand years the world has grown to value love and compassion. This has even caused people to rework their very conception of God—God is now seen as loving because of Jesus."

I am not alone in viewing history and theology in this manner. As sociologist of religion Rodney Stark pointed out in *The Triumph of Christianity*, the Roman Empire was a harsh, unforgiving, and cruel society in which to live. Women were little better than possessions and children were considered undeveloped human beings. Slavery, violence, bloodshed, and revenge mingled with fire, famine, flood, pestilence, and plague. In the midst of the horror, Christians rescued discarded babies, despised abortion, loved their spouses, tended the sick, nurtured the dying, and fed the poor—in the name of and following the example of Jesus. Compassion had begun to shine in the world, and as its light grew, it astonished the Romans and in time revolutionized everything.[4]

Eastern Orthodox, philosophical theologian David Bentley Hart makes a similar point about the concept of innate human dignity: the Christian message was a startling turning point in human history. Because the Son of God took human form, humanity was redeemed. On the first Easter a remarkable and formerly unthinkable truth entered and enlightened the world: each human being had eternal worth.[5]

As a result, slavery would eventually crumble, children would be treated as treasures, and women would be considered as equals. The reformation of civil morality would continue until aristocracy and worth based on birth would eventually wither and the caste system would be seen as inhumane. Revolutions and the civil rights movement would call for freedom, brotherhood, and equality for all—all based on Jesus' initiative.

Now, two thousand years later, our world is no utopia, but at least compassion has entered the tacit belief codes of humanity. Most people understand that war is bad. Killing is out and kindness is in. Defending and feeding the hungry is de rigeur, and helping the homeless is everyone's obligation.

"So," I summed up to the young man, "your position that 'God is love' and that 'Love is the right way to live,' are both right—but your professors failed to give you the true source of those beliefs. Historically, they came from none other than Jesus himself. So to deny Christianity is to deny the very source and basis of the beliefs you hold."

I wish I could tell you that my friends' boy was convinced immediately by my comments and went home repentant, as had the famous prodigal son in a story told long ago.[6] But the social pressure exerted by university professors and lifestyles is enormous, so my young friend went away sad, as also had a famous rich young ruler[7] in the day of Jesus, for he had a wealth—of sophomoric knowledge.

The historical truth is that compassion was birthed in the life and teachings of Jesus, and it grew to its present worldwide stature because of him. Jesus clearly instructed his followers to care for those who are hurting and needy, which began a compassionate revolution of Christianity that has lasted two thousand years. He said,

> When the Son of Man comes in his glory…the righteous will answer him, "Lord, when did we see you hungry and feed you, or thirsty and give you something to drink? When did we see you a stranger and invite you in, or needing clothes and clothe you? When did we see you sick or in prison and go to visit you?"
>
> The King will reply, "Truly I tell you, whatever you did for one of the least of these brothers and sisters of mine, you did for me."[8]

This is what motivated Mother Teresa to leave her comfortable lifestyle as a nun in a school for wealthy girls and begin her mission to minister to the poorest of the poor, the sick and dying in the streets and slums of Calcutta. She knew they were bearers of the image of God and in each one, no matter how sick or deformed, she saw the face of Jesus.

Mother Teresa said, "I have found the paradox, that if you love until it hurts, there can be no more hurt, only more love."[9] This is revolutionary love, sacrificial love, world-changing love. In an era that denies the reality of God, people across cultures are drawn to Mother Teresa and cannot explain the power of such love except that it comes from God himself. Today her order, the Missionaries of Charity, carries on her work around the world.

Of course, the Sisters' efforts are only understandable within a Christian, theistic worldview. And that, I believe, is a good reason to lean toward theism and away from atheism.

If you care about compassion and if you research the source of the remarkable compassion revolution that has swept our world, I believe you will find yourself more closely aligned with Mother Teresa than with western academic and political elites. But that should be no surprise, for the cultural elites in Jesus' day were not aligned with him either. In fact, they crucified him then, and their ilk likewise persecute his followers today.

But if human history teaches us anything, it's that cultures and its elites come and go—but *love endures forever*. And yes, those three words are a quote from the Bible too, about forty-four times to be specific. But it makes sense only if God exists, because in order to actually exist, eternal love and personhood need God to be real. So if you believe in love, like my young collegian friend, that's a pretty good reason to believe in God.

Fascinating converts from atheism to theism: Malcolm Muggeridge

Thomas Malcolm Muggeridge was a journalist, teacher, satirist, and the editor of *Punch* magazine from 1953–1957. *Punch* was known for its sophisticated and intellectual humor, and Muggeridge was the embodiment of both, which led to his popularity on British radio and TV.

Muggeridge began his adulthood as an avowed socialist and atheist. His father, Henry Thomas Muggeridge, a Fabian socialist, taught his son "to regard socialism as the one thing that mattered."[10] Malcolm learned this lesson well, so the young socialist journalist traveled to the USSR in 1932 as a correspondent for the *Manchester Guardian*. But his discovery there of a severe famine in the Ukraine—and the Soviet government's cover-up of the crisis—opened his eyes to the horrors and lies of socialism. As a result, Muggeridge jettisoned Marxist socialism but not its attendant atheism. In fact, in 1936 he wrote *The Earnest Atheist,* which was a literary biography of one of his own erudite and satirical heroes, Samuel Butler.

But as the years wore on, Muggeridge struggled with his atheism. As an intellectual journalist whose only commitment was to the pursuit of truth, he came to realize there were many aspects of religion he admired. In 1958 Muggeridge wrote in his diary: "Christianity, to me, is like a hopeless love affair. It is infinitely dear and infinitely unattainable. I…look at it constantly with sick longing." Muggeridge understood the need for belief in God as a foundation for culture, but he could not step over the line because he simply lacked faith. Any conversion would have to be a real one, not just a romantic hope. As late as 1966 he was a self-professed "religious maniac without a religion." "I don't believe in the resurrection of Christ, I don't believe that he was the son of God in a Christian sense." I am "enchanted by a religion I cannot believe."[11]

But in 1970 Muggeridge filmed a documentary about Mother Teresa in Calcutta, India, and was staggered by this little nun who was caring for the sickest of the sick and the poorest of the poor—the very people the intellectuals and socialists wrote about and cared for in theory. Yet here was love in action, social concern incarnate at a level that put all other social theorists to shame.

In short order, the life and ministry of Mother Teresa opened Muggeridge's heart to faith in God, then in Christ, and then, on November 27, 1982, Malcolm and his wife, Kitty, became members of the Catholic Church.

So can smart people still believe in God? Muggeridge wrote, "It is one of the fantasies of the 20th century that believers are credulous people, sentimental people, and that you have to be a materialist and a scientist and a humanist to have a skeptical mind. But of course exactly the opposite is true."[12]

CHAPTER 27

I WONDER ABOUT THE WONDER OF HOPE, THEREFORE GOD EXISTS

"If you're going through hell, keep going."[1]

WINSTON CHURCHILL (1874–1965)

It is extremely difficult for us today—indeed it may be impossible—to comprehend the despair and impending disaster that fell upon Great Britain in 1940. Adolf Hitler's Nazi war machine was at full force and its appetite for conquest voracious. The nations of Austria and Poland had been annexed; Denmark, Norway, and the Netherlands had been militarily occupied, and France itself had fallen to the *Wehrmacht*. England stood alone against the apparently invincible Germans, with only the narrow English Channel acting as a temporary buffer. The British were doomed. Theirs would be the next nation to fall. The mood of everyone in the nation was despair. Everyone, that is, except for one man.

One man refused to admit defeat.

One solitary individual would not despair.

One leader never gave up hope.

That person, of course, was Winston Churchill. He rallied his fearful nation in speech after speech, bravely calling his country to fight the "wicked" Hitler and his "immoral" empire. Incredibly, and against all odds, Churchill and his allies defeated the megalomaniacal Führer. Because of this, Churchill is variously referred to as "the leader of the century," "the man of the millennium," and even "the savior of Western civilization."

What did Churchill do to deserve such extraordinary accolades? Among his many brilliant qualities, a key asset was this: he never gave up hope. Like other notable leaders, Churchill sensed that "a leader is a dealer in hope"[2] (Napoleon) and that "everything that is done in the world is done by hope"[3] (Martin Luther). Churchill discerned that England could survive if he could awaken hope within the hearts of his downtrodden Brits.

Churchill was an optimist. This may come as a surprise to many who assume he was merely a blunt and bully politician with a perpetual scowl on his face. On the contrary, Churchill was hopeful to the core—even in his paintings he preferred bright colors and said he felt "genuinely sorry" for the browns.[4] "All will come right"[5] was one of his favorite phrases, echoing the Christian mystic Julian of Norwich who said, "All shall be well, and all shall be well, and all manner of things shall be well."[6] Plus, he rarely completed a wartime speech without a stirring appeal for optimism. In the shadow of the rising threat of nuclear weapons at the end of his career, Churchill said, in his last major speech, "Meanwhile, never flinch, never weary, never despair."[7]

Are jokes about optimism permitted in a book about God?

The optimist says, "The glass is half full."

The pessimist says, "The glass is half empty."

The realist says, "This glass is twice as big as it needs to be."[8]

What an amazing man. There was very little evidence in 1940 that his small, isolated nation could defeat the much larger enemy as David defeated Goliath, Cortés overcame the Aztecs, or Washington bested King George. Churchill's clarion call for hope enlivened and emboldened a nation—actually several nations—and led to the defeat of the Nazis.

Yet does hope make sense if there is no God? This is a more difficult question than it first appears. If all reality is accidental, if there is no inherent purpose to life, and if there is no divine hand guiding history toward a better future or a desired destiny, then what possible reason do we humans have to hope? As Robert G. Ingersoll, the theist turned agnostic orator (and one-time associate pastor under American revivalist Charles G. Finney) said, "Hope is the only universal liar who never loses his reputation for veracity."[9] Or as the marine biologist Jacques Cousteau put it, "If we were logical, the future would be bleak indeed. But we are more than logical. We are human beings, and we have faith, and we have hope, and we can work."[10] For a materialist, there is no compelling reason to assume the future will be better than the past or to put any stock in human progress. Hope in the face of great odds is illogical and deceptive. Here's the rub, though: at times it is helpful and maybe even necessary to hope, because otherwise we are left with debilitating despair.

It may surprise you that philosophers have a lot to say about despair. The French existentialists of the early twentieth century, such as Jean-Paul Sartre and Albert Camus, are a clear example. For these philosophers, despair, both personally and collectively, was the result of "a loss of hope." For individuals, despair occurs when one of the "pillars" by which a person has defined him or herself comes crashing down, such as when an athlete becomes disabled or a beauty queen ages. For society as a whole, hope is lost collectively when we realize there are no objective pillars upon which to construct human identity. Thus, the existentialists considered despair to be the natural and inevitable human condition.

Because of this, some existentialists questioned why humans should choose to exist at all. They proposed that the logical response to despair ought to be suicide—which is why Camus began "The Myth of Sisyphus" with, "There is but one truly serious philosophical problem, and that is suicide."[11]

Yet the will to live is a powerful force, so Camus worked to find an acceptable rationale to reject suicide. In fact, "The Myth of Sisyphus" is Camus' strenuous argument that an absurd leap of faith to embrace one's meaningless life is a better choice than suicide. But was he successful, or was he just pushing his own absurdist boulder up a different hill?

Bertrand Russell and Ludwig Wittgenstein,[12] the British fathers of analytic philosophy, which dominates American academic philosophy today, also dealt with despair. Wittgenstein, who some consider to be the top philosopher of the twentieth century, did so on a personal level, having frequent bouts with despair and various debilitating phobias. Russell dealt with despair on a metaphysical level and opined,

> Such, in outline, but even more purposeless, more void of meaning, is the world which Science presents for our belief...Only on the firm foundation of unyielding despair, can the soul's habitation henceforth be safely built.[13]

So there you have it: our existence is purposeless, void of meaning, and founded on despair. If there is no God, then there is no compelling reason for hope.

So why should Brits have toiled in the coal mines, in the factories, and on the farms to defeat Hitler? Why should American youths have sailed to engage the enemy at Iwo Jima or on the beaches of Normandy—knowing that many of them would not return home alive? If history teaches us anything, it is that sooner or later every nation falls. Why, then, from the materialist perspective, ought anyone make the ultimate sacrifice for something that will not last?

This question applies not just nationally but also individually. Why should we hold on to hope that our children will grow up to be happy, that our marriage will last the trials and temptations of a debauched culture, or that our cancer surgery will be successful and will garner us a few more years on this rock orbiting through space? If there is no point to the race, no finish line, no victor's crown, and no spectators in the stands, then why run at all?

Yet we all run this race of life with fervency and with hope. "Don't give up hope!" we tell our kids. "Hope for the future!" our candidates promise. A leading cancer hospital in Southern California is named "City of Hope." Why is this?

Maybe the explanation of our ceaseless inclination to hope is that God implanted within us the urge to hope because we are his image-bearers. The God of Christianity is a being of hope: "May the *God of hope* fill you with all joy and peace as you trust in him, so that you may overflow with hope by the power of the Holy Spirit."[14] Thus, hope is not an irrational, existential leap in the face of contrary evidence (as the philosophers concluded), but it is a rational and relational posture because we see the same quality in our heavenly Father. Hope is a clue to the inherent meaning of life as well as to the intrinsic character of God.

Thus, reasons for hope are abundant within a theist worldview. We are beings designed by a loving God of hope who created us within a meaningful universe and who preprogrammed us to hope. As the prophet Jeremiah said, God desires to give us "hope and a future."[15]

Alexander Pope famously put it this way, "Hope springs eternal within the human breast."[16] This is a remarkable statement, for Pope had every reason to despair. In his lifetime, Catholics, like Pope, were not allowed to go to college, vote, or hold public office. Even his name would have made life difficult in an era of anti-Catholic sentiment. In addition, Pope suffered from many ailments that left him physically deformed (hunchbacked) and in chronic pain. Yet as a Christian he found eternal reasons to hope.

Hope is an intuitive predisposition that motivates us—despite the circumstances. No matter how dark the night or how dismal the diagnosis, we humans still cling to hope. Maybe we are more than *Homo sapiens*; maybe we are *hope-o* sapiens. We never give up hope. Because of this, even when things get tough and dark, we should, as Churchill lectured the students at an English prep academy on October 29, 1941, "Never, never, never give up."[17]

Given the evidence of unquenchable human hope, might this not be a clue that points toward the existence of God? Could our reliance on hope open our minds to the possibility that naturalism alone is insufficient to explain what drives each of us deep inside? I think it does. I hope that, as you ponder this, it may strike you that the fact that you have hopes and dreams leads you to lean toward theism. Belief in God is not a leap-of-faith hope; it is a conclusion drawn from the fact of hope.

Poet and Polish President Vaclav Havel on hope:

"Hope is a state of mind, not of the world...Either we have hope or we don't; it is a dimension of the soul, and it is not essentially dependent on some particular observation of the world or estimate of the situation. Hope is not prophecy. It is an orientation of the spirit, and orientation of the heart; it transcends the world that is immediately experienced, and is anchored somewhere beyond its horizons."[18]

—VÁCLAV HAVEL (1936–2011)

CHAPTER 28

I WONDER ABOUT THE WONDER OF HUMAN DIGNITY, THEREFORE GOD EXISTS

"If I regarded my life from the point of view of the pessimist, I should be undone. I should seek in vain for the light that does not visit my eyes and the music that does not ring in my ears. I should beg night and day and never be satisfied. I should sit apart in awful solitude, a prey to fear and despair. But since I consider it a duty to myself and to others to be happy, I escape a misery worse than any physical deprivation."[1]

HELEN KELLER (1880–1968)

In Nazi Germany during the winter of 1938-39, a baby was born blind and missing an arm and a leg. The father, a German citizen named Knauer, wanted his baby to be "put to sleep," but the hospital would not allow it. So Knauer wrote to Adolf Hitler, asking for his help. Hitler previously had received several similar requests but had been waiting for just the right case to launch his "cleansing" euthanasia plans. Hitler responded to Knauer's letter by dispatching his personal physician, Karl Brandt, to assess whether the child was worthy of life. Upon examination, Brandt decided that the child was indeed not worthy of life, and he instructed the hospital doctors to end the child's life without fear of legal consequences, which they did.

This event began the horrific and systematic killing of thousands of disabled children and adults by the Nazis, under the oversight of the government and the medical establishment. The program began with an August 18, 1939, decree demanding that all physicians, nurses, and midwives report any infant or child, three years of age or less, having severe mental or physical disabilities. These children were then relocated to special pediatric clinics, ostensibly to serve and help them. In reality these were killing wards where these helpless children were murdered by the medical staff through lethal medications or starvation. Soon the age range was extended to seventeen years, and it is estimated that over five thousand German children perished in this manner.

Moreover, the program was soon extended to include disabled adults as well, and became known as *Aktion T4*, a shortened version of the street address that housed the central office of the program. T4's internal records reported 70,273 disabled persons were eliminated at the gassing facilities between January 1940 and August 1941. The program then was halted due to public outcry, but a second phase continued in a more secret fashion. In all, an estimated 200,000 disabled Germans were killed by their own government and medical personnel during the Nazi reign.

In his book *The Nazi Doctors*, Robert Jay Lifton quotes Baby Knauer's father as saying that Dr. Brandt assured him and his wife that "we wouldn't have to suffer from this terrible misfortune because the Führer had granted us the mercy killing of our son. Later, we could have other children, handsome and healthy, of whom the Reich could be proud."[2]

Shockingly, a very similar view was expressed by Princeton bioethics professor Peter Singer, who wrote in his 1980 book *Practical Ethics*,

> When the death of a disabled infant will lead to the birth of another infant with better prospects of a happy life, the total amount of happiness will be greater if the disabled infant is killed. The loss of the happy life for the first infant is outweighed by the gain of a happier life for the second. Therefore, if the killing of the hemophiliac infant has no adverse effect on others it would…be right to kill him.[3]

Singer is a utilitarian, which means that his view of ethics is governed by the maxim: the greatest good for the greatest number is the only way to determine ethical behavior. Thus, all morality is a result of calculations about what will produce the most happiness for the most people. But even this is hard to calculate, because he does not view human life as morally more valuable than animal life. For instance,

Singer uses the term *speciesism* to signify a prejudice for one species over another, and he claims that humans have no moral right to be speciesists (to elevate their species over another), which is why he is a vegetarian. Other atheists, such as Richard Dawkins, support Singer's abrogation of speciesism, comparing it to the racism that led to slavery in previous centuries. Singer even goes so far as to support zoophilia—sex with animals—as long as it causes the animals no harm.

But as philosopher Tom Regan noted, such a position could also be used to promote pedophilia. Such is the moral morass and depths of depravity to which we descend when we try to define the self from a materialist position. It matters not to me that Karl Brandt was a medical doctor or that Peter Singer has degrees in philosophy. It seems to me they are morally disabled. I wonder: if a government passed laws approving the euthanasia of the morally disabled, would Singer have felt forced to drink his own hemlock, so to speak?

Thankfully, the vast majority of humans alive today know that Brandt's and Singer's views are hogwash—complete and utter nonsense, no matter how many degrees are behind the perpetrators' names. Thank God that some of the disabled people throughout history were not euthanized by their parents or their government, for their contributions to society have been immense. Consider, for example, that Einstein was dyslexic. Franklin Roosevelt had polio in both legs. Stephen Hawking has motor neuron disease. Helen Keller was deaf and blind. Beethoven was deaf. And the list could go on and on.

Thank God that legislation has been passed asserting and protecting the rights of the disabled, such as the Americans with Disabilities Act of 1990 (USA), the Disability Discrimination Act of 1995 (UK), and other such laws in South Africa, India, and Australia. In fact, one of the strongest political groups in Singer's home country of Australia is Dignity for Disabled, which also has chapters worldwide, including America.

Does your worldview, dear reader, support the rights of the disabled to live? If you are aghast at what the Nazis did to the disabled in the late thirties and early forties—and I hope you are—I ask you to deeply consider: why are you so aghast? Why was the Nazi T4 program so wrong? So immoral? So wicked?

Singer also famously claimed that since a child is not able to feel satisfaction or frustration before about eighteen months after birth, both abortion[4] and infanticide are permissible before that time. He also opines that this justifies the right to euthanize those on the other end of life—the elderly. For Singer, euthanasia is appropriate when the quality of one's life produces more pain and problems for a community than benefits. His own mother, who suffers from Alzheimer's disease, was kept alive due to the wishes of Singer's sister. He confessed that if he were solely responsible, she might not be allowed to continue to live. (And remember, the Nazis also had a euthanasia program for the infirm elderly.)

So there are huge moral issues to consider on both ends of the human life spectrum, as well as on the able-disabled spectrum. These issues are quite difficult to sort out from an atheistic framework: why can't we euthanize disabled infants like we do disabled infant farm animals, or sickly senior citizens as we do elderly pet dogs and cats? What is so different about humans, even humans in extremely poor health?

From a theistic, Christian perspective the answer is easy: only humans were created in the image of God, and even the loss of good health does not negate that fact.

My friends Roger and Nancy knew this. Their son Jeremy was born a hemophiliac, which impacted their family life greatly. He was unable to play sports, ride a bike, or do many things that healthy kids enjoy. Singer reasons that Roger and Nancy could have chosen to abort Jeremy in order to have a happier family life. Of course, only someone without personal experience of such a child could ever suggest such a monstrous alternative. Even though Jeremy lived for only fourteen years, Roger and Nancy wouldn't trade those years for anything.

If you believe in the dignity of the disabled and dying, that is a very logical—and, I might add, humane—reason to lean toward theism.

The incredible and inspiring life of Nick Vujicic

If anyone had reasons to feel hopeless or depressed, Nick Vujicic had them—or, rather, was missing them. Nick was born with tetra-amelia syndrome, a rare medical disorder involving the lack of arms and legs. Yes, Nick was born without any limbs at all. His autobiography is called, surprisingly, *Life Without Limits: Inspiration for a Ridiculously Good Life*. Today he is a bestselling author, globally famous inspirational speaker, husband, and father of two children.

Growing up is difficult for all children, but just imagine what it must have been like to have no arms or legs. Nick struggled with loneliness and depression as a child, constantly wondering why he was so different from other children.

"At age eight I thought that I should commit suicide. Why? Because I didn't have hope…At age 10, I tried to drown myself in 6 inches, or 15 centimeters of water, in my home. I told my dad I just wanted to relax, but really, I wanted to end my life. I had enough. I had enough. Ok?

"The first two times I rolled over…And the third time…I realized at that moment that if I actually went through with committing suicide, I would leave a greater burden for my parents than they already had. So when I saw in my mind my mom and my dad and my brother crying at my grave if I went through with it, that one thought saved me.

"If my parents never told me that I was beautiful the way I was. If my parents never told me that I was special and that I was loved, I wouldn't be here today."

Nick Vujicic learned to believe that he was beautiful, as his parents told him, and he learned to believe in the love of God, as his parents also told him. Now he is traveling the world, meeting presidents and heads of state, talking before hundreds of thousands annually—telling them all that they are beautiful and that God's love is real. His life is a living testimony that all humans have dignity, a concept that, as we have seen in light of the atheists who would have recommended Nick's death as a newborn, is best understandable in a theistic worldview.

PART FIVE

FEELING HOMESICK AT HOME

Bertrand Russell, in the second volume of his autobiography, included this letter he wrote in 1918:

> Even when one feels nearest to other people, something in one needs obstinately to belong to God and refuse to enter into any earthly communion—at least that is how I should express it if I thought there was a God. It is odd, isn't it? I feel passionately for this world and many things and people in it, and yet...what is it all? There *must* be something more important, one feels, though I *don't believe* there is. I am haunted. Some ghosts, from some extra mundane regions, seem always trying to tell me something that I am to repeat for the world, but I cannot understand the message.[1]

This was a startling confession from Russell, the stoic atheist philosopher who was famous for courageously facing the meaninglessness of existence in a godless universe. Yet here he revealed that he felt "haunted," that is, that there "*must* be something more important" (italics his) to life that he was hearing but not understanding. Why were the passions and joys of this life not enough for Russell?

To my mind, the best explanation of this is what C.S. Lewis called, so provocatively, "the sweet poison of the false infinite."[2] The problem with earthly happiness is that it is a finite experience for beings who were created for the infinite. As Thomas Carlyle wrote, "Man's unhappiness, as I construe it, comes of his greatness; it is because there is an Infinite in him, which with all his cunning he cannot quite bury under the Finite."[3]

According to Christian theology, humans are not mere mortals, alive for a few brief years on earth as the materialists would suggest, experiencing ultimately meaningless moments compared to the vast reaches of space-time. No—we are special creatures designed by an eternal God to experience joy *forever*. As the Westminster Catechism puts it, "Man's chief end is to glorify God and to enjoy him forever."[4] This will occur in what is called heaven, which is a place of uninterrupted and unending joy, however hard that may be for us to imagine. In a strange twist, it is similar to what John Lennon wrote of in his song "Imagine"; he had the intuition right but the location wrong. According to most theists, complete peace, sharing, and wholeness will happen in heaven, not on earth.

If this is true, it explains why we humans have longings that cannot be satisfied by finite things or experiences: we have been designed for infinite joy, so moments of happiness are nice but ultimately fleeting. Each earthly moment of happiness is like one tiny bite of an extraordinary dessert, and the taste is so delicious that we crave more. The exquisite after-desire hints that more must exist somewhere—but we cannot reach the banquet hall that we intuit must be real.

Sadly, some people jump to the conclusion that the first taste is all there is, that momentary flavor is the apex of the experience. So they seek one small, miniscule taste after another, thinking this is all there is to life and happiness. These little bites taste sweet, but if one focuses exclusively on them, one will miss the grander banquet to which they point. The tastes, when idolized as ends in themselves, eclipse the greater banquet of which they are only a small part. They thus become "sweet poisons" masquerading as "false infinites."

But could our tastes, dreams, and desires be pointing to more? Might they contain a hidden message, subtle clues that point toward the existence of God? Could our hunger for a pain-free existence, community, and transcendence also reveal a hidden thirst for God? As Marilynne Robinson put this, "Our limits are entirely consistent with our transcending them."[5]

Are these hungers actual evidence that can help us understand why, as G.K. Chesterton said, we can feel "homesick at home"?[6] These are the questions we will ponder during the last three days of our thirty-one-day journey.

CHAPTER 29

I LONG FOR A WORLD WITHOUT PAIN AND SUFFERING, THEREFORE GOD EXISTS

"You don't become true friends by going to the circus together but only by going through hell together. And remaining friends."[1]

WILLIAM J. O'MALLEY (1931–)

Before one of our weekend services a couple stopped me in our church lobby with downcast faces. They said, "Rick, do you know what today is?"[2]

"No," I responded.

"Today is the one-year anniversary of our granddaughter's drowning in a pool. You did the memorial, remember?"

"Yes, I remember the memorial, but I had forgotten the exact date. I'm again so sorry for your loss." We then shared together a few special moments of tears, memories, and prayers, and then I watched in awe as they walked away, hand in hand. Couples who survive such an event—and remain happily married—are truly extraordinary people.

I was still thinking about and praying for them as I stepped behind the podium to deliver my message. I was deeply sad for their *sorrow anniversary*, as I came to call it. Every year, for the rest of their lives, this date will bring pain and grief. As I looked out upon more than a thousand faces, it hit me that every single family has probably experienced similar pain in life—and some more than once. I thought, *What amazing, resilient people you all are—that you can be hurt so deeply yet carry on. What sadness and sorrow you must carry beneath the veneer of your Sunday smiles. What a testimony to your faith that you still choose to follow God after such dark valleys.* On that Sunday, my respect for "average Christians" grew a thousandfold.

That morning it hit me that every adult probably has several sorrow anniversaries. Everyone experiences—either personally or within their close circle of family and friends—major distress-inducing events such as the death of a family member or friend, the agony of watching a loved one battle a disease, or the rending of a marriage through unfaithfulness or divorce. Sadly, the list could go on and on.

Which is just the problem: Why are our lives so filled with sadness and sorrow? Why so much suffering and pain?

For many atheists, this is *the big roadblock* to believing in God. To paraphrase David Hume, if God is both all-powerful and all-loving, then why does he allow so much sadness and sorrow in our lives? Why doesn't God calm the hurricanes and tsunamis, prevent disabilities in newborns, and cure our loved ones' diseases? For my above-mentioned friends, why didn't God nudge someone to check on their little granddaughter before she wandered over and fell in the pool? How could God just remain silent and do nothing?

To be sure, these are emotional questions at heart, not logical (even though Hume's argument takes the surface form of a syllogism). Answers to the problem of suffering can be given, such as the free-will defense or the Philip Yancey/Paul Brand solution that pain is "the gift no one wants."[3] But very few people are persuaded by such answers while in the throes of loss and grief. Rational answers do little to comfort broken hearts. People lose their faith not because of logic but due to pain—intense personal suffering that trumps all reasonable arguments.

This is why some believers in God abandon their faith. Ted Turner, for instance, was distinctly religious as a boy and planned on becoming a missionary. But when he was fifteen years old, his younger sister, Mary Jane, became ill with a painful, fatal disease. He prayed for God to heal her, but instead she continued to suffer for years and finally died. During that time, Turner's Christian faith also died. He embraced atheism and later famously called Christianity "a religion for losers."[4]

A similar example is Bart Ehrman, the James A. Gray Distinguished Professor of Religion at the University of North Carolina at Chapel

Hill and a bestselling author—of books attacking the reliability of the Bible. He too grew up as a believing Christian, but his faith in the Bible collapsed during graduate school at Princeton under the onslaught of textual criticism. In subsequent years, his study of the problem of suffering led to his abandonment of Christianity and theism. In his words, "The problem of pain destroyed my faith."[5]

Others, though, go through the crucible of suffering with their faith in God still intact. A stellar example of this is Elie Wiesel, the famed Holocaust survivor, author, and recipient of the 1986 Nobel Peace Prize. In a 2006 interview Wiesel revealed that he is often asked, "How can you still believe in God?" His response is, "There are all the reasons in the world for me to give up on God. I have the same reasons to give up on man, and on culture, and on education. And yet...I don't give up on humanity, I don't give up on culture...I don't give up on it. I have the reasons. I don't use them...Look, I have faith. It's a wounded faith."[6]

Other notable examples of people whose faith has endured incredible suffering includes Christians such as C.S. Lewis (who wrote *A Grief Observed* after his wife, Joy, died of cancer) and Joni Eareckson Tada. She wrote, "When quadriplegia ambushed my life, it felt as though God were smashing me underfoot like a cigarette butt. Chronic pain on top of quadriplegia became the extra plate I could not handle, and my anger turned into deep despair."[7] Yet her faith survived this trial, and people worldwide have found comfort in her example of trust in God in the face of pain.

Yet another example is Harvard-trained Nicholas Wolterstorff, who was a respected Christian philosopher when his twenty-five-year-old son, Eric, died in a mountain climbing accident. Suddenly, this esteemed Christian intellectual was confronted by the greatest challenge of his life—how to reconcile his intense, unrelenting agony with his lifelong faith in a loving God. His struggles, questions, and conclusions are recorded in *Lament for a Son*, which I consider to be the best—and most moving—theistic book about human suffering. Wolterstorff wrote,

> What is suffering? [I know] when suffering happens. What it *is*, I do not know...I understand nothing of it. Of pain,

> yes: cut fingers, broken bones. Of sorrow and suffering, nothing at all. Suffering is a mystery as deep as any in our existence...
>
> We are one in suffering. Some are wealthy, some bright; some athletic, some admired. But we all suffer. For we all prize and love; and in this present existence of ours, prizing and loving yield suffering. Love in our world is suffering love...Suffering is for the loving. If I hadn't loved him, there wouldn't be this agony...
>
> In the valley of suffering, despair and bitterness are brewed. But there also character is made. The valley of suffering is the vale of soul-making.[8]

I agree 100 percent with Wolterstorff, especially on three counts. First, suffering happens to us all. We all experience grief and sorrow. In Shakespeare's *Romeo and Juliet*, all dialogue ends with Prince Escalus's grim pronouncement, "All are punished!"[9] but he could as well have said, "All suffereth!"

This is the lesson I have learned from the precious church members I have been privileged to serve. Just yesterday I officiated at the gravesite memorial of a delightful Christian woman whose life suddenly ended at age forty-eight due to a ruptured aorta. Her Filipino family taught me volumes about suffering and grief, for they were unafraid to show their sorrow. I have never attended a service with such wailing. (We evangelical Christians tend to have "Celebration of Life" memorials rather than funerals. But in the process, could we be denying and repressing some of our grief?)

As her casket was lowered into the ground, her nine-year-old son cried "Mommy, Mommy, don't leave me, Mommy!" over and over—and it struck me as healthy. No one told him to stop crying or that big boys don't cry. Instead, they joined him in his grief.

This boy did nothing to deserve this fate. Everyone suffers in this life; no one is exempt. As Ralph Waldo Emerson said, "Sorrow makes us all children again—destroys all differences of intellect. The wisest know nothing."[10] I've seen tough Marines cry uncontrollably and little old ladies keep a stiff upper lip. I've seen some people shed a few tears, others cry rivers; some cry softly and almost silently, others wail loudly; some stiffen up, others shake uncontrollably. As Christian psychologists Tim Clinton and Gary Sibcy put this, "Sooner or later, life trashes our trophies."[11]

Second, suffering both destroys us and yet has the power to remake us, which Wolterstorff calls soul-making. If our faith is somehow able to survive, we can become closer to God and others in the process. Concerning God, William O'Malley has written, "Those who believe that they believe in God, but without passion in their hearts, without anguish in mind, without uncertainty, without doubt, without an element of despair even in consolation, believe in the God *idea*, not God himself."[12]

Indeed, in Christian theism we encounter not only a God who allows suffering but one who knows suffering. In Isaiah 53, though written hundreds of years before Jesus was born, the Messiah of Israel is prophesied to be a *suffering servant*. In addition, Psalm 22, from which Jesus quoted on the cross centuries after it was written, is an uncanny description of crucifixion itself, even though death by crucifixion wasn't even invented yet.

This is a completely unique belief in all human history: a God who chose to suffer with and even die for his creation—all out of love. Somewhere in this profound event we find that deep love and real suffering comingle—in the very being of God. As Wolterstorff wrote, love and suffering go hand in hand, or rather, heart in heart. We can't have one without the other. We love and suffer because we are created in the image of God, who also loves and suffers.

Soren Kierkegaard on God, suffering, and love

"I am seeing evermore clearly that all who God has loved...all had to suffer in the world...this is the Christian doctrine: being loved of God means loving God and suffering."[13]

In a similar vein, M. Scott Peck said, "The truth is that our finest moments are most likely to occur when we are feeling deeply uncomfortable, unhappy, or unfulfilled. For it is only in such moments, propelled by our discomfort, that we are likely to step out of our ruts and start searching for different ways or truer answers."[14] I have certainly found that my deepest relationships are with those who have traveled—through and beyond—the valleys of sorrow with me, as this chapter's opening quote by O'Malley affirms.

Suffering does something in us that nothing else can do, especially not within an atheist perspective: it invites us to rise above our bestial level and participate in the divine. Suffering, though inescapable, becomes endurable if we can glimpse not just positive earthly outcomes from it but also the presence of a Deity who suffers with us—whose very Being is also stained by tears.[15] Incredible as it may sound, suffering is a part of personhood—and even a part of the divine Person. Could this be one reason why God created creatures with free will: he allowed humans to rebel and cause him pain because his agape love was the only thing strong enough to transform their individualism into community, their solitary lives, bent only on survival, into profound fellowship focused on sacrifice, unselfishness, and service?

Here is what I am suggesting: animals suffer without meaning whereas humans suffer to be purged of the idolatry of self so we can find our place in an eternal, others-focused community—which is what the Trinity models for us and what heaven will be for us. I realize this is a big pill to swallow, but it is no harder than the pill that suffering has no ultimate meaning. This is why our sorrow anniversaries can be redemptive rather than just painful and occasions that cause us, more and more each year as we approach the finality of our own deaths, to lean toward theism.

Resources on dealing with suffering and pain

Since pain and suffering are difficult experiences that, if unresolved, lead some to abandon faith in God, I include here several books that I have found to be emotionally and intellectually helpful in traveling through this "valley of the shadow of death."[16]

- Nicholas Wolterstorff, *Lament for a Son* (Grand Rapids, MI: William B. Eerdmans, 1987).
- C.S. Lewis (written under the pseudonym N.W. Clerk), *A Grief Observed* (New York: Seabury Press, 1961).
- Peter Kreeft, *Making Sense Out of Suffering* (Ann Arbor, MI: Servant Books, 1986).
- Philip Yancey, *Where Is God When It Hurts?* (Grand Rapids, MI: Zondervan, 1977).
- H. Norman Wright, *Recovering from the Losses of Life* (Grand Rapids, MI: Fleming H. Revell, 1991, 1993).

CHAPTER 30

I LONG FOR LASTING LOVE AND COMMUNITY, THEREFORE GOD EXISTS

"Hell is yourself, and the only redemption is when you put yourself aside to feel deeply for another person."[1]

TENNESSEE WILLIAMS (1911–1983)

Years ago I came upon a slim book and was so taken by the ending that I have never forgotten the words. In a bed-and-breakfast inn where my wife and I were sharing a quiet getaway, I noticed the small volume lying on a shelf, but the ink on the book's spine was so faint that it took special focus to make out the title: *Eve's Diary*. I was surprised to read, on the title page inside, that it was written by Mark Twain, the acclaimed author, humorist, and self-described atheist. Why was this infamous Bible-scoffer interested in retelling a story from the Bible?

Twain wrote this short piece for the 1905 Christmas edition of *Harper's Bazaar*. Though highly critical of both the Bible and Christianity, Twain found enough inspiration in the Genesis story of Adam and Eve to write several small books, including this one, *Extracts from Adam's Diary*, and others. *Eve's Diary* is a fictional account of the first couple's story, written from the perspective of Eve from the moment of her creation until just after her death.

The book was banned from a library in Charlton, Massachusetts, because the illustrations of the unclothed couple (by Lester Ralph) were censored. Twain railed against the duplicity that his book should be banned but the Bible itself allowed to stay. In one copy of the book, Twain handwrote the comment, "Clothes make the man, but they do not improve the woman."[2]

Interestingly, I barely remember the book having pictures. Instead, I recall Eve's special fondness for the beauty within Eden, and also her awareness of the importance of love. But the sentence that captured me was the book's last. After Eve died, Adam buried her and said these final, poignant words: "Wherever she was, there was Eden."[3]

There it is—one of my all-time favorite quotes. Poetically it summarizes that we humans are created for community. Even after their banishment from the garden utopia, Adam still found his paradise "wherever she was"—that is, in a person rather than a place.

In other words, Eden can only be cohabited, not inhabited. After all, before Eve was created, it still was not good for Adam to be alone. He was designed to be in a human relationship where they both could experience lasting love.

And so are you and I.

But today, sadly, many relationships do not endure. Nor do some marriages, friendships, or families. Nor church relationships, business partnerships, or political ties. I say these things not pointing a finger at others but confessing my own shortcomings. At one time I thought our church would never go through a split, coworkers and I would be on good terms for life, and close friendships would survive severe trials. How naïve I was.

The older I get, my Eden revolves mostly around my Eve. My wife is becoming more and more of my world, which is a good reason to marry well. As Amy and I age, we two more and more become one. At the same time, it seems that lasting friendships become more and more rare (and hence more valuable).

We humans just seem to be better at damaging relationships than we are at nurturing them. Love often does not last, in this fallen world of ours, because we people are so difficult. As pastors sometimes quip, ministry would be easy if it weren't for the people. Along the same lines, while Dostoyevsky "half-jokingly said that though he loved humanity, he couldn't stand individuals,"[4] Sartre said it with a straight face: "Hell is other people."[5]

Here's the problem: we seem to be hardwired for love and created for community. But on this earth, every person is imperfect. Actually, that's a gross understatement. We are far from perfect. Each of us is a magnificent sinner, both in quantity and quality. Sinning is really the only thing every human being does well. As G.K. Chesterton said, the fall was the one doctrine that needed no proof.[6] Because of this, what we desire most—lasting love—is exceptionally difficult to attain.

This is a lot to chew on, so let's divide our concerns into two key questions we'll attempt to answer in this essay: How are we created for community? And why do we tend to destroy the very thing we desire?

Let's take the "created for community" question first. The notion that we are relational beings is a common belief, affirmed in thinkers as diverse as Martin Buber and Sigmund Freud. This belief is a deeply intuitive, tacitly held belief that needs no justification for most people—the misery of loneliness is proof enough. And it's effective: a firm belief in the value of community has transformed societies through the efforts of people like Mohandas Gandhi and Martin Luther King Jr.

King's vision of equality, for instance, went beyond confronting racial injustice to the creation of what he called "the beloved community."[7] In his famous speech at the steps of the Lincoln Memorial, King said,

> I say to you today, my friends, that in spite of the difficulties and frustrations of the moment, I still have a dream... I have a dream that one day on the red hills of Georgia the sons of former slaves and the sons of former slave owners will be able to sit down together at a table of brotherhood...I have a dream that my four children will one day live in a nation where they will not be judged by the color of their skin but by the content of their character...
>
> From every mountainside, let freedom ring. When we let freedom ring, when we let it ring from every village and every hamlet, from every state and every city, we will be able to speed up that day when all of God's children, black men and white men, Jews and Gentiles, Protestants and Catholics, will be able to join hands and sing in the words of the old Negro spiritual, "Free at last! Free at last! Thank God Almighty, we are free at last!"[8]

King's dream involved not just freedom from racism but also freedom for community—a community that transcended the differences that so often divide us. In the words of C.S. Lewis, "There is no way to save one's humanity except by giving it in fellowship to others."[9]

This is the vision that drove Lewis. His biographer, Walter Hooper, suggested the central premise of Lewis's works is "All men are immortal," but Lewis scholar Gilbert Meilaender modified that to: "All human beings are made for life in community with God (and thereby with one another)."[10] Combining the two, we might encapsulate Lewis's thought by saying: Humans are designed for eternal life in community with God and one another. (Which is pretty close to the opening words of the previously referenced Westminster Shorter Catechism: "Man's chief end is to glorify God and to enjoy him forever.") For Lewis, this results in the eternal "revelry of insatiable love,"[11] which is what all humans long for—lasting love and communion with others.

Which leads us to the second question mentioned above: if we all desire love, then why is community so difficult to maintain? The answer again is our monumental sinfulness, rooted in pride and selfishness, for community is the opposite of self-centeredness. "Real transformation is the opposite of self-improvement,"[12] and requires—both personally and corporately—the dethronement of ego. As Eberhard Arnold wrote in 1927,

> The sickness of the world lies in [the] isolation of the accentuated ego. An individual who feels no pain but his own cannot identify with the world's suffering. He cares only for himself, fights only for his own existence, and seeks only his own improvement and happiness. In this way, he increases the suffering of others. He is a parasite that endangers the whole. He has severed himself from the reality and unity of life. He has cut himself off from the whole, and must finally perish.[13]

Which, sadly, is exactly the self-interest paradigm that pervades postmodern America. People are told, "You have a right to be happy," and "Be true to yourself," which means nothing more than "be selfish."

But rather than increasing community and family bonds, today's pervasive selfishness is breaking them.

As the Bible says, we reap what we sow.

Which is, according to C.S. Lewis, what heaven and hell are all about. Heaven is simply the place where those who want to love God and others—and are willing to dethrone their own egos to do so—are gathered in everlasting love and community. Hell, conversely, is the place where those who choose ego over community find just that: eternal aloneness and bitterness.

In his fabulous novel about heaven and hell, *The Great Divorce*, Lewis even suggests that in the afterlife those in hell can choose to go to heaven if they want to (Evangelical Christians can gasp here!), but only one chooses to do so. Most choose to remain in hell because their pride has rendered them incapable of humble repentance. As Lewis superbly puts this, "There are only two kinds of people in the end: those who say to God, 'Thy will be done,' and those to whom God says, in the end, 'Thy will be done.' All that are in hell, choose it. Without that self-choice there could be no hell. No soul that seriously and constantly desires joy will ever miss it. Those who seek find. To those who knock it is opened."[14]

Here is the conundrum: the atheist desires lasting love, all the while knowing that nothing lasts in a materialistic universe. On the other side, Christian theists also desire lasting love, but they have reason to believe in its existence because of the eternity of God—who not only is the source of eternity but also the source of community. Plus, for Christians the problem of sin and human imperfection is solved by the atonement of Christ. It all comes together in a neat package—which is delightful because *coming together* is what we all want to begin with. Of course, this happens in heaven, the eternal paradise, the reconstituted Eden.

Which brings us back to Mark Twain. There is some speculation that Twain wrote *Eve's Diary* to his wife, Livy, after her death in 1904. Twain once said, "*Eve's Diary* is finished—I've been waiting for her to speak, but she doesn't say anything more." Was Twain wishing his wife were still alive—that is, was he revealing our ingrained longing for immortality?

A good marriage is the epitome of community. In the Bible it is even compared to the relationship between Christ and his bride, the church. In this sinful world of ours, spouses have the best chance to experience a little bit of Paradise, and this little bit is a foretaste of what is to come. Twain was so close to grasping this, but the master storyteller had, in the end, a failure of imagination. His cynicism prevented him from recognizing the hints that his soul was trying to tell him.

So, our sorrow over broken relationships may be telling us something: like Twain, when all is said and done—and our grand achievements mean less to us than our close relationships—we find ourselves longing for Eden, that is, heaven. Because we desire lasting love and unselfish community, our longings may be good reasons to lean toward theism.

A philosopher discusses our inability to implement real community

"The ideals of human love and community expressed [by Jesus and the apostles] are so lofty that nowhere other than the New Testament are they presented or expected to be implemented. Indeed, Jesus himself offers complete unity among his followers as a miracle…that only he could bring about."[15]

—THOMAS DUBAY

CHAPTER 31

I LONG FOR IMMORTALITY AND ETERNITY, THEREFORE GOD EXISTS

"Perhaps they are not stars, but rather openings in heaven where the love of our lost ones pours through and shines down upon us to let us know they are happy."[1]

ESKIMO PROVERB

If there is no God, why have so many humans, not only now but throughout human history, believed in an afterlife?

After all, nothing is more certain—and final—than death. And nothing is more difficult to verify than the hereafter.

Yet across cultures and across the millennia, most humans have sensed that when a human life ends, it doesn't really end. We have very little physical evidence to support that intuition, yet some humans have spent most of their lives—and the lives of countless slaves and servants—preparing for their afterlives. Think of the Egyptian pharaohs and their massive pyramids, or consider the Terracotta Army buried near the mausoleum of Qin Shi Huang, the first emperor of China. Over 8000 soldiers, 670 horses, and 150 chariots were fashioned from clay to protect the emperor in his next life. Or consider the burial rituals across the globe, involving everyone from Eskimos to Aborigines and located from Asia to Africa to the Americas. Wherever one looks in human history, humans spend an inordinate amount of time and treasure preparing for life after death.

The brute fact, which is the evidence I wish to consider in this essay, is that most people genuinely believed—and still believe—that death is not the end of life. As Pulitzer Prize-winning poet Robert Hillyer said,

"I believe in my survival after death. Like many others before me, I have experienced 'intimations of immortality.' I can no more explain these than the brown seed can explain the flowering tree. Deep in the soil in time's midwinter, my very stirring and unease seem a kind of growing pain toward June."[2]

We discussed the issue of grief in chapter 29, but here I want to focus on another implication of the reality of grief—the longing for an afterlife. Here is the key: while I have seen many people grieve, I have never heard anyone who lost a close loved one say, "Well, death is no big deal. We all are just evolutionary accidents, so it doesn't matter to me." No—from both theists and atheists I have heard the emotions of grief and the common lament: "Why? Why did this happen? She (he) shouldn't have died so soon (or at all)."

Whenever someone dies at what is considered a young age, whether two, twenty-two, or even fifty-two (what we consider to be young depends on our own reference point), loved ones feel not just a deep sense of loss but also a sense of injustice, that this early death should not have been. This is especially true for parents who have lost children. I have heard many grieving parents say something like, "This was not supposed to happen. Parents aren't supposed to bury their own kids. This is so wrong."

But if there is no God, if life is just an accidental event, and if human life is no more valuable ultimately than animal or insect life, is it rational to grieve so deeply? Is it rational to mourn at all? We don't grieve when a tree in our yard dies (we may be sad, but we don't deeply grieve), and we don't mourn when a chicken or cow is killed for our chicken tenders or hamburgers. It is true that some people deeply mourn the passing of their family pets, but even they would tell you their grief is not as deep as that of a parent who has lost a child. What is it about death that hurts so deeply, that brings about unwanted and unexpected emotions?

When C.S. Lewis's wife, Joy Davidman, died of cancer after their marriage of only four years, his grief was immense. Lewis said, "No one ever told me that grief felt so much like fear."[3] Yes, grief is fearful territory that no one would wish on another.

Why is this? Why does the death of a loved one hurt so deeply? Why does it take so long to recover from grief? (No, not recover, because some never completely do.) Why does it take so long to be able to function semi-normally and experience quasi-joy again? There is simply no rational, materialistic answer. In fact, the older we get and the more frequent the deaths of our family members and friends, the more we should become acclimated and used to grief. If death were just a natural, inevitable phenomenon, then we should get better at handling it with age. Yet that is seldom the case. In addition, our culture is not improving in its ability to comprehend and embrace death. Instead, we are becoming experts at avoiding and suppressing any contact with death. We are becoming less and less comfortable with the reality of death, not more.

Atheist Ernst Becker wrote an insightful, Pulitzer-Prize-winning book titled *The Denial of Death*. Becker's book is essentially a response to the issue: why is it that we humans struggle so much with death? If we are mere creatures like all other creatures on planet Earth, why do we mourn? These questions led him to a deeper issue: why, if we are bestial beings, do we have such feelings of importance and transcendence? His frank answer was startling: feelings of importance and transcendence are "normal neuroses"[4] that enable us to face the reality and finality of death. In other words, we are all crazy, but our craziness allows us to exist in the face of our monumental nonimportance and ultimate nonexistence. For Becker, the only way to live meaningful atheistic lives is *to lie to ourselves and our loved ones* in order to believe, against the relentless logic of materialism, that we each are important.

But maybe our difficulty with death is not irrational. Maybe our hearts know something that our minds can't figure out. Maybe the grief in our hearts is revealing to us something real. When death interrupts love and friendships, maybe we grieve so profoundly because we deeply sense, in a depth of understanding that our brains cannot fathom, that death is not what is supposed to happen. Could it be that our extreme discomfort with death is evidence that we are not mere material, temporary beings? Might we be, as Christians believe, immortal beings cloaked in mortal bodies?

Qoheleth, the writer of Ecclesiastes in the Bible, claimed that God has "set eternity in the human heart."[5] Could it be that our repulsion and revulsion at death is ontological, that is, it is hardwired into our very souls and psyches? Throughout my pastoral journey, I have yet to see nonreligious relatives who did not display a level of profound despair when a loved one passed away. Could this be evidence that we are not temporary but eternal beings? Grief could be the evidence for transcendence that atheists are demanding, evidence that points to the existence of life after death.

A headstone in a cemetery in Ireland reads, "Death leaves a heartache no one can heal; love leaves a memory no one can steal." If that is true, I wonder how atheists and antisupernaturalists can explain it within their materialist framework. Why does death hurt so much when we have known for a lifetime that it was coming? And why is love so memorable if it is nothing more than an evolutionary adaptation for the survival of the species? Think about it. The imprint never vanishes and it fuels our passions long beyond love's inception. In the end, I believe the experience we have all shared—the profound and persistent pain we feel when mourning the loss of a loved one—has no adequate explanation except the reality of a transcendence that is disallowed within materialism.

On the other hand, theism provides a more-than-adequate explanation for this phenomenon. The fact that we mourn necessitates an explanation beyond the confines of naturalism; it requires a supernatural explanation. The Bible teaches that we are not mortal but immortal beings. We will live forever. Grief is the deep and sensible notion that death should not be, that it is *not right* that we be separated from our loved ones. But grief is only a temporary experience for Christians, who believe that we will be reunited with loved ones in heaven, where "there will be no more death or mourning or crying or pain, for the old order of things has passed away."[6] For me, no other explanation of grief suffices.

Plus, we look forward to an afterlife that is better than this one, an eternal experience of harmony. It has various religious names such as heaven, nirvana, jannah, tengoku, or ouranos. But no matter the language, all express the hope for a better existence than the one we had on earth (even those religions that teach reincarnation hope for a better next life, though it is on earth rather than somewhere else).

Why do we think an afterlife will be better than this one? Surely the influence of Jesus and his teachings about heaven have influenced western culture—such as his promise to the penitent thief on the cross, "today you will be with me in paradise,"[7] and his promise to his followers, "In my Father's house are many mansions…I go to prepare a place for you."[8]

We long for something better, purer, longer-lasting. In a word, we long for *transcendence*. We long to transcend the earthly burdens of mortality and sin, and we long to be changed into something glorious. The apostle Paul waxes eloquent as he describes this:

> So it will be with the resurrection of the dead. The body that is sown is perishable, it is raised imperishable; it is sown in dishonor, it is raised in glory; it is sown in weakness, it is raised in power; it is sown a natural body, it is raised a spiritual body…
>
> I tell you a mystery: We will not all sleep, but we will all be changed—in a flash, in the twinkling of an eye, at the last trumpet. For the trumpet will sound, the dead will be raised imperishable, and we will be changed. For the perishable must clothe itself with the imperishable, and the mortal with immortality.[9]

Was Paul right? If so, this is one of the most important truths each person must grasp in life: death is not our intended end—heaven is.

But what will our new existence in heaven be like? Sadly, we have no way to even conceive of our future glory so we are limited to analogous thinking. We are like caterpillars destined to change into butterflies, acorns before transforming into oaks, or even babies before birth.

C.S. Lewis wrote often and deeply about the inchoate awareness of immortality that resides in human hearts, and also provided humorous analogies about what heaven might be like. In *Miracles* he wrote,

> I think our present outlook will be like that of a small boy who, on being told that the sexual act was the highest

> bodily pleasure, should immediately ask whether you ate chocolates at the same time. On receiving the answer "No," he might regard absence of chocolates as the chief characteristic of sexuality. In vain you would tell him that the reason why lovers in their carnal raptures don't bother about chocolates is that they have something better to think of. The boy knows chocolate: he does not know the positive thing that excludes it. We are in the same position.[10]

In another book, *Mere Christianity*, Lewis wrote, "The happiness which God designs for his higher creatures is the happiness of being freely, voluntarily united to Him and to each other in an ecstasy of love and delight compared with which the most rapturous love between a man and a woman on this earth is mere milk and water."[11]

To quote Lewis again, this time from *The Weight of Glory*,

> We want something else which can hardly be put into words—to be united with the beauty we see, to pass into it, to receive it into ourselves, to bathe in it, to become part of it...This is why the poets tell us such lovely falsehoods. They talk as if the west wind could really sweep into a human soul; but it can't. They tell us that "beauty born of murmuring sound" will pass into a human face; but it won't. Or not yet. For if we take the imagery of Scripture seriously, if we believe that God will one day *give* us the Morning Star and cause us to *put on* the splendor of the sun, then we may surmise that both the ancient myths and the modern poetry, so false in history, may be very near the truth as prophecy. At present we are on the outside of the world, the wrong side of the door. We discern the freshness and purity of morning, but they do not make us fresh and pure. We cannot mingle with the splendours we see. But all the leaves of the New Testament are rustling with the rumour that it will not always be so. Some day, God willing, we shall get *in*.[12]

Conversely, Lewis points out that on this earthly plain we are like the

Danaids in Greek mythology, "attempting to fill sieves with water."[13] We long for lasting love, life, and meaning, but they slip through our grasp—though the momentary touch reveals to us their reality.

So our longings for immortality and transcendence, on the positive side, and our grief and sadness over the death of a loved one, on the negative side, provide clear hints that we are designed for eternity. We are indeed like caterpillars, seeds, babies waiting to be born. We are athletes trained for the big league, artists ready to create our masterwork, authors about to write our magnum opus. Like kids outside the front gates of Disneyland, we sense the joy and life on the other side of the gate, and we want in. Plus, we loathe the pain and grief on this side of the gate, and we want out. Is it any coincidence that the Bible too talks about the pearly gates?[14]

Deep in our hearts we sense this life is just a prelude, not the finale; we dream for love to last and never cease. What kind of longing is that? It is a completely irrational and absurd longing if we are just material, temporary beings. But if we are divinely created beings, our longings for immortality and eternity are deep signposts, hidden within our very souls, that point toward the real existence of God.

Theologian N.T. Wright on the beautiful promises of this present world

"The beauty of this present world...has something about it of the beauty of a chalice, beautiful in itself but more hauntingly beautiful in what we know it's to be filled with; of that of a violin, beautiful in itself but particularly because we know the music it is capable of. Another example might be the engagement ring, which is meant as it is to delight the eye but which is meant even more to delight the heart because of what it promises."[15]

CONCLUSION

Which of these thirty-one surprising reasons to believe in God is powerful enough to persuade an ardent nonbeliever to abandon atheism? Or to pose this question another way: which reason would convince Ivan Karamazov?

Ivan Karamazov is the most brilliant, embittered atheist in all of world literature. In a famous chapter titled "The Grand Inquisitor" in Fyodor Dostoyevsky's *The Brothers Karamazov* (sometimes called the greatest novel ever written), Ivan challenges his brother Alyosha's Christian beliefs. Ivan's anti-God diatribe to a nameless Prisoner is often seen as the ultimate argument against the existence of God.

Ivan's arguments are celebrated and debated by both nontheists and theists—but seldom is the Prisoner's response to the Grand Inquisitor noted. After the Grand Inquisitor is through with his extended anti-sermon, the Prisoner responds with...*a simple kiss*.[1]

No words, no arguments, no condemnations. Just a loving gesture in response to the most unloving speech ever rendered. This is pure genius on Dostoyevsky's part. All the arguments in the world—including, of course, the thirty-one surprising reasons discussed in this book—may not convert someone who has been twisted and tortured by pain; even the best reasons might not penetrate the armor of someone deeply wounded by the evil forces in this world.

But love can. After all, it was the wordless argument from Mother Teresa that shattered the atheist worldview of Malcolm Muggeridge.

This also is the ultimate apologetic: in spite of all the suffering and injustice in the world, in spite of all of the ugliness and hatred, it still is a fact that *undeserved, forgiving love exists*. It exists in the teachings and example of Jesus, it exists in his disciples who follow him, and it exists in the cultures that have been stamped by his influence. But self-sacrificing, Christlike love is craziness in secularism's me-first, look-out-for-number-one culture. Dostoyevsky knew this also: that anyone who lived in a truly Christlike manner would be considered insane by his or her family and friends. This is why another of Dostoyevsky's books is titled *The Idiot*.

Christlike love is idiocy in a materialist world (as Nietzsche understood). But for some of us, such love has awakened us from the sleep of secularism into the awareness of deeper meanings to life and existence. We have felt the kiss of God's presence in the forgiving embrace of a spouse or when cradling a newborn infant; we've caught glimpses of hidden messages within sunsets and ocean vistas; we've heard divine echoes that sound out from behind beauty, justice, human suffering—and even sports heroes and zombies. The Sacred shyly makes its presence known through myriad mediums, for Love is not overbearing. Yet when these "shadows of heaven"[2] are added together, they comprise a pretty weighty set of reasons to believe in God.

ONE FINAL, PHILOSOPHICAL CONFESSION

To sum up this book, these heavenly shadows serve two purposes. First, they reveal a world "charged with the grandeur of God"[3] and thereby point toward and reveal the presence of God; that is, they are *surprising reasons to believe in God.* Second, they reveal an *order of existence*, about which I have allowed, by design, a severe defect to persist within the theology of this book. Now that the book is drawing to a close, it's time to confess and correct this defect.

Up until now, I began each essay with the facts of this world (the premises of human experience), and inferred from them the likeliness of the existence of God: we trust our ability to reason, therefore God exists; we hope, therefore God exists; we long for a world without suffering, therefore God exists.

Here is my confession: this ending—"therefore God exists"—is both completely backward and bad theology. Of course, bad theology is the expected result when one begins from a bad premise, such as "It's all about me." In contrast, Christian theology begins with "It's all about God." But since atheists and agnostics are not willing to begin with that premise, Christians cannot start there when trying to explain faith to nontheists. As a result, in this book we use the materials available and start where people are rather than where we wish they were.

In a manner of speaking, "It's all about God" has been the *supreme* hidden and surprising element lurking throughout this book about hidden and surprising things. I have hinted at this in each essay: *who God is* determines who we are and not vice versa. God is love, therefore I am a loving being; God is just, therefore I value justice; God is beautiful, therefore I adore beauty; and so forth. Thus, the final message of these many chapters, taken together, is: *God is, therefore I exist.* The existence of God, properly speaking, comes before our own and his essence shapes our own. Yes, God is revealed in our likes, morals, surroundings, and instincts—but ultimately he is the Cause, not the consequent; the Premise, not the conclusion. Because of this, "therefore God exists" was an expedient designed to give way, in time, to the highest truth of all: *God is,* or as he himself put this, "I AM WHO I AM."[4]

There. I feel better getting that off my chest, at last. Confession is good for mind as well as the soul. The correct order is "God is, therefore..." It's all about God—which explains all about us as well.

ONE FINAL HIDDEN-TREASURE STORY

I began this book with true stories about a buried treasure found in a field in Northern California and a message double-coded into one of Bach's sonatas. Interestingly, there was also a hidden message in the last fugue Bach ever wrote, the final "Contrapunctus" in his *Art of the Fugue.* There the musical theme "B-flat–A–C–B" occurs over and over, up and down, backward and forward, according to the style of fugues. In addition to the melody, there is a completely separate, double-coded message in these notes, a message hidden from those trained to name musical notes only A through G. But the message is clear to those trained in Bach's homeland of Germany, where B-flat is called B, and B is called H (this is why Bach's famous *Mass in B-Minor* is called

H-moll Messe in German).[5] When this different musical notation is applied, the hidden message appears: B–A–C–H.

In other words, just as painters often sign their artwork in a lower corner, Bach signed his name, over and over again, in the very musical notes that comprised the last fugue he ever penned. What creative genius!

Essentially, this book has been an attempt to reveal the even more brilliant, creative genius of God—how the Almighty has signed his name, over and over again, in his magnificent creation and deep within our very being. He is speaking, but is heard only by those who have ears that hear and eyes that see.[6] God is not silent, but he is so very, very subtle.

"The World is filled, and filled with the Absolute. To see this is to be set free."

PIERRE TEILHARD DE CHARDIN[7]

ACKNOWLEDGMENTS

In an earlier draft of this book, I included *gratitude* as one of the thirty-one surprising reasons to believe in God. Though gratitude is not the subject of a chapter in this book, I still believe it is an extremely powerful clue to the existence of God—because it is grounded, both etymologically and historically, in grace.

As the wit G.K. Chesterton expressed so memorably, "I would maintain that thanks are the highest form of thought, and that gratitude is happiness doubled by wonder." Or as he expressed so humorously, "The worst moment for an atheist is when he is thankful and has no one to thank."

One of the benefits of leaning toward theism, then, is that I have the privilege of giving thanks to many, including:

- Don and Gay Stedman, my parents and those to whom this book is dedicated
- My lovely wife, Amy, and our terrific adult kids: Micah, Noah, and Jesse
- My siblings Randy and Teri, as well as their families
- Dean and Marcia Holst, my in-laws, and the extended Holst/Buch clans
- The edit team—and friends—who once again helped me wordsmith various drafts and correct many mistakes: Lori Clark, Nicholas Domich, Glenn Ellis, Erin Fritz, Bev Graham, Vivian Jones, Erik Neilson, Carol Peterson, Alan Reinhart, Steve Rindfuss, Dave Sidnam, Julia Staton, and Randy Watson
- Janet Grant, my esteemed literary agent
- Terry Glaspey, the rest of the team at Harvest House, and editor Rod Morris

- Our friends who served with us at Adventure Christian Church during the twenty-one years I was privileged to serve as founding and senior pastor
- Above all, I give thanks to the God of grandeur, who, as this book has tried to recount, has revealed himself to humans in the beautiful and meaningful array of his handiwork—which is essentially the same as giving thanks to Jesus Christ, the incarnation of all beauty and meaning, who at once is both the reason for and the recipient of all gratitude.

ENDNOTES

INTRODUCTION: SURPRISING REASONS TO LEAN TOWARD THEISM

1. Associated Press, "Northern California Couple's Buried Treasure Goes for Sale," *Mercury News*, May 27, 2014, updated August 12, 2016, www.mercurynews.com/2014/05/27/northern-california-couples-buried-treasure-goes-for-sale/.
2. Michael Winter, "Calif. Couple Unearths Gold Rush Coins Worth $10M," *USA Today*, February 26, 2014, www.usatoday.com/story/news/nation/2014/02/25/california-gold-coins-buried-treasure/5817179/.
3. Antoine de Saint-Exupéry is a French national hero who is honored for his World War II exploits as a pilot and mourned for his disappearance at sea during a reconnaissance mission on July 31, 1944.
4. Antoine de Saint-Exupéry, *The Little Prince* (New York: Harcourt, Brace, and World, 1943), 70.
5. Rainer Maria Rilke, *Letters to a Young Poet,* translated and with a foreword by Steven Mitchell (New York: Random House, 1984), 7-8.
6. David Bentley Hart, *God: Being, Consciousness, Bliss* (New Haven, CT: Yale University Press, 2013), 87.
7. Harry A. Overstreet, "The Hidden World Around Us," in Edward R. Murrow, *This I Believe: The Personal Philosophies of One Hundred Thoughtful Men and Women* (New York: Simon and Schuster, 1952), 131-32.
8. John Lennox, *God's Undertaker* (Oxford: Lion Hudson, 2007, 2009), 191.

PART ONE: THE ECSTASY AND AGONY OF BEAUTY

1. Dr. Darren R. Weissman, *The Power of Infinite Love and Gratitude* (Carlsbad, CA: Hay House, Inc., 2005), 30.
2. David Bentley Hart, *God: Being, Consciousness, Bliss* (New Haven, CT: Yale University Press, 2013), 279-80; 277.
3. As Hart puts this, "Theology begins only in *philokalia*: the 'love of beauty.'" David Bentley Hart, *The Beauty of the Infinite: the Aesthetics of Christian Truth* (Grand Rapids, MI: Wm. B. Eerdmans, 2003), 30.
4. Gilbert Meilaender, *The Taste for the Other* (Grand Rapids, MI: Wm. B. Eerdmans, 1978), 177.
5. William Shakespeare, *The Tragedy of King Lear,* ed. Jay L. Halio (New York: Cambridge University Press, 1992), 225.

CHAPTER 1: SUPERHERO AND FANTASY MOVIES

1. James Herrick, *Scientific Mythologies* (Downers Grove, IL: InterVarsity Press, 2008), 20.
2. E. Michael Jones, *Monsters from the Id* (Dallas, TX: Spence Publishing, 2000).
3. Humphrey Carpenter, *The Letters of J.R.R. Tolkien* (Boston, MA: Houghton Mifflin, 1995), letter 142, p. 172; quoted in https://en.wikipedia.org/wiki/The_Lord_of_the_Rings.
4. Peter Kreeft, *The Philosophy of Tolkien: The Worldview Behind The Lord of the Rings* (San Francisco: Ignatius Press, 2005).
5. Ibid., 181.

6. Revelation 5:5.
7. I am indebted to Dr. Louis Markos for this insight.
8. Jonathan Petre, "J.K. Rowling: 'Christianity Inspired Harry Potter,'" *The Telegraph*, October 20, 2007, www.telegraph.co.uk/culture/books/fictionreviews/3668658/J-K-Rowling-Christianity-inspired-Harry-Potter.html.
9. If you are interested in other ways people today have been influenced—and even fooled—by science fiction, I highly recommend *Scientific Mythologies* by James Herrick.
10. https://en.wikipedia.org/wiki/Ray_Bradbury.
11. http://hollowverse.com/ray-bradbury/. "At play in the fields of the Lord" is the name of a book by Peter Mattheissen and a movie based on that book. It also is very likely an allusion to Matthew 13:24-30 in the Bible, since the plot involves missionary efforts to convert a tribe in Brazil.

CHAPTER 2: HORROR MOVIES AND BOOKS

1. Jones, *Monsters from the Id*, 20.
2. Ibid., 44, 85.
3. Ibid., 87.
4. Ibid., 85.
5. Ibid., 84.
6. Ibid., 59.
7. Ibid., 260.
8. Ibid., xii.
9. C.S. Lewis, *The Great Divorce: A Dream* (London: Geoffrey Bles Ltd., 1946), 27.
10. Anne Rice, *Called Out of Darkness: A Spiritual Confession* (New York: Alfred A. Knopf, 2005), 183.
11. http://annerice.com/ChristTheLord-Profession.html.
12. "Writer Anne Rice: 'Today I Quit Being A Christian,'" *NPR*, August 2, 2010, www.npr.org/templates/story/story.php?storyId=128930526.

CHAPTER 3: MUSIC MOVES MY SOUL

1. Gerald Klickstein, *The Musician's Way* (New York: Oxford University Press, 2009), v; see also Victor Hugo, *William Shakespeare* (Paris: Librairie Internationale, 1867).
2. "The Case of the Divje Babe I Bone," *Oxford Journal of Archaeology*, vol. 25, issue 4, November 2006, 317-33.
3. John Noble Wilford, "Flutes Offer Clues to Stone-Age Music," *New York Times*, June 25, 2009.
4. John Lennon, interview with the *Evening Standard* newspaper, March 4, 1966.
5. Michael Kennedy, review of "A Confidential Matter: The Letters of Richard Strauss and Stefan Zweig, 1931–1935," *Music & Letters*, vol. 59, no. 4, October 1978, 472-75.
6. In fact, Cage preferred the sounds of traffic over ordinary music. He said, "When I hear what we call music, it seems to me that someone is talking. And talking about his feelings, or about his ideas of relationships. But when I hear traffic, the sound of traffic—here on Sixth Avenue, for instance—I don't have the feeling that anyone is talking. I have the feeling that sound is acting. And I love the activity of sound...I don't need sound to talk to me." Quoted by Miroslav Sebestik, "Interview with John Cage," 1991, from *Listen, Documentary by Miroslav Sebestik*, ARTE France Développement, 2003.

7. Michael Caputo, *God: Seen Through the Eyes of the Greatest Minds* (West Monroe, LA: Howard Publishing, 2000), 26.
8. Jeremie Begbie, "The Sense of an Ending," in *A Place for Truth*, ed. Dallas Willard (Downers Grove, IL: InterVarsity Press, 2010), 216-18.
9. Ibid.
10. Genesis 4:21.
11. Numbers 10:1-10.
12. 1 Samuel 16:14-23.
13. Psalm 150:1-6.
14. Colossians 3:16.
15. Revelation 15:2.
16. Revelation 14:5.
17. Quoted in William J. O'Malley, *Connecting with God* (Maryknoll, NY: Orbis Books, 2013), 146-47.

CHAPTER 4: I LOVE BEAUTY AND ART

1. Thomas Dubay, *The Evidential Power of Beauty: Science and Theology Meet* (San Francisco: Ignatius Press, 1999), 3.
2. Charles Saumarez Smith, "The Sacred and the Secular in Contemporary Art," *Standpoint*, December 2016/January 2017, http://standpointmag.co.uk/node/6708/full.
3. Thomas Cathcart and Joe Klein, *Plato and a Platypus Walk into a Bar* (New York: Penguin Books, 2007), 173.
4. David Bentley Hart notes, 'There are even a few texts of Darwinian aesthetics out there, which regrettably attempt to reduce our sense of beauty to a function of sexual selection or to the neurobiology of pleasure or to the modular brain's recollections of sorts of landscapes preferred by our phylogenic forbears. Yet, in the end, the experience of beauty is ubiquitous; it is inseparable from that essential orientation toward the absolute that weds rational consciousness to being. And at some level it is clearly an experience of delight...without any conceivable ulterior purpose." Hart, *God*, 277-78.
5. One atheist who greatly appreciated art and music was Arthur Schopenhauer, who found great delight in art, and especially music. He took art to be key to the liberation of the individual human from the suffering and pessimism he thought one must embrace if there were no God. Art was a momentary release from the burden of existence, an intuitive experience of the universal. However, he saw that liberation through art was temporary at best, and thus ultimately futile. Hans Küng, *Does God Exist?: An Answer for Today* (New York: Doubleday and Co., 1978), 360.
6. Genesis 1:3,10,12,18,21,25,31.
7. Ecclesiastes 3:11.
8. Song of Solomon 6:10; 1 Corinthians 15:41.
9. Genesis 24:16; 29:17.
10. Ezekiel 20:6.
11. Psalm 27:4.
12. "From Atheism to Catholicism, By Way of Truth and Beauty," *Catholic World Report*, March 2, 2015, www.catholicworldreport.com/Item/3726/from_atheism_to_catholicism_by_way_of_truth_and_beauty.aspx.

13. Hart, *God*, 285. For other excellent treatments of beauty and its relation to God, see David Bentley Hart, *The Beauty of the Infinite*, and Dubay, *Evidential Power of Beauty*.

CHAPTER 5: SPORTS FANATICS

1. Cindy Boren, "Aaron Rodgers: 'I Think God Was a Packers Fan Tonight.' Hear That, Russell Wilson?" *Washington Post*, September 21, 2015, www.washingtonpost.com/news/early-lead/wp/2015/09/21/aaron-rodgers-i-think-god-was-a-packers-fan-tonight-hear-that-russell-wilson/.
2. Christopher R. Cotter, "Just How Religious Is 'Sport'?" *Religion and More*, September 30, 2010, https://religionandmore.wordpress.com/2010/09/30/just-how-religious-is-sport/.
3. Arthur Remillard, "Religion and Sports in America," *Oxford Research Encyclopedias*, March 2016, http://religion.oxfordre.com/view/10.1093/acrefore/9780199340378.001.0001/acrefore-9780199340378-e-145.
4. Though we should not discount rituals, for they provide an access to the heart. As W.H. Auden wrote, "Only in rites," he would say, "can we renounce our oddities / and be truly entired [made whole or become a part of the whole]." See Wilfred M. McClay, "Grappling with God: The Faith of a Famous Poet," *Catholic Education Resource Center*, May 15, 2006, www.catholiceducation.org/en/culture/art/grappling-with-god-the-faith-of-a-famous-poet.html.
5. Cotter, "Just How Religious Is 'Sport'?"
6. Galatians 2:2.
7. Ephesians 6:12.
8. 1 Corinthians 9:25.
9. Philippians 3:13-14.
10. 2 Timothy 2:5.
11. 1 Corinthians 9:24-27.
12. Darren Heitner, "Sports Industry to Reach $73.5 Billion by 2019," *Forbes*, October 19, 2015, www.forbes.com/sites/darrenheitner/2015/10/19/sports-industry-to-reach-73-5-billion-by-2019/#2fa01e9a1585.
13. "Global sports market—total revenue from 2006 to 2015," *Statista*, www.statista.com/statistics/194122/sporting-event-gate-revenue-worldwide-by-region-since-2004/.
14. Ecclesiastes 3:11.
15. "Sports in Heaven?" *Desiring God*, June 10, 2014, www.desiringgod.org/interviews/sports-in-heaven.
16. Robert Novak, *The Joy of Sports*, quoted in Raymond J. de Souza, "God Is a Sports Fan," *Catholic Education Resource Center*, January 10, 2013, www.catholiceducation.org/en/faith-and-character/faith-and-character/god-is-a-sports-fan.html.
17. Ibid.
18. de Souza, "God Is a Sports Fan."

CHAPTER 6: HAPPINESS IS A MORAL RESPONSIBILITY

1. A.A. Milne, *The House at Pooh Corner* (New York: Penguin Books, 1928), 172.
2. Aristotle, *Nicomachean Ethics*, book 1, sec 7.
3. Declaration of Independence, 2nd paragraph. It is good to remember that original intent of "pursuit of Happiness" was related to civic duty and the feeling one gets from doing good for others. See http://blog.dictionary.com/happiness/.

4. Henry David Thoreau, *Walden* (Boston: Beacon Press, 1997), 6.
5. Eric Hoffer, *The Passionate State of Mind* (New York: Harper & Bros, 1955), 6.
6. Julian Baggini, *What's It All About?: Philosophy and the Meaning of Life* (New York: Oxford University Press, 2004), 89.
7. Quoted in Orison Sweet Marden, *How to Get What You Want* (New York: Thomas Y. Crowell, 1917), 74.
8. Charles Schulz, United Features Syndicate, October 13, 1960.
9. Dana Meachen Rau, *Albert Einstein* (Minneapolis, MN: Compass Point Books, 2003), 19.
10. Daniel Weis, *Everlasting Wisdom* (Rothersthorpe, UK: Paragon Publishing), 103.
11. Varla Ventura, *Sheroes* (Berkeley, CA: Conari Press, 1998), 150.
12. C.S. Lewis, *Surprised by Joy* (New York: Harcourt, Brace and Co., 1955), 18.
13. Nehemiah 8:10.
14. Dubay, *Evidential Power of Beauty*, 334.
15. John Suppe, "Ordinary Memoir," in Paul M. Anderson, *Professors Who Believe: The Spiritual Journeys of Christian Faculty* (Downers Grove, IL: InterVarsity Press, 1998), 65-73.
16. Ibid.

CHAPTER 7: SEX CAN BE OUT OF THIS WORLD

1. Quoted in Philip Yancey, *Rumors of Another World* (Grand Rapids, MI: Zondervan, 2003), 78.
2. Raymond J. de Sousa, "Charlie Sheen's Search for God," *National Post*, February 12, 2011, http://fullcomment.nationalpost.com/2011/02/12/father-raymond-j-de-souza-charlie-sheens-search-for-god/.
3. Ibid.
4. Dennis Prager, *Happiness Is a Serious Problem* (New York: Regan Books, 1998), 88.
5. Pope Benedict XVI, quoted in de Souza, "Charlie Sheen's Search for God."
6. de Souza, "Charlie Sheen's Search for God."
7. Genesis 4:1 (KJV).
8. Genesis 4:1.
9. Psalm 46:10.
10. "Research: Christian Sex Better than Kama Sutra," *World Net Daily*, July 27, 2008, www.wnd.com/?pageId=70669.
11. Genesis 2:24.
12. Genesis 2:25.
13. Ben Witherington, "Rob Bell's *Sex God* Book—A First-Rate Read," *Ben Witherington* (blog), March 2, 2007, http://benwitherington.blogspot.com/2007/03/rob-bells-sexgod-book-first-rate-read.html.
14. Genesis 1:27.
15. Genesis 3:23.
16. Genesis 4:14.
17. Justin Taylor, "Five Things You Didn't Know About 'Jane Roe,'" *Gospel Coalition*, January 22, 2013, https://blogs.thegospelcoalition.org/justintaylor/2013/01/22/5-things-you-didnt-know-about-jane-roe/.

PART TWO: YEARNINGS FOR A BETTER WORLD

1. Marilynne Robinson, *The Givenness of Things* (New York: Farrar, Straus and Giroux, 2015), 41.

CHAPTER 8: HUMAN TRAFFICKING

1. This oft-quoted statement has no known reference in Burke's writings or speeches, but may be an adaptation of his comment: "When bad men combine, the good must associate; else they will fall one by one, an unpitied sacrifice in a contemptible struggle." Edmund Burke, *Thoughts on the Cause of Present Discontents*, 1770.
2. Anatole France, *The Revolt of the Angels* (1914), ch. 27.
3. For instance, evolutionary naturalist Michael Ruse concludes: "Morality is a biological adaptation no less than are hands and feet and teeth. Considered as a rationally justifiable set of claims about an objective something, ethics is illusory. I appreciate that when somebody says, 'Love thy neighbor as thyself,' they think they are referring above and beyond themselves. Nevertheless, such reference is truly without foundation. Morality is just an aid to survival and reproduction...and any deeper meaning is illusory." Michael Ruse, "Evolutionary Theory and Christian Ethics," in *The Darwinian Paradigm* (London: Routledge, 1989), 262-69; quoted in J.P. Moreland, "The Image of God and the Failure of Scientific Atheism," in William Lane Craig and Chad Meister, *God Is Great, God Is Good* (Downers Grove, IL: IVP Books, 2009), 44.
4. I truly mean "universal," as can be seen in the interesting hypothetical: what if extraterrestrial life exists? Does this entail that child abuse is wrong even in alien cultures? Is the mass murder of one race of beings by another always wrong, as was portrayed in the movies *Avatar* and *Independence Day*? As director and writer James Cameron himself acknowledged, *Avatar* made a moral, philosophical argument against the mass murder of one species by another. He clearly wanted viewers to feel that it is wrong for one alien race to exterminate another, and therefore, by extension, it is wrong for humans to exterminate any animal species here on earth. (The movie also makes many other transcultural moral arguments, such as the immorality of betrayal and of antienvironmentalism. Imagine that—Cameron's movie is an extended argument for this book.) In *Avatar*, the perpetrators of evil were humans, while in *Independence Day* the bad guys were aliens. So from both angles, this chapter's argument is illustrated: mass murder with the goal of extinguishing a separate race or species is always wrong. Furthermore, this is a supracultural moral law—it even applies to extraterrestrials.
5. This oft-quoted statement has no known exact reference in the writings of Dostoyevsky, but instead is a summary by Jean Paul Sartre of "the formulation of Dostoyevsky" which Sartre considers "the starting point of existentialism." J.P. Sartre, *Existentialism and Humanism* (London: Methuen, 1948, 1970), 33. However, there are several references in Dostoyevsky's *The Brothers Karamazov* that may have led to Sartre's summary. One such possible reference is: "Ivan Fyodorovitch added in parenthesis that the whole natural law lies in that faith, and that if you were to destroy in mankind the belief in immortality, not only love but every living force maintaining the life of the world would at once be dried up. Moreover, nothing then would be immoral, everything would be lawful, even cannibalism. That's not all. He ended by asserting that for every individual, like ourselves, who does not believe in God or immortality, the moral law of nature must immediately be changed into the exact contrary of the former religious law, and that egoism, even to crime, must become not only lawful but even recognized as the inevitable, the most rational, even honourable outcome of his position." Dostoyevsky, *The Brothers Karamazov*, 1912, trans. Constance Garnett (New York: Signet Classics, 1957), 72.

   Another possible reference is: "If there is no immortality, then all things are permitted." See also Dostoyevsky, *Brothers Karamazov*, bk. 2, chap. 6; bk. 5, chap. 4; bk. 11, chap. 8.

6. This is not to claim that God is the source of all morality, just universal morality. For instance, different cultures may very well create their own, culturally limited moral norms. One culture may approve of polygamy (the ancient Hebrews), for instance, whereas another culture may not. I would suggest that God is not the source of this moral system, but it arose simply within cultures as a tradition of preference—and was finally replaced by monogamy due to the Christian ethic that placed a higher value on women.
7. William J. Murray, *My Life Without God* (Nashville: Thomas Nelson, 1982), 232-33.

CHAPTER 9: CRUELTY TO ANIMALS

1. David P. Gushee, *The Sacredness of Human Life: Why an Ancient Biblical Vision Is Key to the World's Future* (Grand Rapids, MI: Wm. B. Eerdmans, 2013), 388.
2. Lisa Abend, "In Spain, Human Rights for Apes," *Time*, July 18, 2008, www.time.com/time/world/article/0,8599,1824206,00.html.
3. Carol E. Lee, "PETA Miffed at Obama's Fly 'Execution,'" *Politico*, June 18, 2009, www.politico.com/story/2009/06/peta-miffed-at-obamas-fly-execution-023886.
4. "I learned that all moral judgments are 'value judgments,' and that none can be proved to be either 'right' or 'wrong.' ...I discovered that to become truly free, truly unfettered, I had to become truly uninhibited. And I quickly discovered that the greatest obstacle to my freedom, the greatest block and limitation to it, consists in the unsupportable 'value judgment' that I was bound to respect the rights of others. I asked myself who were these 'others'? Other human beings, with human rights? Why is it more wrong to kill a human animal than any other animal...?" Ted Bundy, quoted in Harry V. Jaffa, *Homosexuality and the Natural Law* (Claremont, CA: The Claremont Institute Center for Political Philosophy and Statesmanship, 1990), 3-4.
5. A similar encounter is recounted in Prager's book, *Think a Second Time* (New York: HarperCollins, 1995), 76-77.
6. Gary L. Francione and Anna E. Charlton, "The Case Against Pets," *Aeon*, https://aeon.co/essays/why-keeping-a-pet-is-fundamentally-unethical?utm_source=Aeon+Newsletter&utm_campaign=0935483c82-Daily_Newsletter_8_September_20169_5_2016&utm_medium=email&utm_term=0_411a82e59d-0935483c82-68726381.
7. Genesis 1:27.
8. Exodus 20:10.
9. Exodus 23:4-5.
10. Proverbs 12:10. The question may be asked, "Why would God, in the Bible, forbid the consumption of some animal meat while at the same time permitting that of others?"

    For instance, Christopher Hitchens makes the unique assumption that it is *similarities between pigs and humans* that led human religions to ban porcine consumption, which resulted in what he called "why heaven hates ham." He suggests that pigs "were too uncomfortably reminiscent of the human" and thus laws against eating ham "probably originates in a nighttime of human sacrifice and even cannibalism at which the 'holy' texts often do more than hint." Christopher Hitchens, *God Is Not Great* (New York and Boston: Twelve Hachette Book Group, 2007), 40. (Truly, nontheists grasp at straws when they try to explain Divine reasoning, which by definition is beyond human discovery without revelation.)

    Hitchens's suggestion is ironic because the opposite is, in fact, the case. As Ian S. Markham points out in *Against Atheism*, "The truth about food laws is that two themes emerge: the first is an eco-friendly affirmation of life; and the second is the holiness and separateness from the nations." Ian S. Markham, *Against Atheism* (West Sussex, UK: Wiley-Blackwell, 2010), 25.

Markham quotes Jacob Milgrom's commentary on Leviticus 1–16 in favor of an interpretation diametrically opposite that of Hitchens's, that Israelite dietary laws were not subconscious denials of death, but instead were purposeful assertions of life. Concerning Jewish dietary laws, Milgrom explains their "purpose is to teach the Israelite reverence for life by (1) reducing his choice of flesh to a few animals; (2) limiting the slaughter of even these few permitted animals to the most humane way; and (3) prohibiting the ingestion of blood and mandating its disposal upon the altar or by burial as acknowledgement that bringing death to living things is a concession of God's grace and not a privilege of man's whim." Markham, *Against Atheism*, 25.

In short, Jewish dietary laws support rather than deny animal rights.

11. Jacques Cousteau and Susan Schiefelbein, *The Human, the Orchid and the Octopus: Exploring and Conserving Our Natural World* (2007), quoted in Seth Capo, "Jacques Cousteau: The Voice of a Silent World," *Vision*, Spring 2013, www.vision.org/visionmedia/biography-jacques-cousteau/67427.aspx.

CHAPTER 10: I'M EMBARRASSED BY THE BAD BEHAVIOR

1. Martin H. Manser, *The Westminster Collection of Christian Quotations* (Louisville, KY: Westminster John Knox Press, 2001), 313.
2. Quoted in *The Historical Jesus: Five Views*, ed. James K. Beilby and Paul Rhodes Eddy (Downers Grove, IL: InterVarsity Press, 2009), 84.
3. Mohandas Gandhi: *Gandhi: An Autobiography* (Boston: Beacon Press, 1993) 68; see also Mahatma Gandhi, *Gandhi on Christianity*, ed. Robert Ellsberg (Maryknoll, NY: Orbis Books, 2003), 5.
4. Gandhi, *Gandhi on Christianity*, 29.
5. Terrence Rynne, *Gandhi and Jesus* (Maryknoll, NY: Orbis Books, 2008), 27.
6. Kevin Glenn, *Hand Over Fist* (Bloomington, IN: Westbow Press, 2014), 111.
7. Celsus, *Celsus on the True Doctrine*, trans. R. Joseph Hoffman (New York: Oxford University Press, 1987), 91.
8. *Benjamin Franklin's The Art of Virtue*, ed. George L. Rogers (Eden Prairie, MN: Acorn Pub., 1996), 81.
9. John F. Nash, *Christianity: The One, the Many*, vol. 1 (Bloomington, IL: Xlibris, 2007), xi.
10. John Stevens Cabot Abbott, *Napoleon at St. Helena* (New York: Harper and Brothers, 1850), 245.
11. Katherine Whitehorn, *View from a Column* (London: Eyre Methuen, 1981), 121.
12. Thomas Cathcart and Joe Klein, *Plato and a Platypus Walk into a Bar* (New York: Penguin Books, 2007), 94.
13. Kimberly Winston, "Richard Dawkins Stands by Remarks on Sexism, Pedophilia, Down Syndrome," *Washington Post*, November 18, 2014, www.washingtonpost.com/national/religion/richard-dawkins-stands-by-remarks-on-sexism-pedophilia-down-syndrome/2014/11/18/a2915cd8-6f64-11e4-a2c2-478179fd0489_story.html.
14. Some atheists have recently argued, following Bertrand Russell, that there were serious defects in Christ's moral behavior, such as his cruelty to a herd of pigs and his cursing of a fig tree. My rejoinder is that if Russell could find only these two behaviors to prove his point about Jesus' less than moral behaviors, he certainly was grasping at straws. See Bertrand Russell, *Why I Am Not a Christian* (New York: Simon and Schuster, 1957), 17-19.

15. Claudia Dreifus, "Interview with the Dalai Lama," *New York Times*, November 28, 1993.
16. Matthew 26:31.
17. Ray Monk, *Bertrand Russell: The Ghost of Madness* (New York: The Free Press, 2001), 311. "I grow morbid & reflect what a failure I have made of life, as a husband & as a father. I have tried to think the fault was other people's but the repetition seems to show that it can't be."
18. Larry Taunton, *The Faith of Christopher Hitchens: The Restless Soul of the World's Most Notorious Atheist* (Nashville, TN: Thomas Nelson, 2016), 108.
19. Stanley Hauerwas, "The Virtues of Alasdair MacIntyre," *First Things*, October 2007, www.firstthings.com/article/2007/10/004-the-virtues-of-alasdair-macintyre.

CHAPTER 11. PROTECTING OUR ENVIRONMENT

1. Henry David Thoreau, Letter to Harrison Blake, May 20, 1860, published in *Letters to Various Persons* (Boston: Ticknor & Fields, 1865).
2. Robert Redford, address at Yosemite National Park dedication ceremony, 1985.
3. Tim Reid, "Save the World One Square at a Time—and Annoy Bush's Brain," *London Times*, April 24, 2007.
4. Quoted in Lawrence A. Beer, *A Strategic and Tactical Approach to Global Business Ethics* (New York: Business Expert Press, 2010) 56.
5. Quoted in Derrick Johnson, *End Game, Vol. 1, The Problem of Civilization* (New York: Seven Stories Press, 2006), 395.
6. Genesis 1:29; 2:16-17; 9:1-4.
7. Genesis 1:28.
8. Genesis 2:15.
9. John Muir, *My First Summer in the Sierra*, 148-49; quoted on http://escholarship.org/uc/item/1835687g#page-4.

CHAPTER 12: I DESPISE NEEDLESS VIOLENCE

1. Anthony St. Peter, *The Greatest Quotations of All Time* (Bloomington, IN: Xlibris, 2010), 166.
2. These are discussed—and rebutted extensively—in David Bentley Hart, *Atheist Delusions: The Christian Revolution and Its Fashionable Enemies* (New Haven, CT: Yale University Press, 2009), 3-18; see also chapters 7, 8, and 9.
3. Arthur Miller, *The Crucible* (New York: Penguin Books), 1953.
4. John Lennon, "Imagine," released on the record album *Imagine* on September 9, 1971.
5. Rudolph J. Rummel, "Death by Government," www.hawaii.edu/powerkills/NOTE1.HTM.
6. For more information on the Crusades, Inquisition, and witch trials, see Rodney Stark, *The Triumph of Christianity* (New York: HarperCollins Publishers, 2005), chapters 13, 15, and 18. Also see Dinesh D'Souza, *What's So Great About Christianity?* (Washington, DC: Regnery Publishing, 2007), chapters 18 and 19.
7. "The last paragraph of the Manifesto of the Communist Party reads: 'The Communists disdain to conceal their views and aims. They openly declare that their ends can be attained only by the forcible overthrow of all existing social conditions. Let the ruling classes tremble at a Communist revolution. The proletarians have nothing to lose but their chains. They have a world to win.'" Adam Schaff, "Marxist Theory on Revolution and Violence," from *The Journal of the History of Ideas*, vol. 34, no. 2, April–June 1973; www.jstor.org/pss/2708729.

8. Edward E. Ericson Jr., "Solzhenitsyn—Voice from the Gulag," *Eternity*, October 1985, 23-24.
9. Catharine MacKinnon, *Are Women Human?* (Cambridge, MA: Belknap Press of Harvard University Press, 2006), 58.
10. Bill Harry, *The John Lennon Encyclopedia* (London: Virgin Books, 2001).

CHAPTER 13: I DEEPLY VALUE FREE SPEECH

1. Salman Rushdie, address at Columbia University, December 11, 1991; "1,000 Days 'Trapped Inside a Metaphor,'" *New York Times*, December 12, 1991.
2. Catherine Donaldson-Evans, "Father of Marine Killed in Iraq Sues Church for Cheering Death, Appeals to Public Online for Help," *FoxNews.com*, October 26, 2007.
3. *This Glorious Struggle: George Washington's Revolutionary War Letters*, ed. Edward G. Lengel (New York: Harper Collins, 2007), 269.
4. These words are often attributed to Voltaire, but are actually a summation of his beliefs by Evelyn Beatrice Hall, writing under the pseudonym Stephen G. Tallentyre, *The Friends of Voltaire*, 1906.
5. Declaration of Independence, 2nd paragraph.
6. John Reed, *Ten Days that Shook the World* (New York: Boni and Liveright, 1919), 270-71.
7. Daniel Mahoney, "The Conservative Foundations of the Liberal Order," quoted in Bruce S. Thornton, "Protecting Democracy from Friend and Foe" in *City Journal*, March 4, 2011; www.city-journal.org/html/protecting-democracy-friend-and-foe-9648.html.
8. James Madison, quoted in Thornton, "Protecting Democracy from Friend and Foe."
9. Mallory Ortberg, "The Convert Series: Leah Libresco," *The Toast*, November 12, 2015, http://the-toast.net/2015/11/12/convert-series-leah-libresco/.

CHAPTER 14: I BELIEVE IN THE JUSTICE

1. Bianca Jagger, source unknown.
2. C.S. Lewis, *Mere Christianity* (New York: Collier Books, 1943), 45.
3. "Biographies of Nazi Leaders: Adolf Eichmann," *The History Place*, 1997, www.historyplace.com/worldwar2/biographies/eichmann-biography.htm.
4. "Adolf Eichmann," *Wikipedia*, https://en.wikipedia.org/wiki/Adolf_Eichmann.
5. "Of all the antitheistic arguments, only the argument from evil needs to be taken seriously. But I believe, paradoxically enough, that there is a *theistic* argument *from* evil, and it is at least as strong as the antitheistic argument from evil... What is deeply disturbing about horrifying kinds of evil?...wickedness strikes us as deeply perverse, wholly wrong, warranting not just quarantine and the attempt to overcome it, but blame and judgment. But could there really be any such thing as horrifying wickedness if naturalism were true? I don't see how... It can't accommodate appalling wickedness." Alvin Plantinga, "A Christian Life Partly Lived," in *Philosophers Who Believe: The Spiritual Journeys of 11 Leading Thinkers*, ed. Kelley James Clark (Downers Grove, IL: InterVarsity Press, 1993), 72-73.
6. John Rist, "Where Else?" in *Philosophers Who Believe*, 87,89.
7. Ibid., 95,98.
8. Ibid., 101.

PART THREE: SHAFTS OF GLORY

1. Carl Sagan, *Cosmos* (New York: Random House, 1980), 1.
2. Psalm 19:1-3.

CHAPTER 15: I'M AMAZED AT THE EXISTENCE

1. Bertrand Russell, quoted in John F. Post, "Mystery, Ultimate Explanation, Sufficient," at http://people.vanderbilt.edu/~john.f.post/fesec21-24.htm.
2. Martin Heidegger, *An Introduction to Metaphysics* (New York: Yale University Press, 1959), 61.
3. Stephen Hawking, *A Brief History of Time* (New York: Bantam Books, 1988), chapter 12.
4. Ibid., 193.
5. Stephen Hawking, 1994 debate with Roger Penrose at Cambridge, transcribed in Stephen Hawking and Roger Penrose, *The Nature of Space and Time* (Princeton, NJ: Princeton University Press), 26.
6. Hawking, *Brief History of Time*, chapter 8.
7. Stephen Hawking and Leonard Mlodinow, *The Grand Design* (New York: Bantam Books, 2010).
8. Stephen Hawking and Leonard Mlodinow, "Why God Did Not Create the Universe," *Wall Street Journal*, September 3, 2010.
9. Hannah Devlin, "Hawking: God Did Not Create Universe," *London Times*, September 2, 2010.
10. Radio interview with Alister McGrath and Justin Brierley on *Unbelievable?*, September 25, 2010.
11. Milton K. Munitz, *The Mystery of Existence* (New York: Appleton-Century-Crofts, 1965).
12. René Descartes, *Principia Philosophize* (Principles of Philosophy), 1664, Part 1, Article 7.
13. Vera Kistiakowsky, quoted in *Cosmos, Bios, and Theos,* eds. H. Margenau and R.A. Varghese (LaSalle, IL: Open Court, 1992), 52.
14. Roger Penrose, interview in the film *A Brief History of Time*, 1991.
15. Michael Caputo, *God: Seen Through the Eyes of the Greatest Minds* (West Monroe, LA: Howard Publishing, 2000), 66.
16. David Bentley Hart, *God: Being, Consciousness, Bliss* (New Haven, CT: Yale University Press, 2013), 108-9.

CHAPTER 16: I'M STAGGERED BY THE GLORY

1. Paul Davies, *The Cosmic Blueprint: New Discoveries in Nature's Creative Ability to Order the Universe* (New York: Simon and Schuster, 1988), 203.
2. Paul Davies, *The Mind of God: The Scientific Basis for a Rational World* (New York: Simon and Schuster, 1992), 232.
3. Hugh Ross, "Fine-Tuning for Life in the Universe," *Reasons to Believe*, August 29, 2006, www.reasons.org/fine-tuning-life-universe-aug-2006.
4. Francis Collins, quoted in Timothy J. Keller, *The Reason for God* (New York: Dutton, 2008), 130.
5. Hugh Ross, *The Creator and the Cosmos* (Colorado Springs, CO: NavPress, 1993, 1995), 115.
6. Ibid., 177.
7. Lee Strobel, *The Case for a Creator* (Grand Rapids, MI: Zondervan, 2004), 133.
8. Ibid., 135.

9. Arno Penzias, quoted in *Cosmos, Bios, and Theos*, 83.
10. Edward Harrison, quoted in Ross, *Creator and the Cosmos*, 123; see also E. Harrison, *Masks of the Universe* (New York: Collier Books, Macmillan, 1985), 252,263.
11. George Greenstein, *The Symbiotic Universe: Life and Mind in the Cosmos* (New York: William Morrow, 1988), 26-27.
12. Robert Jastrow, *God and the Astronomers* (New York: W.W. Norton, 1978), 116.
13. Robert Griffiths, quoted in Ross, *Creator and the Cosmos*, 123.
14. John Barrow and Frank Tipler, *The Anthropic Cosmological Principle* (Oxford: Oxford University Press, 1986).
15. Though their notion of God is not orthodox, they nonetheless must be counted among the scientific atheists that have converted to theism. Tipler wrote, "When I began my career as a cosmologist some twenty years ago, I was a convinced atheist. I never in my wildest dreams imagined that one day I would be writing a book purporting to show that the central claims of Judeo-Christian theology are in fact true, that these claims are straightforward deductions of the laws of physics as we now understand them. I have been forced into these conclusions by the inexorable logic of my own special branch of physics." Frank Tipler, *The Physics of Immortality* (New York: Doubleday, 1994), preface.
16. Martin Gardner, quoted in Ross, *Creator and the Cosmos*, 129.
17. For instance, Davies said in an interview (after explaining that he holds to neither the multiverse view nor the intelligent-design view), "I have my own preferred view, which is that the universe has engineering [*sic*] its own bio-friendliness through a sort of feedback loop that operates in both directions in time." Paul Davies, quoted in "The Self-Made Universe," *MSNBC*, April 19, 2007, www.ignaciodarnaude.com/textos_diversos/Davies,Self-Made%20Universe.htm. See also Paul Davies, *Cosmic Jackpot* (New York: Houghton Mifflin Harcourt, 2007); also published as *The Goldilocks Enigma*, 2008.
18. *Ockham's razor* is a methodological principle from the philosophy of science stipulating that if two explanations for an occurrence exist, then the simpler one should be given priority. Ockham's razor doesn't guarantee that the simpler explanation will be correct, but just suggests that it is best to eliminate assumptions that are not necessary. In a nutshell, simpler is better.
19. http://nobelist.tripod.com/id1_1.html (italics added).

CHAPTER 17: THE MARVEL OF LANGUAGE

1. Kofi Annan, address at the Global Knowledge 97 conference in Toronto, June 22, 1997; http://deepsky.com/~madmagic/kofi.html.
2. *Windtalkers*, directed by John Woo, Hollywood: MGM Studios, 2002.
3. Howard Connor, quoted in "News and Information," *Central Intelligence Agency*, 2008, www.cia.gov/news-information/featured-story-archive/2008-featured-story-archive/navajo-code-talkers/.
4. William Dembski, *Intelligent Design* (Downers Grove, IL: InterVarsity Press, 1999), 47.
5. Quoted in James Hannam, *The Genesis of Science: How the Christian Middle Ages Launched the Scientific Revolution* (Washington, DC: Regnery Publishing, 2011), 349.
6. "Plymouth experiment's monkeys type no Shakespeare-like text," May 10, 2003, http://lubbockonline.com/stories/051003/ent_051003027.shtml#.WK35bBiZOCQ.
7. Doug Gross, "Digital monkeys with typewriters recreate Shakespeare," CNN, September 26, 2011, http://www.cnn.com/2011/09/26/tech/web/monkeys-typewriters-shakespeare/

8. For an entertaining account of the Infinite Monkey Theorem, see "Infinite Monkey Theorem," *Wikipedia*, https://en.wikipedia.org/wiki/Infinite_monkey_theorem.

9. To be accurate, I must point out that Collins believes the complexity of the DNA code is explainable by theistic evolution rather than intelligent design. See Francis S. Collins, *The Language of God: A Scientist Presents Evidence for Belief* (New York: Free Press, 2006).

10. Francis Collins, quoted in Mark Mittelberg, *The Questions Christians Hope No One Will Ask* (Carol Stream, IL: Tyndale, 2010), 42.

11. Pearcey, *Total Truth*, 194-95.

12. Frederick Ferre, *Basic Modern Philosophy of Religion* (New York: Scribner's, 1967), 161; quoted in *The Hand of God*, ed. Michael Reagan (Philadelphia: Templeton Foundation Press, 1999), 102.

13. John 1:1.

14. An example of this is the statement of George Wald, Nobel Laureate and professor of biology at Harvard University: "It has occurred to me lately—I must confess with some shock at first to my scientific sensibilities—that both questions [the origin of consciousness in humans and of life from nonliving matter] might be brought into some degree of congruence. This is with the assumption that mind, rather than emerging as a late outgrowth in the evolution of life, has existed always as the matrix, the source and condition of physical reality—that stuff of which physical reality is composed is mind-stuff. It is mind that has composed a physical universe that breeds life and so eventually evolves creatures that know and create: science-, art-, and technology-making animals. In them the universe begins to know itself." George Wald, "Life and Mind in the Universe," *International Journal of Quantum Chemistry: Quantum Biology*, Symposium 11 (1984): 1-15.

15. Robert Browning, "Paracelsus."

16. 1 John 4:8.

17. William Shakespeare, *A Midsummer Night's Dream*, act 3, scene 1, p. 7.

18. Albert Einstein, quoted by Antonina Vallentin in *Einstein: A Biography* (New York: Doubleday, 1954), 24.

19. A.N. Wilson, "Why I Believe Again," *New Statesman*, April 2, 2009, www.newstatesman.com/religion/2009/04/conversion-experience-atheism.

CHAPTER 18: MATHEMATICS AND NUMBERS

1. Morris Kline, *Mathematics: The Loss of Certainty* (New York: Oxford University Press, 1980); see also Morris Kline, *Mathematics and the Search for Knowledge* (New York: Oxford University Press, 1985).

2. Quoted in Anthony Walsh, *Science Wars* (New Brunswick, NJ: Transaction Publishers, 2013), 31.

3. Quoted in James Bradley and Russell Howell, *Mathematics Through the Eyes of Faith* (New York: HarperCollins, 2011), 8,179. See also David Skeel, *True Paradox* (Downers Grove, IL: InterVarsity Press, 2014), 44; Vinoth Ramachandra, *Subverting Global Myths* (Downers Grove, IL: InterVarsity Press, 2008), 184-85; and John D. Barrow, *The Constants of Nature* (New York: Pantheon Books, 2002).

4. This is because math is more than mere tautologies (since math is based on axioms) and because "we can understand mathematics only by our tacit contribution to its formalism." Michael Polanyi, *Personal Knowledge* (Chicago: University of Chicago Press, 1958, 1962), 187-88.

5. Ibid., 189.

6. Quoted in Bradley and Howell, *Mathematics Through the Eyes of Faith*, 10.

7. Ibid., 225.
8. Charles Thaxton and Nancy Pearcey, *The Soul of Science* (Wheaton, IL: Crossway Books, 1994), 28-29.
9. Kathleen Norris, *Amazing Grace: A Vocabulary of Faith* (New York: Riverhead Books, 1998), 377.
10. *God Created the Integers,* ed. Stephen Hawking (Philadelphia: Running Press, 2005).
11. J.J. O'Connor and E.F. Robinson, "Leopold Kronecker," University of St. Andrews, Scotland, 1999, www-history.mcs.st-andrews.ac.uk/Biographies/Kronecker.html.
12. Stephen Hawking, interview on British television, June 2010, quoted by Laura Roberts, "Stephen Hawking: God Was Not Needed to Create the Universe," *The Telegraph,* September 2, 2010, www.telegraph.co.uk/news/science/science-news/7976594/Stephen-Hawking-God-was-not-needed-to-create-the-Universe.html.
13. Norris, *Amazing Grace,* 290.
14. Frank Wilczek, *A Beautiful Question: Finding Nature's Deep Design* (New York: Penguin Press, 2015), 250.
15. Caputo, *God,* 164.

CHAPTER 19: THE SCIENTIFIC METHOD

1. This oft-quoted statement attributed to Einstein is probably a variant of: "I, at any rate, am convinced that *He* does not throw dice." Albert Einstein, in a letter to Max Born on December 4, 1926, quoted in *The Born-Einstein Letters,* trans. Irene Born (New York: Walker and Company, 1971).
2. Here's a loose definition: the scientific method is a systematic procedure involving the formulation, testing, and modification of hypotheses, while utilizing the techniques of observation, measurement, and experimentation.
3. Thomas Cathcart and Joe Klein, *Plato and a Platypus Walk into a Bar* (New York: Penguin Books, 2007), 140.
4. Thaxton and Pearcey, *The Soul of Science,* 17.
5. Ibid.
6. Joseph Needham, *The Grand Titration* (Toronto: University of Toronto Press, 1969), 327; quoted in Thaxton and Pearcey, *Soul of Science,* 29.
7. Hannam, *Genesis of Science,* 57.
8. Thaxton and Pearcey, *Soul of Science,* 27.
9. Ibid., 26-27. Prominent philosophers and scientists agree on this point. Thaxton and Pearcey explain Alfred North Whitehead's view on this: "As Whitehead puts it, 'faith in the possibility of science' came antecedently to the development of actual scientific theory...This faith, Whitehead explains, rested on certain habits of thought, such as the lawfulness of nature—which in turn, he maintains, came from the Christian doctrine of the world as a divine creation." Ibid., 21.
   This is also pointed out by Nobel Prize laureate biochemist Melvin Calvin: "As I try to discern the origin of that conviction [the fundamental conviction in science that the universe is ordered], I seem to find it in a basic notion discovered 2000 or 3000 years ago, and enunciated first in the Western world by the ancient Hebrews: namely, that the universe is governed by a single God, and is not the product of the whims of many gods, each governing his own province according to his own laws. This monotheistic view seems to be the historical foundation for modern science." Ibid., 25.
10. Ibid., 27.

11. Hannam, *Genesis of Science,* 349.

12. Albert Einstein, quoted in "What Life Means to Einstein: An Interview by George Sylvester Viereck," *Saturday Evening Post,* October 26, 1929, 17.

CHAPTER 20: I NEED REASONS

1. Jill Haak Adels, *The Wisdom of the Saints: An Anthology* (New York: Oxford University Press, 1987), 176.

2. Siddhartha Gautama, *Life*, March 7, 1955, 102.

3. The Dalai Lama, *The Path to Tranquility: Daily Wisdom* (New York: Viking/Penguin, 1999), 140.

4. Quoted in K.L. Seshagiri Rao, *Mahatma Gandhi and Comparative Religion* (Delhi: Motilal Banarsidass Pub., 1978, 1990), 59.

5. *The Works of Thomas Jefferson in Twelve Volumes,* vol. 5, ed. Paul Leicester Ford (New York: Putnam's Sons, 1904), 324.

6. Blaise Pascal, *Pensées,* trans. A.J. Krailsheimer (Baltimore, MD: Penguin Books, 1995), no. 277.

7. Quoted in David Ropeik, *How Risky Is It?* (New York: McGraw-Hill, 2010), 244.

8. Quoted in Steven D. Price, *1001 Smartest Things Ever Said* (Guilford, CT: Lyons Press, 2004), 257.

9. Daniel Dennett, *Breaking the Spell: Religion as a Natural Phenomenon* (New York: Penguin Books, 2006).

10. Keller, *Reason for God,* 136-37.

11. Thomas Nagel, *The Last Word* (New York: Oxford University Press, 1997), 135.

12. Keller, *Reason for God,* 138.

13. Ibid., 136.

14. Alvin Plantinga, *Warrant and Proper Function* (New York: Oxford University Press, 1993, 2000).

15. Thaxton and Pearcey, *Soul of Science,* 42.

16. C.S. Lewis, chapter 3, "The Self-Contradiction of the Naturalist," in *Miracles,* 1st ed. (London: Geoffrey Bles, 1947).

17. Victor Reppert, *C.S. Lewis's Dangerous Idea* (Downers Grove, IL: InterVarsity Press, 2003).

18. A brief synopsis of Alvin Plantinga's "Evolutionary Argument Against Naturalism" can be found in Troy M. Nunley's 2005 PhD dissertation at the University of Missouri–Columbia: "Alvin Plantinga argues that [based on] naturalism it is irrational for a reflective person to hold to the doctrine of naturalism. If naturalism is true, some evolutionary doctrine must also be true and our evolutionary history must be accounted for in terms of only random mutation and natural selection. The probability of our being reliable cognitive agents given these origins is low or, at best, inscrutable. But it cannot reasonably be thought to be high. Consequently, the naturalist cannot reasonably hold to the belief that they are reliable cognitive agents. And since the reliability of their cognitive apparatus has been called into such grave question, naturalists are rationally bound to dismiss any belief accepted on the basis of trust in that apparatus. Specifically, to the extent that the naturalist is rational, they will give up their belief in naturalism." See static1.1.sqspcdn.com/static/f/38692/468365/.../A+Defense+of+Alvin+Plantinga.

19. G.K. Chesterton, *Orthodoxy* (New York: Dodd, Mead and Co., 1908), 25.

20. Job 25:2.

21. Isaiah 1:18 (ESV).

22. "Interview with Alister McGrath," *Zacharias Trust*, November 20, 2013, www.rzim.eu/interview-with-alister-mcgrath-2.

CHAPTER 21: TRUTH IS MORE REAL

1. Alexander Solzhenitsyn, Nobel Prize acceptance speech, 1970, www.columbia.edu/cu/augustine/arch/solzhenitsyn/nobel-lit1970.htm.
2. Kahlil Gibran, *The Prophet* (New York: Alfred A. Knopf, 1923), 54.
3. Richard Rorty, *Philosophy and the Mirror of Nature* (Princeton, NJ: Princeton University Press, 1979).
4. Daniel Dennett, interviewed by Bill Moyers on *The Charlie Rose Show*, June 6, 2006.
5. Francis Schaeffer, *Escape from Reason* (Downers Grove, IL: InterVarsity Press, 1968), 21.
6. *Shakespeare: The Complete Works*, "Measure for Measure," act V, scene 1, ed. G.B. Harrison (New York: Harcourt Brace Jovanovich, 1968), 1129.
7. Isaiah 45:19.
8. John 14:6.
9. "'The Few': Churchill's Speech to the House of Commons," August 20, 1940, *Churchill Society*, www.churchill-society-london.org.uk/thefew.html.
10. http://fakebuddhaquotes.com/three-things-cannot-be-long-hidden-the-sun-the-moon-and-the-truth/.
11. "Friedrich Nietzsche," *Stanford Encyclopedia of Philosophy*, June 7, 2016, http://plato.stanford.edu/entries/nietzsche/. See section 6: "Nietzsche's Unpublished Notebooks."
12. Marcus Aurelius, *Meditations*, IV:3.

PART FOUR: THE MIRACLE THAT IS ME

1. David Bentley Hart, *God: Being, Consciousness, Bliss* (New Haven, CT: Yale University Press, 2013), 158.

CHAPTER 22: I WONDER ABOUT...THE SELF

1. *The Elephant Man*, directed by David Lynch, Hollywood: Paramount Pictures, 1980.
2. Merrick's first name was John in the movie, but in real life his name was Joseph.
3. For an example of how this accidental origin is presented as science, see "The First Living Thing/Curiosity: Mankind Rising," *Discovery*, www.youtube.com/watch?v=z2_-h3I_WXQ.
4. Jesse Jackson, recited on *Sesame Street* Children's Television Series, 1971; see www.youtube.com/watch?v=iTB1h18bHlY.
5. *Zoolander*, directed by Ben Stiller, Hollywood: Paramount Pictures, 2001.
6. John Searle, *Freedom and Neurobiology* (New York: Columbia University Press, 2007), 4-5, quoted in J.P. Moreland, "The Image of God and the Failure of Scientific Atheism," in William Lane Craig and Chad Meister, *God Is Great, God Is Good* (Downers Grove, IL: IVP Books, 2009), 34.
7. Quoted in William J. O'Malley, *Connecting with God* (Maryknoll, NY: Orbis Books, 2013), 2.

CHAPTER 23: I WONDER ABOUT...FREE WILL

1. Leo Tolstoy, *War and Peace*, trans. Richard Pevear and Larissa Volokhonsky (New York: Alfred A Knopf, Vintage Classics), 1201.

2. Michael Caputo, *God: Seen Through the Eyes of the Greatest Minds* (West Monroe, LA: Howard Publishing, 2000), 8.
3. Many atheistic scientists and philosophers do not admit to being determinists. For instance, the atheist philosopher Daniel Dennett wrote a book attempting to defend free will, delightfully (in my opinion) called *Elbow Room* (though the book is not as good as the title). Yet, when we arrive at the core of his book, his point seems to be that we all have choices, but in each case there really is only one choice we can make. This is a semantic solution that seems to deprive the word *choice* of its true meaning. My point, again, is that if one subscribes to materialism and to the notion that the human brain is an organic computer, then it is very difficult to convincingly defend the notion of free will. Daniel Dennett, *Elbow Room* (Cambridge, MA: The MIT Press, 1984).
4. Charles Dickens, *A Christmas Carol* (New York: Bantam Classics, 1843, 1986), 16.
5. Philip Vander Elst, "From Atheism to Christianity: A Personal Journey," *Bethinking*, 2011, www.bethinking.org/is-christianity-true/from-atheism-to-christianity-a-personal-journey.

CHAPTER 24: I WONDER ABOUT...DOUBT

1. William Shakespeare, "Troilus and Cressida," in *Shakespeare—the Complete Works,* ed. G.B. Harrison (New York: Harcourt Brace Jovanovich, 1948), 988.
2. *The Writings of Henry David Thoreau,* ed. Bradford Torrey (Cambridge, MA: Riverside Press, 1837, 1906), 346.
3. Hart, *God,* 216-25.
4. Ibid., 220-21.
5. David Hume, *An Inquiry Concerning Human Understanding* (New York: Liberal Arts Press, 1955).
6. Kathleen Norris, *Amazing Grace: A Vocabulary of Faith* (New York: Riverhead Books, 1998), 67, 202-3.

CHAPTER 25: I WONDER ABOUT...EMOTIONS

1. Quoted in Igor and Irena Kononenko, *Teachers of Wisdom* (Pittsburgh, PA: Rose Dog Books, 2010), 236.
2. Leo Buscaglia, *Speaking of Love and the Art of Being Fully Human* (DVD).
3. 1 Corinthians 13:13.
4. Quoted in Darlene Mininni, *The Emotional Toolkit* (New York: St. Martin's Griffin, 2005), 54.
5. C.S. Lewis, *The Four Loves* (New York: Harcourt and Brace, 1960), 53.
6. Quoted in Daniel Goleman, *Working with Emotional Intelligence* (New York: Bantam Dell, 1998), 61.
7. Daniel Goleman, *Emotional Intelligence: Why It Can Matter More than IQ* (New York: Bantam Books, 1995).
8. Ibid., 36.
9. Harold Kushner, *When Bad Things Happen to Good People* (New York: Avon Books, 1981), 107-8.
10. Daniel B. Allender and Tremper Longman III, *The Cry of the Soul* (Colorado Springs, CO: NavPress), 50.
11. Rick Stedman, *Praying the Psalms* (Eugene, OR: Harvest House Publishers, 2016), 118.
12. Quoted in David Foster, *Accept No Mediocre Life* (New York: Time Warner Book Group, 2005), 162.
13. See my discussion of this in Stedman, *Praying the Psalms*, 77.

14. Nikos Kazantzakis, *The Saviors of God: Spiritual Exercises*, "The Action/The Relationship Between God and Man" (New York: Simon and Schuster, 1960), 56-57.
15. 1 John 4:8.
16. Nicole Cliffe, "How God Messed Up My Happy Atheist Life," *Christianity Today*, May 20, 2016, www.christianitytoday.com/ct/2016/june/nicole-cliffe-how-god-messed-up-my-happy-atheist-life.html.

CHAPTER 26: I WONDER ABOUT...COMPASSION

1. Dalai Lama, *The Art of Happiness* (New York: Riverhead Books, 2009).
2. Friedrich Nietzsche, *Twilight of the Idols and the Anti-Christ* (London: Penguin Books, 2003), 33.
3. Marilynne Robinson, *The Givenness of Things* (New York: Farrar, Straus and Giroux, 2015), 213.
4. Rodney Stark, *The Triumph of Christianity: How the Jesus Movement Became the World's Largest Religion* (New York: HarperCollins, 2011), 105-152.
5. David Bentley Hart, *Atheist Delusions: The Christian Revolution and Its Fashionable Enemies* (New Haven, CT: Yale University Press, 2009), 166-82, 199-215.
6. Luke 15:11-32.
7. Matthew 19:16-22.
8. Matthew 25:31,37-40.
9. Quoted in Paul Coughlin and Jennifer Degler, *No More Christian Nice Girl* (Minneapolis, MN: Bethany House, 2010), 91.
10. Dinesh D'Souza, "Conversion of a Cynic," *Crisis Magazine*, August 1, 1984, www.crisismagazine.com/1984/conversion-of-a-cynic.
11. "A Spiritual Evolution: Malcolm Muggeridge's Conversion Experience," *The Words Group*, www.thewords.com/articles/mugquest.htm.
12. Quoted in D'Souza, "Conversion of a Cynic."

CHAPTER 27: I WONDER ABOUT...HOPE

1. *The Definitive Wit of Winston Churchill*, ed. Richard M. Langworth (New York: Public Affairs, 2009), 203.
2. *Napoleon: In His Own Words*, ed. Jules Bertaut (Chicago: A.C. McClurg, 1916), 52.
3. *The Table Talk of Martin Luther*, ed. William Hazlitt (London: Bell and Daldy, 1872), 146.
4. "I cannot pretend to feel impartial about the colours. I rejoice with the brilliant ones, and am genuinely sorry for the poor browns." This Churchill quote first appears in "Painting as a Pastime" in *Strand Magazine*, December 1921 and January 1922.
5. Winston Churchill, "Speech to the Allied Delegates," St. James Place, London, June 12, 1941.
6. Julian of Norwich, *Revelations of Divine Love* (Brewster, MA: Paraclete Press, 2011), ix.
7. Winston Churchill, from his last major speech in the House of Commons, March 1, 1955.
8. Thomas Cathcart and Joe Klein, *Plato and a Platypus Walk into a Bar* (New York: Penguin Books, 2007), 17.
9. Robert G. Ingersoll, speech given in 1892.
10. Quoted in Marcia Ford, *Finding Hope* (Woodstock, VT: Skylight Paths Publishing, 2007), 92.
11. Albert Camus, "The Myth of Sisyphus" in *The Myth of Sisyphus and Other Essays* (New York: Vintage Books, 1955), 3.

12. This is not to suggest that Wittgenstein was an atheist. As Hans Küng notes, "Throughout his life Wittgenstein personally defended religion against its destructive, positivistic despisers." Wittgenstein himself wrote in his Notebooks on July 8, 1916: "To believe in a god means to see that the facts of the world are not the end of the matter. To believe in God means to see that life has a meaning." Hans Küng, *Does God Exist?: An Answer for Today* (New York: Doubleday and Co., 1978), 506.

13. Bertrand Russell, "A Free Man's Worship," in *Why I Am Not a Christian and Other Essays* (New York: Simon and Schuster, 1957), 106.

14. Romans 15:13 (italics added).

15. Jeremiah 29:11.

16. *The Poetical Works of Alexander Pope* (London: James and Co., 1826), 46.

17. Winston Churchill, speech to Harrow School on October 29, 1941. Churchill, I must point out, is considered by some today as an agnostic, possibly even an atheist (see William Manchester and Paul Reid, *The Last Lion: Winston Spencer Churchill: Defender of the Realm, 1940–1965*). Others disagree with this conclusion, citing his many references to God in his writings, the worship service he designed and shared with Franklin D. Roosevelt on the battleship *Prince of Wales*, as well as his own funeral service, which he himself planned to be clearly Christian. My own conclusion is that Churchill was not a church-going man, but he clearly had a deep Christian worldview that supported his optimism.

18. Quoted in O'Malley, *Connecting with God*, 152-53.

CHAPTER 28: I WONDER ABOUT...DIGNITY

1. Helen Keller, *The Story of My Life and Optimism* (London: Hodder and Stoughton, 1911; reprint Whitefish, NY: Kessinger Publishing, 2010), 54.

2. Robert Jay Lifton, *The Nazi Doctors* (New York: Basic Books, 1986), 115-16.

3. Peter Singer, *Practical Ethics*, 2d ed. (New York: Cambridge University Press, 1980, 1993), 186.

4. When considering abortion, the following quote is sobering: "Countries that allow selective abortion (China, India, Azerbaijan, Georgia, and Armenia, among others)—so that parents can give birth to boys instead of girls—are responsible for a daunting population trend. According to *Unnatural Selection* by Mara Hvistendahl, 163 million girls who should have been born in the past 30 years were not" ("A Shocking Statistic," in *Reader's Digest*, September 2011, 65). Sadly, the movement to provide abortions as a method of protecting women's rights has resulted in the selective deaths of millions of girls who thereby were prevented from becoming women themselves.

PART FIVE: FEELING HOMESICK AT HOME

1. Bertrand Russell, *The Autobiography of Bertrand Russell* (Boston: Little, Brown and Company, 1968), 125-26; quoted in J.P. Moreland and Kai Nielsen, *Does God Exist?: The Debate Between Theists and Atheists* (New York: Prometheus Books, 1993), 74.

2. C.S. Lewis, *Perelandra* (New York: Macmillan, 1944), 81.

3. Thomas Carlyle, *Sartor Resartus* (London: Chapman and Hall, 1831), 131.

4. *The Westminster Shorter Catechism* (Phillipsburg, NJ: P&R Publishing, 1970), 1.

5. Marilynne Robinson, *The Givenness of Things* (New York: Farrar, Straus and Giroux, 2015), 259.

6. G.K. Chesterton, *Orthodoxy* (New York: Image Books, 1959), 79-80.

CHAPTER 29: I LONG FOR A WORLD

1. William J. O'Malley, *Connecting with God* (Maryknoll, NY: Orbis Books, 2013), xi.
2. Parts of this chapter are taken from my book *Praying the Psalms*, chapter 5, used by permission of Harvest House Publishers, Eugene, OR., 2016.
3. See Peter Kreeft, *Making Sense Out of Suffering* (Ann Arbor, MI: Servant Books, 1986) and Philip Yancey, *Where Is God When It Hurts?* (Grand Rapids, MI: Zondervan, 1977).
4. Ann O'Neill, "The Reinvention of Ted Turner," *CNN*, November 17, 2013, www.cnn.com/2013/11/17/us/ted-turner-profile/.
5. Bart Ehrman, "How the Problem of Pain Ruined My Faith," *Beliefnet*, www.beliefnet.com/columnists/blogalogue/2008/04/why-suffering-is-gods-problem.html.
6. "Elie Wiesel on His Beliefs," *CrownHeights*, August 10, 2006, http://crownheights.info/general/2897/elie-wiesel-on-his-beliefs/.
7. Joni Eareckson Tada, foreword to Daniel B. Allender and Tremper Longman III, *The Cry of the Soul* (Colorado Springs, CO: NavPress, 1994), xi.
8. Nicholas Wolterstorff, *Lament for a Son* (Grand Rapids, MI: Wm. B. Eerdmans, 1987), 89,97.
9. *Shakespeare: The Complete Works*, ed. G.B. Harrison (New York: Harcourt, Brace, Jovanovich, 1968), 509.
10. Ralph Waldo Emerson, from his personal journal, January 28, 1842. Quoted in Rosemarie Jarski, *Words from the Wise* (New York: Skyhorse Publishing, 2007), 221.
11. Tim Clinton and Gary Sibcy, *Attachments: Why You Love, Feel and Act the Way You Do* (Brentwood, TN: Thomas Nelson Publishers, 2002), 260.
12. O'Malley, *Connecting with God*, 2.
13. Quoted in Michael Caputo, *God: Seen Through the Eyes of the Greatest Minds* (West Monroe, LA: Howard Publishing, 2000), 51.
14. Quoted in O'Malley, *Connecting with God*, 18.
15. John 11:35.
16. Psalm 23:4 (ESV).

CHAPTER 30: I LONG FOR LASTING LOVE

1. Johann Christoph Arnold, *Escape Routes: For People Who Feel Trapped in Life's Hells* (Walden, NY: Plough Publishing House, 2002), 15.
2. "Eve's Diary," *Wikipedia*, https://en.wikipedia.org/wiki/Eve%27s_Diary.
3. Mark Twain, "Eve's Diary," in *The Complete Short Stories of Mark Twain*, ed. Charles Neider (Garden City, NY: Doubleday and Company, 1957), 294.
4. Arnold, *Escape Routes*, 8.
5. Jean-Paul Sartre, *No Exit and Other Plays* (New York: Vintage Books, 1989), 45.
6. Quoted in John Patrick, "The Necessity of Trust," in Paul M. Anderson, *Professors Who Believe: The Spiritual Journeys of Christian Faculty* (Downers Grove, IL: InterVarsity Press, 1998), 37.
7. Quoted in Vinoth Ramachandra, *Subverting Global Myths* (Downers Grove, IL: InterVarsity Press, 2008), 123.
8. Martin Luther King Jr. gave his "March on Washington Address," which is often called his "I Have a Dream" speech, on August 28, 1963, in Washington DC; www.mlkonline.net/dream.html.